Scandals of '51

BY THE SAME AUTHOR

Have Jump Shot Will Travel
A Mile Above the Rim
Maverick (with Phil Jackson)

SCANDALS of '51

How the Gamblers Almost Killed College Basketball

Charles Rosen

Holt, Rinehart and Winston   New York

Published simultaneously in Canada by Holt, Rinehart and Winston of Canada, Limited.

LIBRARY OF CONGRESS CATALOGING IN PUBLICATION DATA

Rosen, Charles.   Scandals of '51.

   1. Basketball—United States—History. 2. Bribery—United States. 3. Basketball players—United States—Biography. 4. College sports. I. Title.
GV885.7.R67   364.1'63   77-25355

FIRST EDITION

DESIGNER: Susan Mitchell

PRINTED IN THE UNITED STATES OF AMERICA
10 9 8 7 6 5 4 3 2 1

With love to

SUSAN, DARRELL, AND ALEXANDRA

There are no heroes and no villains.
There are only victims.

—Dalton Trumbo

Scandals of '51

Manhattan College is unaccountably located on the crest of a hill in the Bronx. The school is run by the Christian Brothers, a Jesuit teaching order, and its architecture has a decidedly medieval flavor. Flying buttresses abound. There are shady glens, cobblestoned walks, and a bell tower.

It is nine o'clock on a Sunday evening—January 14, 1951. The campus lies wet and subdued under a light rain. Clusters of robed figures march silently off to chapel. A few undergraduates pass from the library to the dormitories. A nun kneels briefly before an icon. Several young men in Manhattan College varsity jackets bounce across the campus, headed down the hill for a few beers. . . . And a huge figure keeps a gaunt vigil in the campus parking lot.

His name is Junius Kellogg. He paces the sidewalk and listens to his watch. Waiting usually comes easy for Junius but he is jittery. Junius was one of a family of eleven back home in Portsmouth, Virginia. He was raised poor, patient, and Christian. Junius also did a forty-month infantry tour in World War II. He attends Manhattan College under the GI Bill of Rights. Junius is twenty-three years old and a very popular figure on campus. He is also 6 feet 8 inches tall and a mild curiosity. The official National Collegiate Athletic Association Guide for 1951 features a separate section highlighting the basketball doings of America's "Colored Colleges." Junius Kellogg is the first black man ever to play for the Manhattan College varsity basketball team, the Jaspers. The New York sportswriters call Junius a "black giant" and "an elongated Negro center." They bemoan his inconsistency on the court but they laud his potential. With the graduation of last season's co-captains, Hank Poppe and John Byrnes,

Junius is the mainstay of a Manhattan College team on its way to a fine 16 and 6 season. But Junius doesn't want to think about basketball. It hurts too much. He rechecks his watch. He pokes his attention down the street and spots the detectives parked comfortably under a broken street lamp. Junius sighs and shifts his weight. He is waiting for Hank Poppe.

It's been only three days since Junius last saw Poppe, and their meeting was a shocker. Poppe blatantly offered Junius $1,000 in his hand to "dump" an upcoming basketball game against De Paul University. Junius was quick to refuse but Poppe begged him to reconsider. "Just think it over," Poppe said. "I'll meet you in the parking lot Sunday night at nine." Junius was frightened. But Junius lost little time in reporting the conversation to Kenny Norton, Manhattan's basketball coach. Norton could barely believe what he heard and he immediately started the information up the college's chain of command. It wasn't until early the next morning that Brother Bonaventure Thomas, Manhattan College's president, approved the idea of calling in the police. Junius spent the entire weekend being questioned and instructed by detectives from the Bronx District Attorney's office. Junius was still numb. He was told to play along with Poppe.

A pair of headlights sweeps the street, and Junius stiffens. The car pulls to a stop in front of him. Hank Poppe smiles from behind the wheel as Junius opens the door and climbs inside.

"Let's go get a couple of brews," Poppe suggests.

"Sure," Junius says. His skin shrivels.

Poppe drives down the hill and leads Junius into a bar on Broadway and 242nd Street. The two athletes are greeted warmly by the patrons, most of them Manhattan College students. There is a hockey game on the television set and Junius and his ex-teammate slide into a secluded booth.

"Did you think it over?" Poppe asks.

"Yeah," says Junius. His mouth is suddenly dry. "I've changed my mind. I'm ready to go along with the pitch."

"Good," Poppe says with a quiet satisfaction. "You won't be sorry."

Junius grimaces, nods, and remembers his instructions. "How do I fix a game?" he asks. "Exactly what do I have to do?"

Hank Poppe scored 1,027 points in his varsity career. He is the second highest scorer in the school's history. Poppe leans back and sips his beer. "It's easy," he says. "You can miss a rebound once in a while. After you do get a rebound don't look to pass it down court. Hang on to it and give the defense a chance to set up. Then you can try shooting your hook shot a little hard. And don't really try to block the other guy's shot. Throw the ball away when you get the chance. Just remember that Manhattan doesn't have to actually lose the game. All you have to do is control the margin of victory. It's easy, Junie. Everybody's doing it. Everywhere. All over the country. The pros too. But whatever you do, Junie, don't stink up the joint. Make it look like you're trying."

Poppe is confident and buoyant. Since his graduation last spring, Poppe has been doing manual labor. He tells Junius about all the money they'll both be making. Poppe pays for the beer and drives Junius back to the campus.

"I'll see you before the De Paul game on Tuesday," Poppe says, "to let you know the final arrangements. Don't worry about it, Junie. It's easy."

Junius is kept up until well past midnight being debriefed by the detectives.

The Manhattan–De Paul game is part of a college double-header, and Madison Square Garden is sold out. Outside the arena, on Eighth Avenue, the ticket scalpers herd their eager customers into orderly lines. The number of available tickets rapidly dwindles and the negotiations turn into a frantic auction. The bids reach $50 for a $5 seat, but with few exceptions, the scalpers save their last precious ticket to use themselves.

In 1951 college basketball is king, and the pro game is

nowhere. Collegiate basketball is the perfect bridge to span the football and the baseball seasons. The fledgling National Basketball Association still has franchises in places like Waterloo, Anderson, and Sheboygan. The only time the pros ever draw a full house is when a Harlem Globetrotters game is on the program. Superstars like George Mikan and "Jumping Joe" Fulks play in the NBA and are certainly worth seeing. But the pros play for money while the college kids play for Boola Boola and for the Gipper. The undergrads are incredibly talented athletes on their own—Bob Cousy, Ed Macauley, Paul Arizin, Dick Groat, Gene Melchiorre, Bill Spivey, the fabulous Sherman White, and the McGuire brothers. The colleges play to SRO houses all over the country. But Madison Square Garden is the mecca. Unfortunately, the Garden is also the clearinghouse for New York City's gambling establishment. Even the popcorn vendors regularly know the point spread. And the word leaks out on Tuesday evening. Every tinhorn in town knows that the fix is on for the Manhattan–De Paul game.

A BOOKIE REMEMBERS: "Everybody was betting on De Paul with the points. Guys who never bet more than ten bucks in their life suddenly wanted to get down for three hundred dollars. They were breaking their necks running up the stairs to make their bets."

Junius Kellogg is warming up with the rest of his teammates. Junius is nervous and he has trouble making even the simplest of shots. The basketball feels like a shot put. Game time is still several minutes away but the fans are already in a frenzy. Junius sees Hank Poppe standing at courtside, waving and beckoning to him.

"Manhattan is favored by ten points," Poppe says. "So make sure you win by less. I'll meet you in the men's room in Gilhooley's bar over on Eighth Avenue right after the game. I'll have your money."

The ball game begins and the fans turn into shrieking aborigines. At least two-thirds of them have money riding on the contest. The fans greet each shot with horseplayers' enthusiasm. Junius is so unnerved that his game falls apart. He fumbles easy passes and is a step behind everyone else. "Fix!" the fans start yelling. "Dumper!" they scream. Kenny Norton is quick to appraise the situation. He pulls Junius from the game and limits his star's playing time. Without their big man, the Jaspers falter. The Manhattan bettors are shouting obscenities and racial epithets. Junius winds up with only 4 points. But his substitute converts all eight of his field-goal attempts and Manhattan hangs on to win, 62–59. The De Paul money also wins.

Junius showers quickly and hurries over to the rendezvous with the detectives a discreet distance behind. Once again Junius waits, but this time Poppe fails to show. There is a conference and squad cars are ordered out to round up Poppe.

Hank Poppe is arrested in his home in Queens at 3:00 A.M. He talks freely to the police, and John Byrnes is apprehended two hours later. Byrnes makes no statement. He is apparently not involved in Poppe's attempt to fix Junius Kellogg. As Wednesday morning breaks, three other men are arrested—Cornelius Kelleher, Benjamin Schwartzberg, and Irving Schwartzberg. Kelleher is the front man. The two brothers are bookmakers, felons, and ex-cons. In the presence of Junius and Kenny Norton, Poppe, Byrnes, and the three gamblers are interrogated by an assistant D.A. They are booked on varying counts of bribery and conspiracy. They are in violation of Section 382 of the Penal Code, which makes it illegal to attempt to bribe a participant in any sporting event.

Investigation reveals that Poppe and Byrnes were first approached by Kelleher before the 1949–50 season got under way. Both players succumbed to the gambler's inducements and were paid $40 a week to tide them over until the season began. Poppe and Byrnes were then paid $3,000 each to make certain that Manhattan lost ball games against Siena (December 3, 1949), Santa Clara (December 29, 1949), and Bradley (January 12, 1950). All of the games were played at

Madison Square Garden. Poppe and Byrnes earned an additional $2,000 each for helping Manhattan to *exceed* the point spreads against St. Francis and New York University.

Max Kase breaks the story on Thursday morning, January 18, in the *New York Journal-American*. The news blows a blizzard of outrage and retribution across the country. Max Kase reports that "a first blush of sympathy for the corrupted weaklings has given way to a cold rage because of their lack of loyalty to their school and a calloused greed for their Judas pieces of silver."

Irving Marsh of the *New York Herald Tribune* is convinced that "basketball is through as a big-time sport." The *Chicago Tribune* blames the scandal on the New Deal. The *Daily Worker* ties the news in with "profiteering chairmen of Wall Street corporations" and "bankers and big-shot politicians grabbing war contracts."

Arthur Daley, *The New York Times*'s award-winning journalist, is especially vindictive: "All scandals are ugly and this is a particularly vicious one because it touches the presumably untouchable. . . . The personal preference here would be boiling in oil for all fixers."

Life magazine publishes an incriminating series of action photographs purporting to illustrate instances of collaboration. One sequence shows Poppe hustling downcourt on a solo breakaway in the game against Siena. Poppe misdribbles the ball, pushing it beyond his reach and over to the side, where a Siena player makes the recovery. Another spread shows Byrnes flubbing an uncontested rebound with the ball landing in the hands of a startled Bradley player. Everybody is outraged for a couple of days.

Howard Hobson of Yale University provides a rare voice of compassion: "The faith of our youngsters in these All-American idols has been shattered. . . . Yet it is difficult to sit in judgment on these boys when there are so many others indirectly responsible."

"This racket is not purely local," Kenny Norton warns. "I loathe the whole stinking business. I can't believe that gamblers got next to my kids."

The New York Times cautiously canonizes Junius Kellogg: "We may be overly trustful, but we fancy Junius Kellogg, with his immediate dismissal of the idea of playing less well than he could is the rule, not the exception, in collegiate sports." As if to reconvince the public, the same editorial goes on to simplistically redefine the aims and values of intercollegiate sports: "To build physical and moral health and inspire good sportsmanship, while playing the game as well and as hard as possible." But the *Times* is too late. The amateurs are already street pros.

Junius Kellogg is accorded a rally in the Manhattan College quadrangle. Professors, students, clergy, and maintenance people press against the hastily erected platform. "I never gave that bribe offer a thought," Junius tells them. The crowd finds release in a roaring, thankful, loving ovation.

Prevention becomes the byword. Both the *Kansas City Star* and the *Nashville Tennessean* reveal they will henceforth be providing only local basketball scores over the phone lest any gamblers be aided. The *Milwaukee Journal* announces it will give no scores over the phone. New York City Police Commissioner Thomas F. Murphy lets it be known that thirty plainclothesmen will be stationed at strategic points throughout Madison Square Garden in an effort to keep the arena free from gamblers and bookmakers. Commissioner Murphy also presents Junius with a scroll of honor in recognition of his "integrity, honesty and valuable assistance."

There is a flurry of activity around City Hall and the smell of smoke spreads. Sports fans wonder who is next. But the LIU team remains undefeated and both St. John's and CCNY are playing well. So the Garden scalpers are still in business.

Dr. Tristam W. Metcalfe, the president of LIU, issues an invitation to the heads of Columbia, Fordham, NYU, Manhattan, St. John's, Brooklyn College, St. Francis, and CCNY to attend a discussion on the gambling menace in metropolitan collegiate basketball. The meeting is attended only by Dr. Metcalfe and Brother Bonaventure Thomas.

At the arraignment, Byrnes, Kelleher, and the brothers

Schwartzberg plead not guilty, and Hank Poppe makes an admission of guilt. "I would give a million dollars to be out of this fix," Poppe says. "I just did the wrong thing. I guess I was weak." The D.A.'s office reports that Poppe has signed a waiver of immunity and has volunteered to help in whatever way he can. The police also hint at a series of new arrests. Several All-American and All-NBA players and a couple of referees sleep with worms in their dreams.

The dam is about to break. It may be that the war is over. That the Japanese have been A-bombed, that Hitler is dead, and that the junior senator from Wisconsin has the Commies on the run. It may be that President Truman doesn't take any crap from anybody. It may be that the country is prosperous. But things aren't the same anymore. There's another war brewing in some place named Korea. College kids are crooked. The Brooklyn Dodgers have a black man playing second base and hitting .340. And it's getting harder and harder to tell the bad guys from the good guys.

Most contemporary sports come fully equipped with exotic creation myths. There are youthful octogenarians in Coney Island who swear that the curiously designed walls of the fabled Aztec temples were once upon a time used for games of handball. The American Indians are known to have played a version of lacrosse several hundred years before Columbus. The Indians' rules included an unlimited playing field and thousands of players on each side. Instead of balls, the high-scoring Indians used human heads and averaged over a hundred fatalities a game. The sport of baseball is rumored to have been invented by either Abner Doubleday or Jiminy Cricket. Bowling was evolved by trolls in upstate New York. But the sport of basketball has a much neater and more orderly history.

In the year 1891, Dr. James Naismith was an alumnus and a faculty member of the International Young Men's Christian Association Training School in Springfield, Massachusetts. Naismith was a thirty-year-old native Canadian with an undergraduate degree from the prestigious McGill University and three years of divinity school. He had a stylish handlebar mustachio, a T-square jaw, a cleft in his chin, and he wore his hair parted a rakish inch to the left.

Naismith taught physical education at the Springfield school, and the curriculum was simple. In the fall, the students studied football outdoors. They were instructed in baseball come the spring. Gymnasium activity during cold weather consisted of either marching, calisthenics, or apparatus work. In the autumn of 1891, one particular class voiced their displeasure with the boring indoor fare. Their teacher was replaced but the class remained incorrigible. The second teacher also had to be removed, and Naismith was asked to take over the unruly class. He discovered that the class was composed of several dozen rambunctious football and soccer players, and he soon realized that a game situation was the only possible solution. Naismith had the students play rugby indoors, but they bruised each other from head to toe. Next he tried soccer, but they smashed windows and shinbones. When he attempted a modified game of lacrosse, the enthusiastic students beat each other with their sticks.

Then one night Naismith had a brainstorm. He scribbled a few sketches and transcribed a few hasty rules. Early the following morning, Naismith salvaged two peach baskets from the janitor and nailed them to either end of the gym. An overhead balcony dictated that each basket was a fortuitous ten feet above the floor. "A player cannot run with the ball," Naismith said. "Passing the ball is the only way it can be legally advanced. There is no shouldering, holding, pushing, tripping, or striking allowed." Naismith had half the class face one of the baskets and the other team face the other way. He threw a soccer ball onto the floor and said, "Go." The players were earnest and adventuresome. It was difficult to tell who was on offense and who was on defense. But the resulting mayhem was neat enough for Naismith and satisfying enough for the young athletes.

The game caught on quickly. The Central and Armory Hill branches of the Springfield YMCA played the first basketball game between two distinct teams in March of 1892, battling to a 2–2 tie. Naismith was an honored guest at the first women's game, which pitted the local Springfield girls against a squad of women teachers. One of the players, Maude Sherman, so impressed him with her moves without the ball that he asked her to marry him. A pair of women's colleges, Vassar and Smith, were quick to add basketball to their regular physical educational activities. Amos Alonzo Stagg, one of Naismith's colleagues, took the game with him when he left Springfield to teach at the University of Chicago. But Vanderbilt University fielded the first men's varsity in a game against the Nashville YMCA in March of 1893.

The game had instant appeal, and with the country's YMCA's acting as a pipeline, basketball spread west over the prairies and south into the mountains of Kentucky. It wasn't long before basketball reached New York City, where it received a passionate nurturing and a feverish refashioning. Most of the city's universities adopted the sport and organized varsity teams. On April 24, 1896, a YMCA tournament for the Championship of America was staged in the heart of Brooklyn. All but two of the entries were from New York and East District defeated Brooklyn Central 4–0 for the title. The new sport found especially rabid devotees in those sections of the city that were settled by immigrants: Brownsville, the East Bronx, and Williamsburg. There were Irish-bar teams and Polish Social Club teams. Basketball games often had the intensity of race wars. The "personal foul" was invented. In Brooklyn and on the Lower East Side, the Jews played in settlement houses instead of YMCA's. As the competition increased, some teams made innovations. The Chicago West Side YMCA boasted the game's first big man, a 6-foot-4-inch player. The same team also introduced another revolutionary weapon, the short pass. Other teams hired "ringers," most of them college kids.

When the YMCA's governing body decided to drop the sport because of its growing roughness, most of the dedicated players were left without a place to play. One alternative was to form a team, rent a gym, and charge admission. Sometimes there was enough money left over to split among the players. As a result, the first pro league, the National Basketball League, was organized in 1898 in Philadelphia. It lasted for five years. The better ballplayers would sell their services to the highest bidder before every game. A team's roster was very unstable and wildcat teams were the rule. The only other available option for the basketball enthusiast was an increasing list of colleges with varsity basketball teams.

The initial all-collegiate male contest was played between Hamline College and the Minnesota State School of Agriculture. The Porkies crushed the Aggies, 9–3. Then for many years, the Ivy League teams dominated the college scene. Yale made a successful road trip in 1900, bringing the gospel to the hinterlands. In 1908 Wabash College of Indiana claimed the world's championship but basketball on campus was still a second-class operation. Other collegiate athletes sneered and called the game "round ball," and basketball was generally looked upon as an excellent off-season conditioner for more manly, brain-denting sports.

Then, from the cold and hungry streets of the Lower East Side, came one of the most influential apostles of basketball. A man who would fuse the collegiate and the pro games, providing a vital boost for them both.

Kareem Abdul-Jabbar hails from the New York metropolitan area. So does Julius Erving. Yet in 1976, an official proclamation from the Boys' Athletic League named Nat Holman as the greatest basketball product ever to come out of the city. There is no question that Nat Holman was an authentic founding father.

A FRIEND REMEMBERS: "Sometimes Nat acts as though he's sore that Dr. Naismith beat him to the punch."

Nat Holman was born in 1896, the fourth of ten children of Russian immigrant parents. Papa was a hard worker and soon saved enough of a pittance to buy a small grocery store on Norfolk Street. With seven sons, help was cheap and dependable. The Holman boys all followed the same routine. They awoke before the sun to open, clean, and stock the store. They stayed up late cleaning and replenishing the shelves. But Papa also insisted on the virtues of a formal education. The boys always did their homework. In a time when a high school diploma was a rarity, seven of the Holman children went on to college.

It was a crowded, busy household. And sometimes the growing boys got into each other's way. They heatedly competed for attention and survival, but they didn't dare compete with Papa's iron hand. One after another, all seven brothers turned their spirited natures to the game of basketball. They lived and imbibed the game at the University Settlement House, which was only blocks from their apartment. Their first collective basketball was an old vegetable sack stuffed with paper.

A BROTHER REMEMBERS: "Aaron played on a great New York University team in 1920. Morris captained the CCNY squad in 1918. We all played and we were all good. But Nat was the ace."

At twelve Nat was playing for the local settlement house against grown men, and the tiny court left an indelible mark on his basketball philosophy. The playing area measured 70 feet by 40 feet and any player foolish enough to take off in a burst of straightaway speed was in imminent danger of splattering himself against a wall. Defense consisted of a five-man barrier standing from sideline to sideline. In such cramped quarters, goals could only be earned by jockeying and weaving, by acquiring a relentless repertoire of subtle and deceptive movements. Nat Holman was the most artful dodger of them all.

Nat entered the High School of Commerce in 1912 and also showed himself to be a gifted all-around athlete, playing baseball and being named to the all-city soccer team. Nat went on to be a three-letterman at NYU. In 1917 he turned down a professional baseball contract offered by the Cincinnati Reds. But money and sports were no strangers to Nat. Most of New York's college basketball players were in the habit of picking up a few surreptitious dollars by playing under assumed names for pro teams on weekends. Nat was an outstanding hoopster at NYU so his fee was a hefty $6 a game. Then World War I erupted on Nat's athletic career and terminated his college days. After a discharge from the navy, Nat jumped into professional basketball with both feet. But he also took the precaution of accepting a position as CCNY's varsity coach in 1919.

As the 1920s dawned, America was on the threshold of the "Golden Age of Sports," and there soon developed two dominant pro basketball teams in New York: the Whirlwinds and the Celtics. Both clubs made substantial bids for Nat's services. The Celtics were a bunch of tough Irish kids from Twenty-third Street and Ninth Avenue, and Nat opted for the Whirlwinds. The rules of the game had been standardized but the competition was still brutal. There were no backboards but double dribbles and "walking" violations no longer counted as personal fouls. Shooting became a factor. Games were often played inside huge steel cages where the ball was never out of bounds. The referee's primary function was to wipe the blood off the ball.

In 1921 the Whirlwinds and the Celtics played a famous grudge series that led to inflamed passions and wagers involving large sums of money. The Whirlwinds took the first game 40–27 before 11,000 fans in New York's Seventy-first Regiment Armory. The Celtics evened the score with a 26–24 victory. But the deciding game had to be canceled because of strong rumors that some of the players were in the pay of gamblers. At the conclusion of the season, Nat and a teammate, Chris Leonard, jumped to the Celtics. The Celtics were now able to offer their players guaranteed annual salaries and the pro game became almost respectable.

Nat was a great passer, an excellent shooter, and a clever improviser. He was responsible for having the Celtics' biggest player position himself in the "pivot," close to the basket with his back to the hoop. This allowed the Celtics to create a picking, cutting, give-and-go offense. The team changed its name to the "Original Celtics" and barnstormed the country taking on all comers. Nat was the smallest player on the Celtics, but the most dynamic. His self-assured style of play could be counted on to rile up an already hostile crowd. There were many times when Nat had to concentrate on the game while at the same time trying to avoid being hatpinned in the backside by irate courtside spectators. Nat

14

was the game's biggest draw, and the Original Celtics won 720 of 795 games from 1920 to 1928.

AN OLD PRO REMEMBERS: "Nat had flair, talent, intelligence, and an unquenchable arrogance. He spoke with a phony English accent, and his sentences were always laced with literary references. The customers would pay to see Nat fall on his face but they were always disappointed. Nat Holman was to basketball as Babe Ruth, Red Grange, Jack Dempsey, and Bill Tilden were to their sports. But being a professional basketball player was a difficult way to make a living back in those days. We played about a hundred games a year. We'd come into a city with six guys and hire a local kid to play with us. We'd play Friday night and beat the yokels by a narrow margin. Then we'd get some bets down, play them again on Sunday afternoon, and kill them. We'd collect our money and get the hell out of town. The Original Celtics were doing the same kind of thing when Nat was playing with them. Only we didn't call it point shaving. We called it survival."

Nat showed as much aptitude and enthusiasm for coaching as he did for playing. He drove his CCNY players hard and turned out winning teams year after year. Then in 1920, a game between CCNY and NYU drew 10,000 fans, and college administrators from coast to coast were forced to take another look at their basketball programs.

College football was the big moneymaker up till then. The football teams supported all the other varsity activities, and in some universities even paid for libraries, books, and distinguished professors. But football teams need expensive equipment and huge stadiums. As the twenties roared along, the stock market boomed and real estate values skyrocketed, but the price of sneakers, jockstraps, and uniforms remained the same. Colleges began to see the financial advantages of making intercollegiate basketball a big-time sport. It wasn't long before the college game began to match gate receipts with the pro game. Sometimes the collegiate and professional rosters were remarkably similar.

A PHYSICIAN REMEMBERS: "When I was playing college ball in the mid 1920s, we used to play pro games every Saturday night in places like New Haven, Bridgeport, Passaic, and Paterson. Everybody was doing it. The college coaches knew but there was nothing they could do or say. One year, my entire college varsity team used colors for our assumed names. Joe Brown. Jim White. George Blue. We all came from poor families, and a dollar was a lot of money in those days. We even bet on the college games we played in. We'd go up into the stands before the game and place bets with kids from the other school. The coach knew what we were up to so we always bet on our own team to win. But it was all penny-ante stuff."

Nat Holman's CCNY teams ruled Eastern college basketball while the Original Celtics continued to trounce all their opponents. The Celtics attracted 24,000 spectators to an afternoon-evening doubleheader in Cleveland. They drew 9,000 fans at Chattanooga. Everybody could now afford to make money legitimately. Nat was the star and he was paid the unheard-of salary of $12,500 a year.

In 1925 a Washington laundry tycoon named George Preston Marshall decided to put his money behind a professional basketball league. Marshall's idea was sound, but the independent Celtics refused to cooperate. They were too busy making too much money to have any part of Marshall's American Basketball League. The Celtics added further insult by routing the ABL's teams in exhibition games. Finally the ABL moved to blacklist the Celtics, forbidding any of its teams to play them. Suddenly, the Celtics' biggest dollar dates were gone, and the team was left with no choice but to join the ABL midway through the 1926–27 season.

The Celtics ran away with the second-half title, winning 19 of 20 games. The following year, the Celtics easily won both halves of the ABL championship and then trounced Fort Wayne in a playoff series. Marshall was the owner of the Washington franchise and he spent more than $65,000 in salaries trying to hire players good enough to beat the Celtics.

But Marshall's efforts were fruitless, and the Celtics bragged they would force him into bankruptcy.

The Celtics were so good that the fans around the league gradually began to lose interest and attendance dropped. In a desperate attempt to restore competitive balance, the ABL broke up the Celtics and parceled out their players to the other teams. Nat Holman and Joe Lapchick found their way to the Cleveland Rosenblums and quickly stamped their new team with the Celtic mold. The Rosenblums made such a shamble of the league opposition that the ABL finally had to cease all operations in 1929.

Nat had one last fling with the old gang later that same year, when the Original Celtics were temporarily reunited to play a series against the Renaissance Big Five, a black team that claimed the world's championship. Nat outscored the Ren's star "Cappy" Ricks 15–6 in the opener, and the Celtics blasted the black team. Nat played briefly for teams in Syracuse and Chicago before retiring from active play in 1933 to devote all of his time to coaching.

NAT HOLMAN ON COACHING: "I have no patience with mediocrity. I'll string along with a sophomore but after a boy has had a full year of my teaching, I want a passing grade, just like the teacher of mathematics or history. As the French say, 'By dint of great hammering one becomes a blacksmith.' You correct mistakes by pounding at them. Easygoing guys who don't demand the best from their players don't win many games."

ONE OF NAT'S BOYS REMEMBERS: "Nat had total commitment. He pushed himself as hard as he pushed his players. He based everything on merit. Whoever did the best job with the least mistakes got to play. Nat was tough and a lot of players hated him."

By the early thirties, the game was making its move and several metropolitan colleges were fielding teams good enough to challenge CCNY's supremacy. One of the best of these new teams, if the least known, was the Long Island University Blackbirds, coached by the scholarly and ambitious Clair Bee.

Clair Bee was born in West Virginia and first ventured into the New York area while pursuing a master's degree at Rutgers. During the course of his formal education, Bee accumulated four graduate degrees, including a CPA. And Clair Bee studied basketball like Branch Rickey studied baseball. Bee was credited with introducing the 1-3-1 zone defense, the 3-second rule, and, later on, suggesting the 24-second clock that would save the National Basketball Association. After Rutgers, Bee found employment at tiny Rider College in nearby Trenton, New Jersey, where he coached baseball and football as well as basketball. From 1926 to 1931 the Rider basketball team lost a total of only seven games. In his spare time, Bee wrote treatises on zone defenses and looked around for another situation more suited to his expansive genius.

Long Island University was a privately endowed school of 1,500 students, struggling to gain respectability in an industrial section of Brooklyn. Its classes convened in factory buildings, in lofts, and even in a rented hall above a bowling alley. The LIU board of directors recognized the value of sports as a builder of student morale and had already launched a football team. The squad finished its only season with a 6 and 2 record, but the sport proved too expensive to survive the Great Depression. Bee was hired by LIU in 1931 to revive the football team, coach the baseball team, and stimulate school pride. His salary for the next fifteen years would be $3,500 a year. Whatever the sport, Bee was always a tyrant at practice. "I do all the talking," he'd tell his teams. "If you want to say something, write a book and I'll read it." Bee certainly read enough himself to know where to find the players needed to pump life into LIU's athletic program.

ONE OF CLAIR'S BOYS REMEMBERS: "Breathing and winning had the same importance to Clair Bee. The day before a football game, Bee would head for a coal mining town in Pennsylvania and recruit a team to represent LIU. But all the other coaches were doing the exact same thing."

Bee was also LIU's baseball coach for several years. Two of his more celebrated protégés were Marius Russo, who later pitched for the New York Yankees, and Ken Norton, Junius Kellogg's coach at Manhattan College.

ONE OF CLAIR'S BOYS REMEMBERS: "Bee brought some shady baseball players with him from Rider. And in 1933 he had a baseball player named Barnes who wasn't even enrolled at LIU. Then there was one day in 1935 when Bee desperately needed a pitcher for a game against Princeton. Ken Norton had a sore arm and Marius Russo had pitched the day before. Bee came up with a guy named Mike DiVito, who happened to be enrolled in NYU at the time. DiVito was at NYU on a baseball scholarship but was temporarily ineligible because of low grades. DiVito pitched and won the Princeton game for the Blackbirds. Later that same season, DiVito regained his eligibility for NYU and pitched for them in a game *against* LIU. But shenanigans like this were commonplace. Most of the New York coaches came from the same neighborhoods. Some of them had relatives who came over on the same boat. It was a closed fraternity and nobody would ever think of ratting."

In 1932, when LIU's holdover basketball coach resigned to look after his business interests, Bee gladly assumed the extra job. The Blackbirds played their home games in a minuscule gym rented from the Brooklyn College of Pharmacy that seated only eight hundred. Bee's first team was 7–11 in mediocre competition, but Clair Bee knew lucky numbers when he saw them.

The following year, everything began to come together. Archie Kameros enrolled as a predental student and paid his own way. Leo Merson walked into Bee's office with an unsolicited application for a basketball scholarship. Bee had only to take pains to procure the services of his star player, Julie Bender. For years, Bender was a nonmatriculated student in LIU's night school and theoretically ineligible to play varsity ball. Clair Bee had a super team on his hands and a chance to put all of his theories to a practical test. In 1933 the Blackbirds were 27–1. LIU would win 77 of 80 ball games over the following three seasons. All of the local coaches came to see LIU play but none of them dared to schedule the Blackbirds. Nat Holman said that CCNY would never play Bee's team because of LIU's lax academic standards. Other coaches claimed that the Blackbirds' schedule was loaded with patsies.

But the game was busting out at the seams. Columbia and Fordham were the only two metropolitan universities with gymnasiums seating more than 1,200 people. No other local schools could make their varsity basketball teams pay for themselves. NYU repeatedly played to overstuffed gyms and lost $3,000 a year. Manhattan College played in the smallest, dingiest gym of them all, one that in 1977 still stands as the Jaspers' home court. Legend has it that one night in the early thirties, a boy reporter named Ned Irish tore his pants while fighting his way in through a window to cover a game in Manhattan's jam-packed gym. Irish instantly became convinced that college basketball should be made more accessible to the public. Irish wrote for the *New York World-Telegram*, and his convictions gained official support during the winter of 1931.

Jimmy Walker, the mayor of New York, asked Irish and several other sportswriters to arrange a college basketball program to raise funds for the relief of the city's unemployed. A tarpaulin was stretched on the floor, a pair of temporary baskets were wheeled in and tied down, and on December 31, 1931, a capacity house watched six New York colleges play a triple-header at Madison Square Garden. Similar shows in the subsequent two winters drew just as well. Irish quit his job at the newspaper and became the "Boy Promoter." He rented the Garden for the night of December 29, 1934, and put together another collegiate basketball attraction. A crowd of 16,188 showed up to see NYU defeat Notre Dame, 25–18, and Westminster beat St. John's, 37–33. The next season, eight college doubleheaders booked by Irish drew almost 100,000 customers. It wasn't long before Irish could guarantee a "Golden Percentage" to good collegiate teams further and further afield. The Garden became synonymous with quality, big-time, big-pressure college basketball. Every schoolboy in the country dreamed about playing there.

Ned Irish didn't cut LIU into the pie until February 1936, when he matched the upstart Blackbirds against a top-ranked team from Duquesne. Bee's club engineered a 2-point upset and LIU's check for the game was worth more than an entire season's receipts at the Brooklyn gym. In December 1936, LIU took part in one of the most famous of the Garden's early intersectional games. LIU was riding a forty-three-game winning streak but Stanford University had the great Hank Luisetti, the inventor of the daring one-handed shot. The purists watched in dismay as Luisetti's off-the-ear wizardry easily shot down the Blackbirds by 14 points.

"That's not basketball," Nat Holman pontificated. "Before I ever coach that type of game, I'll quit." The one-handed shot was too fancy and too uncontrollable. But other coaches were impressed with its accuracy and its quick release. They began to teach the new shot along with the two-hand set shot, the right-hand lay-up and the left-hand lay-up.

Clair Bee scheduled enough games in the Druggist's Den (the Brooklyn Pharmacy gym) to insure winning records for his teams (LIU would be 217 and 3 on the tiny court over the next twenty years). But Madison Square Garden became the Blackbirds' unofficial home ground.

CLAIR BEE REMEMBERS: "Now the boys were exposed to the hard, brassy atmosphere of show business. They looked around the jammed arena and all they saw was the Broadway crowd. Their own schoolmates were in the peanut gallery, temporarily out of sight and mind. They were surrounded by a sea of strange faces peering at them as though they were livestock exhibits."

Bee spent his portion of the new income on basketball scholarships, flashy equipment, a training table, road trips, and office overhead. He expanded the sports publicity staff and hired more scouts. The more LIU spent, the more they had to earn. And there was money enough for everybody. Ned Irish soon became a very wealthy and influential man. Nat Holman became a tenured full professor. Clair Bee was made assistant to the president at LIU. The game was bigger than anyone had ever expected. Bigger than life.

But there was a specter dogging each dribble. A whisper behind every missed shot.

3

He started making book in a telephone booth in the corner candy store, but nowadays he's strictly legit. He owns a half-dozen trotters. He is accorded testimonial dinners for his efforts in raising moneys for charities. He is in his early sixties but his head still sports a shock of thick black hair. The wrinkles in his face are clean and benign. "People bet for a lot of different reasons," he says. "Some of them are trying to predict and influence the future. Some of them are trying to show that they're smarter than everybody else. Gambling is the ultimate ego trip. People very rarely bet just to win money."

According to figures published by Gamblers Anonymous, one of every four adult Americans is a compulsive gambler, and 60 percent of us gamble in some form or another. Except for the gaming casinos of Las Vegas and Atlantic City, legal bets can only be made on horses, dogs, jai alai players, and bingo cards. Almost half of the five billion dollars wagered every year in the United States is bet illegally with bookmakers. Illicit gambling is just as much an American tradition as political chicanery, padding an expense account, fudging a tax return, or seeing a psychiatrist.

Sporting events have always attracted gamblers. Even the fountain of Western sports, the Greek Olympic Games, collapsed in a rubble of dumpers and fixers. In A.D. 393 the Emperor Theodosius ordered the games abandoned because many of the athletes were in league with wizards and gamesters. The corruption was so virulent that the Olympics were not revived for another 1,500 years. Most American sports followed suit and were swaddled in greenbacks and weaned in scandal.

Baseball first appeared in the New World in 1859, and

within a few short years the sport was teetering with terminal rascality. Gamblers brazenly conducted their business deals in the stands and in the dugouts. Bribed players threw ball games in the clumsiest fashion and went unpunished. Finally, some degree of control was brought to the sport when the National League was formed in 1876. A stern Victorian gentleman named William A. Hulbert was chosen to head the operation. In the second year of the National League's precarious existence, it was discovered that four Louisville players were deliberately losing games. Hulbert acted quickly and suspended the guilty parties for life. The news barely rippled the front pages, but baseball was saved.

For the next forty-three years, baseball fanatics would swear their oaths on the heads of their children and on the sanctity of the national pastime. Then in the winter of 1920, the country was shocked to hear that a Chicago gambler named Arnold Rothstein had fixed the 1919 World Series. The infamous Chicago Black Sox featured two of baseball's most talented players: "Shoeless" Joe Jackson, a bona fide .400 hitter, and Eddie Cicotte, a consistent 20-game winner. The owners were in a dither lest their golden assets turn to lead, and they scoured the country looking for a public figure of unimpeachable honesty. Seasoned observers predicted the sport's demise. But in 1921 Judge Kenesaw Mountain Landis was appointed Commissioner of Baseball and given supreme powers. The venerable Landis immediately suspended the guilty players and banned several others who were known to consort with gamblers. Landis ruled with an iron gavel, and baseball's plastic virginity was repaired and renewed. But the judge's justice was very judicious indeed. He knew enough not to throw the baby out with the dirty bath water.

ARTHUR DALEY REPORTS: "Late in 1919, the Detroit Tigers were playing the Cleveland Indians. Cleveland was assured of a second-place finish, while the Tigers were still battling for third-place money. The Indians didn't much care if they won or lost, but the Tigers were up for the game. Players on both sides bet on Detroit to win. Ty Cobb and Tris Speaker were both involved. Once the facts were known, Judge Landis exonerated everybody."

The Black Sox were washed in public and several states passed legislation making it a crime to offer bribes to athletes. The professional ballplayer was like a john caught with his pants down in a whorehouse: He faced humiliation but not criminal prosecution. Baseball players and gamblers continued to be cozy bedfellows.

WILLIAM BARRY FURLONG REPORTS: "It wasn't too many years ago when I learned that four Major League baseball players were betting against their own team and playing less than enthusiastically. It was my opinion that one of the players, in effect, confirmed this to me in a telephone call. The newspaper for which I was writing was not interested in pursuing an investigation, and the players were quickly traded to another ball club. Fix attempts are much more common than most people suspect. The sports establishment usually prefers to get rid of a problem rather than solve it and risk giving the game a bad name."

Baseball's most recent impropriety occurred in 1970 when Denny McLain, a 30-game winner for Detroit, confessed to having bet regularly on the Tigers to win. McLain was scolded and told to sit in a corner for the first half of the following season.

The history of boxing is the history of tank jobs done in tank towns. Horse racing is as straight as the clubhouse turn. Even the imported sport of ice hockey is not without a blemish. It was disclosed in 1948 that Don Gallinger of the Boston Bruins had bet on his own team. Gallinger received no bribe and the Bruins scored an upset victory, but the player was banned for life.

The first professional football teams were barnstormers who usually left town a long dropkick ahead of the sheriff.

There was also some hanky-panky connected with the 1946 championship game between the New York Giants and the Chicago Bears. As late as 1951, the *New York World-Telegram* was reporting that District Attorney Frank Hogan had evidence of a master betting ring that had been fixing pro football games for many years. The story died an unnatural death and was never heard again. And in 1963, a pair of NFL All-Stars named Alex Karras and Paul Hornung were suspended for a year for betting on their own teams.

The ex-bookie lives in a redbrick row of attached houses in Brooklyn Heights. He can almost see the Fifty-ninth Street Bridge from his window. He has been married and divorced twice. He has a married daughter and a son who is a dentist in Philadelphia. He has three grandchildren. His house is soft and worn. A schnauzer prowls the rugs.

"Back when I was working," he says, "no book in his right mind would quote a price on a pro football game. There were just too many rumors flying around. A lot of guys bet on college football but at least 80 percent of my handle was college basketball. It was the same all over the country. There's no question that the invention of the point spread was what turned basketball into such a hot attraction. It was just so easy to use. Let's say UCLA is playing a real stiff team. Before the point spread, bets on basketball games were made on straight odds just like horse racing. So UCLA might have been 2–1 or 5–2 to win. Under the new system, the weaker team is spotted a certain number of imaginary points. Let's say the spread, or the 'line,' is UCLA minus 20 points. If UCLA wins by 19 or less, all the bets against them are good. If they win by 21 or more, the UCLA money collects. If UCLA happens to win by 20, it's called a 'push' and everybody gets their money back. The point spread was the greatest discovery since the zipper."

In addition to facilitating betting, the point spread had another distinctive advantage. Under the old odds betting, the only possible fix was a loss. The point spread made it possible for players to be dumping and still win the game. Bookies always work on a commission basis. The established betting odds for all transactions was 11–10: a bettor had to wager $11 to win $10. "If I got an eleven-thousand-dollar bet on UCLA," the ex-bookie explains, "then I gotta get the same amount going the other way. If I can balance my accounts I make one buck for every ten I handle. Like clockwork. No matter who wins the game."

But the bookies were not satisfied with their vigorish and they found new ways to make more money. They instituted a procedure known as "middles betting" that was supposed to do away with the annoyance of a "push." If UCLA was favored by 20 points, the bookies would actually quote a "line" of 19–21 points. This meant that a bettor who wanted UCLA had to accept a handicap of 21 points. A bettor favoring the underdog got only 19 points. If UCLA chanced to win the game by 20 then the bookies pocketed all the bets on the table.

Up until 1960, the official point spread emanated from a group of experts known as the Minneapolis Clearinghouse, a secret if not sinister organization. The man who ran it, Leo Hirschfield, liked to boast that he belonged to the "best Jewish country club in Minneapolis," and that he habitually hobnobbed with some of the area's most respectable citizens.

"There were always rumors," the ex-bookie says, "even way back when. The bettors would suddenly come running in with fistfuls of money. Maybe they heard something from somebody's brother-in-law. But they each knew they had a sure winner. When their bets turned up bad it was easy to convince themselves that their team was in the bag. Losers have a hard time facing up to their own bad judgment. So there were always a lot of betting stampedes and a lot of stories. Some of them were even true."

From 1926 to 1930, the best college team in the East was fielded by a well-known Catholic university. During that stretch, the team compiled a winning percentage of over .900. Most of the players were Jewish graduates of the settlement houses. "Those guys never belonged in a college like that," the ex-bookie recalls. "Most of them eventually were kicked out of school because they were dumping. They hung together for a few years and then formed a barnstorming professional team."

In March 1931, Max Posnack, the captain of the St. John's team, was offered a bribe to throw a home game against Manhattan. When college basketball struck paydirt in the Garden, the rumors of scandal grew even thicker. The *New York Herald Tribune* was already sounding the alarm less than one month after Ned Irish catered the Garden's first college doubleheader: "Basketball has been adopted by those unerring feelers of the public pulse, the betting commissioners. Fifty thousand dollars, the peak of the betting to date, changed hands on the recent Temple-NYU game at the Garden."

The point spread swelled the take on college games, and it wasn't long before the mob muscled in. Betting syndicates began assigning agents to college campuses to try and sniff out any news that might influence a game or a line. Any information from a sprained ankle to a team party was useful. In the early forties, an NYU player was asked by several junior executives of Murder Incorporated to fix a game. The goons suggested broken bones and bruised relatives, and the player complied. There were occasional rumors about NYU, Manhattan, and St. John's. But there were *always* rumors about LIU.

ONE OF CLAIR'S BOYS REMEMBERS: "Clair Bee was in the merchant marines during the war, and Red Wolfe took over the LIU basketball team. Wolfe used to be a great player with the old South Philadelphia Hebrew Association, the famous SPAH's. Wolfe was also very friendly with a book in the Bronx named Mike Mansfield, who informed him one night that the Blackbirds were dumping. Wolfe gathered the team before the game and said, 'I've known most of you since you were born but if you dump I'm turning you in.' The players dumped anyway and Wolfe kept his mouth shut. What else could he have done? Have his own children arrested? All he had to do was blow the whistle and Wolfe also would have become suspect."

The situation was no secret to anybody on the collegiate athletic scene. In 1944 "Phog" Allen of Kansas warned of a coming scandal that would "stink to high heaven." But gate receipts were astronomical and jubilant alumni were funding basketball scholarships by the score. A coach's organization was moved to reprimand Allen for showing "a deplorable lack of faith in American youth and a meager confidence in the integrity of coaches." Ned Irish extended his promotions into arenas in Philadelphia and Buffalo. Irish could now offer a touring college team at least a three-date package. Basketball teams played their way across the country and back without ever seeing a campus. Irish became a vice-president in Madison Square Garden, Inc. The Garden instituted and hosted a prestigious postseason National Invitational Tournament every year.

Then early in 1945, the New York D.A.'s office was tapping the telephone of a man whom they suspected of receiving stolen goods. Quite by accident, they discovered that the supposed fence was also involved in fixing college basketball. Surveillance was stepped up and the full plot was quickly uncovered. Five members of the Brooklyn College basketball team were implicated along with several gamblers. Each player had already been paid $1,000 and promised another $2,000 if he laid down in an upcoming game against Akron. It was also learned that one of the ballplayers was not even a registered student at the school. The gamblers were arrested, the ball game was canceled, and the players were expelled in disgrace. "This involved only a local crowd," the D.A. said, but nobody believed him. The city's lawmakers amended the bribery bill to include gamblers who made bribe offers to amateur sportsmen. Betting rumors persisted, but the college game continued to grow.

World War II was drawing to a close. Business boomed in

anticipation of the end of the war. Players from Georgetown and George Washington universities were approached by gamblers. A player from the University of Colorado had a pistol held to his head and $500 stuffed into his pocket. And Nat Holman's CCNY Beavers were dumping.

In 1945 a player named Paul Schmones was the star of the City team. One of his teammates, Lenny Hassman, was a veteran dumper who realized that Schmones's cooperation was essential if business as usual was to continue. Hassman came to Schmones with an invitation to join in the fun. But Schmones took the offer straight to Nat. Holman kept the problem a secret. He cited Hassman's weak grades and impending academic probation and dropped him from the squad. Nat felt very righteous about the way he handled the situation.

"Nat was a pip," the ex-bookie says. "He was a genius and he knew it better than anybody. Good old Nat. He's eighty and still going strong. He still talks like a professor. You should call him sometime. He likes talking to writers. Nat's a very rich man these days. I understand he has extensive real estate holdings."

The ex-bookie gets up from his pillow chair and begins to make excuses. Since his retirement he spends most of his afternoons at the track. "Don't let anybody tell you anything different," he says. "America's the greatest country in the whole world."

4

The Neighborhood Development Corporation is situated on a commercially zoned side street in Orange, New Jersey. The windows are posted with anti-drug signs aimed at the kids, but the office is crowded with senior citizens seeking information about Social Security and Medicare. There is a pleasant air of humility about the community center, and everyone who steps through the front door is treated with courtesy and genuine respect. It is not the kind of place where personal tragedies can be dwelt upon. Most of the staff are volunteers and Sherman White is one of them. Sherman used to be the premier basketball player of his generation, but that was more than twenty-five years ago. Since then, his wiry, antelope body has softened. The only touches of youthful agility that have survived are the dancing steps that Sherman uses to climb the staircase to the building's second floor. Sherman weighs around 260 pounds these days, and his tiny office can barely contain him.

"Being angry used to be a big thing in my life," Sherman says. "Being bitter. But as you grow older, you learn you can't live with all that hate. You learn that hatred can destroy you. You have to get involved in something else. You have to get back to normal." Sherman answers the telephone and sets up an appointment to counsel a young man on probation. The youngster has been in trouble ever since his father died several months ago.

"I don't think a lot about the scandals anymore," Sherman says. "Once in a while I meet somebody who just wants to be vicious for no reason. He knows me or knows about me and he wants to turn the knife. I've learned that most people have a mean streak in them. People will be cruel if you give them half a chance. But I'm all finished with feeling ashamed. I've already lived through that. I'm six feet eight inches tall so I could never hide. I did something wrong but I can't carry it around on my back for the rest of my life. Point shaving had a long and distinguished history at LIU. I don't know how far back it went, but I do know we weren't the first to do it. Let's just say it was very widespread. There was one guy on our team who always said the only reason he came to LIU was to shave points and make money. Some guys were ruthless and went at it like a business. The majority of us got hooked because we wanted to belong. We just fell into it. It was like joining a fraternity. Money wasn't even the main thing. We were all too poor to really know what money was. It was the belonging. I know it sounds easy, but that's how easy it happened."

Sherman White was born in Philadelphia on December 16, 1928, and his family moved to Englewood, New Jersey, when he was two. They lived in a rambling house in the black section of town, a home filled with poverty and spirit. Sherman's father labored in an icehouse while his mother tended to the children and the hearth. Sherman's parents were humble Christians, and none of the family ever got into any kind of trouble. The kids were even well behaved in school. As a youngster, Sherman had enough character to avoid his friends' apple-stealing expeditions.

Sherman was always taller, faster, and stronger than his playmates. He was always their leader and sometimes their guide. He was generous and loyal to all his buddies, not just the good athletes.

When Sherman entered Lincoln Junior High School he was almost 6 feet tall. He had big feet, big hands, and a huge, bashful grin, but he was never a pushover. Englewood's black ghetto was rough-and-tumble. The kids who wanted to study had to fight for the privilege. Sherman was never much of a scholar, but he did understand and respect the need that some of his friends had for books and he never gave the students a bad time. He was content to spend his spare time playing basketball in the park. Fletcher Johnson was the second biggest kid in town, and Sherman would outplay him with embarrassing regularity. By the time Sherman was fifteen he was competing against players in their twenties. Sherman may have been the junior member of the game but he was also its leader. People who knew him well wondered at the promise of his youth. People who saw him play said that Sherman White was born to play basketball.

Sherman's father went to night school and studied to make himself a refrigeration engineer. He soon saved enough to buy a house. "Englewood is just across the Hudson River from New York City," Sherman says. "It might as well be a thousand miles away. It's a very small town. My childhood was healthy, loving, and secure. I was very naïve."

Sherman grew to 6 feet 5 inches and he entered Morrow High School in 1944. He earned a spot on the varsity basketball team as a sophomore and was its star performer the following season. Tom Morgan was the coach. He was quick to recognize Sherman's genius and encouraged the youngster to stretch out the boundaries of his talent. Whenever Sherman got careless or lazy, Morgan would have a tantrum and fire curses and oranges at his head. But Sherman loved Tom Morgan and would gladly have dived off a cliff after a loose ball had his coach made the suggestion. As far as Sherman was concerned, anybody even remotely linked with the game of basketball had to possess a spotless soul.

In Sherman's senior year, the team marched through an undefeated season and captured the Northeastern High School championship. Sherman established a New Jersey schoolboy record by scoring 49 points in one game. He was a unanimous selection for the All-State team. Sherman didn't hesitate to share his good fortune with his friends. He taught them all the basketball he had learned from coach Morgan. He forced Fletcher Johnson to jump rope, run sprints, and do push-ups. He showed Fletcher how to rebound. Sherman gently prodded his friend with laughter and with slogans.

"The game is the thing," Sherman would say. "When the going gets tough, the tough get going."

Sherman was a below-average student, graduating 230th in a class of 263. But he was never stupid. Sherman could quote from memory the names and statistics of the country's leading collegiate players:

Jim Smith, Defiance	24.6 ppg
Bob Brightman, Morris Harvey	24.3
George Mikan, De Paul	23.1
Tony Lavelli, Yale	21.3
Walt Dropo, Connecticut	21.0

Despite his difficulties in the classroom, each day's mail brought a parcel of scholarship bids from colleges all over the region. "Chick" Davis, the famous coach of Duquesne University, visited Sherman at school. Davis swooned over Sherman's game but he had to back off when he saw his grades. "I'm sorry," Davis said. "That's okay," said Sherman. "Maybe you can use a great rebounder instead. He's a teammate and a friend of mine." Davis stayed to take another look and offered the scholarship to Fletcher Johnson.

The Siena coach came to his home, but Sherman didn't relish the prospect of spending the next four winters so close to the Canadian border. A scout from LIU also stopped by to see Sherman's face. The scout told Sherman all about the Blackbirds' phenomenal team and dared the youngster to come to Brooklyn for a tryout.

Clair Bee had made a science of basketball and he did the same thing for recruiting. Before Bee used one of his precious scholarships, he wanted to inspect the goods as closely as possible. The LIU tryouts were held twice a year in the old Brooklyn Pharmacy gym. For most of the players, a basketball scholarship was the only way to a college education, and the competition was fierce. Along with two hundred other boys, Sherman had a number pinned to his back. With each succeeding day, Bee and his assistant, Sam Picarillo, pared the group down until there were just enough left to play a regulation game. Surviving into the finals was considered quite an achievement, and scouts from other colleges hung around the gym offering scholarships to Bee's leftovers. Clair Bee was instantly dazzled by Sherman's game.

Sherman had matured into a 6-foot-8-inch youth who demanded his place on the court. He was a brute but he could run like a deer. He would snatch a rebound and be the first man downcourt on the fast break. Sherman also had uncanny accuracy with all of his shots: a rolling hook with either hand, a one-handed push, and a modern-day jump shot. Bee's eyes nearly bounced on the floor when he saw the nineteen-year-old's poise and unselfishness, how well he passed, defensed, and moved without the ball. Bee was understandably excited. Sherman White was the first big man with the skills, the quickness, and the savvy of a guard. He was an Elgin-Baylor-and-a-half. He was a combination of Doug Collins and Rick Barry. When "Dr. J" was still wearing Doctor Dentons, Sherman White's classic game and mirror-smooth inventions helped turn the game black.

Sherman was pressed by Bee and gave a verbal commitment to enter LIU in the fall. His scholarship would include room, board, tuition, and books. As soon as he returned to Englewood, Sherman started talking to everyone he knew and he soon changed his mind. New York was too big, too dirty, and too busy. Tom Morgan was a graduate of Villanova and he suggested that the Wildcats were just the team for Sherman. Sherman wouldn't dream of saying no to his ex-coach and he enrolled in Villanova in September of 1947. Clair Bee was extremely upset.

Villanova was a Catholic school with no other blacks in attendance, and Sherman felt ill at ease. Nor did Villanova offer the physical education major that Sherman had been promised. Sherman played freshman ball and lingered at Villanova for six months. He received two D's, two C's, and an F and he withdrew from school.

Sherman wasn't back in Englewood for a week before he heard from another LIU scout. Clair Bee wanted to know if Sherman was still interested in LIU. Sherman was, and he undertook another trip into the city to speak with Bee. Sherman's appearance coincided with an LIU practice session. The Blackbirds were one of the best outfits in the area and they were on their way to a 19 and 4 season. "Do you think you can make this team?" Bee asked. "Do you think you're good enough?" Sherman jumped at the challenge and was "permitted" to scrimmage with Bee's varsity. Sherman had never competed against such accomplished players but he was easily a standout. Bee reconfirmed the scholarship offer and Sherman became a full-time student at LIU in February 1948. There were only a handful of freshman games left on the schedule, and Sherman played in them all. He soon became fast friends with Leroy Smith, the 5-foot-11-inch jump-shooting sensation of the freshman team.

Clair Bee made some very special provisions for his future star. Bee provided Sherman with a room at a nearby YMCA and tipped the janitor to make sure the gym and the pool were kept open all night. The Y became a natural gathering place for the LIU basketball clique. Their workouts were famous for quality and intensity. The Blackbirds were a seasoned, city-wise bunch. All of them were older and more sophisticated than Sherman and he was happy to take a back seat.

Eddie Gard was as solid a backcourtman as there was in the country. He was heady and shifty. Lay back on him and he'd hit the set shot. Play up on him and he'd drive to the hoop. Gard was the son of a Brooklyn doll manufacturer who learned the game in a settlement house in Williamsburg. While Gard was still in high school, he was contacted by Sam Picarillo and invited to a tryout. Gard's play was impressive, but there was a war on and he opted for the merchant marine after his graduation. Gard chanced to be stationed in Sheepshead Bay along with Lt. Commander Clair Bee. When the war was over, Gard made straight for LIU. Bee wanted him badly but Gard's high school grades were too low. The resourceful Bee induced some of LIU's loyal supporters to send Gard to a prep school so that his grades might be sufficiently inflated. Gard eventually matriculated at

LIU and became a backcourt fixture for the Blackbirds.

Eddie Gard was a stylish, gentle man and Sherman liked him right away. Sherman always felt uncomfortable in New York, and Gard seemed to know all the ropes. The two of them played special games of one-on-one at the Y gym. Sherman would be prohibited from taking Gard into the pivot but he still managed to outquick and outshoot one of the finest guards in the nation. Eddie Gard was lovable, but he was also larcenous. Once he became a member of the LIU varsity, Gard was quick to join a cabal that was fixing the Blackbirds' games. Gard orchestrated the players while Jack Goldsmith dealt with the gamblers.

Goldsmith was another habitué of the scimmmages at the YMCA. He was a veteran of the coast guard who had grown up in the crime-ridden Brownsville section of Brooklyn. Goldsmith was only 5 feet 7 inches but he could launch a deadly set shot from as far out as 45 feet. In his sophomore year, Goldsmith tallied 395 points to become the Blackbirds' leading scorer at the time. The sportswriters called him "The Brownsville Bomber." During the 1946–47 season, Goldsmith's play was brilliant but increasingly erratic. He was seen in the company of thugs and hoodlums from his old neighborhood. He was seen at the track. Goldsmith would pass up playing ball in his senior year to devote more time to his business interests.

Adolf Bigos was a sturdy ex-marine who hailed from Perth Amboy, New Jersey. Bigos had earned five battle stars during a twenty-nine month stint in the European theater and he was a murderous rebounder. Bigos's father owned a successful grocery store and the affable "Dolf" always had cash in his pockets. Other members of the 1948–49 LIU varsity included Leroy Smith, Dick Feurtado, Natie Miller, and Lou Lipman.

Sherman prepared earnestly for his first varsity season. During the summer of 1948 he went to school to make up some of the courses he had flubbed at Villanova. In the afternoons, he would get together with Picarillo and run through some of LIU's plays. Sherman was a substitute once the season finally got under way, but the more he played the better he performed. Sherman enjoyed playing for LIU and for Clair Bee. The Garden was a thrill, a dream come true. Sherman was close to home and his teammates were right guys. Sherman was taking physical education courses and even studying. Everything was going well, but there were a few things Sherman didn't quite understand. There was always a lot of money floating around the team.

DICK FEURTADO REMEMBERS: "My job was to shoot fifty foul shots a day. Once a week I'd go and pick up an envelope at the Bursar's Office. My average salary amounted to eight dollars a week. Sometimes there'd be as much as fifteen dollars in the envelope if I had a good ball game. Then I found out that most of the others were making more than me, so I went to Bee and complained. I told him that my mother was working to support me. Right after that, the school started to send my mother twenty dollars a week."

The Blackbirds practiced four hours a day and three hours on Sunday. There were lengthy road trips and innumerable hours whiled away together. A team is unique in its collective goal orientation. The team wins as a unit and loses as a unit. It is natural and almost inevitable that the younger players on a team take their behavioral clues from the veterans. As the season progressed, Sherman began to "borrow" spending money from Clair Bee. He thought it was the proper thing to do. But Sherman had no idea that his teammates were dumping ball games.

Lou Lipman was much more worldly than Sherman. Lipman was married and a veteran of the last war. But Lipman had no suspicions himself until he was approached by a teammate after a closely fought LIU win at the Garden. "If you'd made one more basket," said the relieved teammate, "you'd have gotten us all shot." Lipman was alarmed and took his aroused suspicions to another teammate. "Keep your mouth shut," Lipman was told. "Or you'll be put in a sack and dumped in the river." Lipman took his advice.

On December 4, 1948, the Blackbirds were set to play Bowling Green at the Garden. Jack Goldsmith shopped around looking to sell the doctored game to the highest bidder. Goldsmith had a reputation for always delivering and he landed a package worth almost $5,000. Goldsmith turned the deal over to Eddie Gard, who quickly lined up the old regulars. Since Lou Lipman had been playing very well lately, Gard also invited him into the pot. Lipman was frightened by the strong-arm stuff he had already heard. The whole idea repelled him and Lipman refused the offer. The Blackbirds were 3-point underdogs, which meant that they had to lose by at least 4 points for the Bowling Green bettors to win. Bowling Green roasted the Blackbirds, 97–64.

Three weeks later, Goldsmith had some more money waiting for his ex-teammates. LIU took another dive and Western Kentucky beat them 83–58 at the Garden. Clair Bee was also in the dark. A shot hits the side of the backboard, a player zigs when he should have zagged, a point spread doubles in two hours.

CLAIR BEE REMEMBERS: "A coach has to believe in his players or he might as well quit."

As the season unfolded, Lou Lipman spurned Gard on three separate occasions. Then Lipman accepted the promise of what he later said was a $300 "come-on bonus" for a game against Duquesne on New Year's Day of 1949. From the opening tip-off, the Blackbirds were woefully inept. They missed easy shots, had several passes intercepted, and generally embarrassed themselves. Only the fine play of Leroy Smith, Jack French, and Herb Scherer kept the Blackbirds competitive during the first half. The fixers defused the problem by monopolizing the ball. Duquesne trounced LIU, 64–55.

DUQUESNE (64)	G	F	P		LIU (55)	G	F	P
Skendrovich	5	3	13	Feurtado	0	1	1
Dahler	3	3	9	Bigos	0	4	4
Mohan	0	0	0	Anderson	0	0	0
Keriek	0	0	0	White	0	1	1
Cooper	7	3	17	Horne	1	2	4
Barry	2	3	7	French	4	2	10
Farrell	0	0	0	Scherer	7	0	14
Manning	5	0	10	Smith	6	4	16
Gallagher	1	0	2	Gard	0	0	0
Cypher	2	2	6	Lipman	2	0	4
				Miller	0	1	1
	25	14	64		20	15	55

With the game over, the Blackbirds gathered around Goldsmith and asked for their money. Goldsmith distributed only a fraction of the money. "Listen," Goldsmith said. "I got a line on another team that's doing business later in the week. Bradley University. I'm going to the bank against them with the points. If you want, I could take your money and bet it for you. I'll double your money. I'll triple it. You can't lose." The players agreed to go along. But Lipman didn't trust his former teammate and he checked Goldsmith's story out with one of the gamblers. Lipman was told that Goldsmith owed a lot of money around town and was simply shortchanging the team. Lipman wanted his $300 and he hounded Goldsmith for ten months until he was paid.

The LIU-Duquesne game also marked a "double fix" on the part of Dick Feurtado. Goldsmith's arrangements called for Feurtado to receive $500 for his efforts. The enterprising Feurtado also sold his services to another gambler for $1,000. Then on March 19, 1949, the Blackbirds had to hustle to beat an inferior Kansas State team by 3 points at the Garden. Goldsmith's stable shared another $5,000 after the game.

Gard, Bigos, Lipman, Miller, and Feurtado played in

galoshes and the Blackbirds' season was a dud. LIU's 19 and 12 record failed to earn a spot in either postseason tournament. Clair Bee was further embarrassed when St. John's, Manhattan, NYU, and CCNY all were chosen for the National Invitation Tournament. All the New York schools were first-round losers and the San Francisco Dons became the NIT champs. The 1948–49 season came to an end when Adolph Rupp's Kentucky Wildcats rocked Oklahoma A & M and captured the NCAA title.

Sherman White's first varsity campaign was hesitant and uneven. He played his way into the starting lineup by midyear and his improvement was rapid and exhilarating. But there were a great many ball games that confused Sherman, that he couldn't quite grasp. There were times when Sherman didn't play well. He still had a lot to learn and the magic was awkward and intermittent. Sherman did manage to average 9.1 points a game and he was named to the All-Metropolitan Second Team. Great things were expected of him.

Sherman spent the entire summer preparing for his junior year. He went back to school on his own initiative to get a head start on the courses he knew would be his most difficult. He played regularly at the YMCA. He attended supervised workouts at the Brooklyn Pharmacy gym. And whenever he could find the time, whenever his burgeoning talent needed to be tested, Sherman escaped the boiling city and headed north to the Catskill Mountains.

"Good morning, ladies and germs. My name is Buster Babich and I'm your host and social director here at Levy's By The Lake. I'll tell a few jokes, sing a few songs, and . . . Wait a minute. Wait a minute. . . . What are you looking, lady? I'm the social director, lady. I'm not your waiter. Furschtast Yiddish, lady? . . . Ha! Can my bubba make meintzer? Is the Pope a Catholic? . . . I'm your host, darling. I'm the tummler. And for you I've got some special tummling already in mind. But listen, everybody. They're already wheeling out the pastry table. Another exclusive feature of Levy's By The

Lake. So let me tell you what we have planned for today and let me get the hell out of here before I get trampled. . . . Right after breakfast, we'll have a hilarious game of Dirty Simon Sez out on the pool deck with yours truly doing the conducting. . . . At eleven o'clock, there's a shuffleboard tournament, also at the pool. There's a cha-cha lesson at noon. . . . Soon, lady. Relax. You're drooling all over your mink coat. . . . Then there's mah-jongg instruction. . . . It's almost ready, everybody. Sit down a second. . . . There's a basketball game at eight o'clock with the bellhops and the kitchen boys playing the Grossinger's All-Stars. There's also a betting pool in case anybody's interested. . . . There a Ping . . . Ladies and gentlemen! Presenting ten yards of confectionary delights! The Levy's By The Lake world famous Viennese Table is now OPEN!!! Enjoy yourselves and I'll see you later."

In the early 1930s, the owner of a Catskill resort learned that several members of the staff were college basketball players from New York. The players periodically organized their own games to stay in shape and the owner, quick to see the possibility of an added attraction, let the guests watch them play. The idea caught on and within a few years, virtually all of the area's two hundred hotels were fielding a liveried basketball team. Ballplayers from all over the country jumped at the chance to earn some extra money, have a good time, and play some very competitive ball. Some of the players applied for the jobs by letter, some simply appeared in May when the hiring was done, but most of them were placed by their coaches.

The waiters, busboys, and bellhops had the most difficult jobs and made the most money. The average salary was $40 a month, and they picked up anywhere from $500 to $1,000 in tips. There were also soft jobs available on the athletic staff: teaching tennis and swimming and organizing the guests into games of softball. The easier jobs paid only $300 a summer and there were never any tips. But the athletic staff could sleep through breakfast and they didn't have to work at all when it rained. Another resort attraction were the scads of lonely and eager young ladies whose husbands worked in the city and vacationed only on weekends. There were some resorts, however, where the ballplayers were expected to do the same amount of work as the other hired hands.

A HOTEL OWNER EXPLAINS: "Guests like to watch basketball games, but they love to eat. If the best basketball player in the world is slow with the roast beef or lets the coffee get cold, then I lose a paying customer."

Some resorts sent their teams on week-long road trips all around Sullivan County. They usually played two games a week and practiced every day. There were no actual leagues, no standings, and no winner at the end of the season. Basketball games featuring the likes of Bob Cousy, Alex Groza, and George Mikan provided wonderful entertainment for a summer's evening. The ball games also kept the guests and their money on the hotel premises. There were few social directors who dared to announce "away" games.

In addition to salaries and tips, the ballplayers had another substantial source of income. A hat would be passed around the stands and guests could pick a number for a dollar.

ONE OF NAT'S BOYS EXPLAINS: "It was a betting pool to match the total number of points scored in the ball game. The players used to split the pot with the winner and pocket an extra ten or fifteen dollars every time we played. But the fix was working even in the summertime. If the chef had number one-fifty-four, we'd make sure that was all the points we'd score. Then we'd eat like kings for a week."

In any given summer, there were perhaps five hundred varsity basketball players employed in the Catskills. In the summer of 1949, one of these players was Eddie Gard. Jack Goldsmith had moved on to bigger and better operations, leaving Gard in control of the dumping machinery. Lou Lipman and Natie Miller had graduated, but Gard could still produce himself and two other starting players, Dolf Bigos and Dick Feurtado. And Eddie Gard was ambitious. He wasn't too thrilled about having to shop around for a deal before every ball game. He was looking for something more reliable, more convenient, and less dangerous. He was looking for someone with enough money to finance a city full of corrupt teams; someone with enough imagination to try and fix every single ball game played in the Garden. Eddie Gard dreamed of having a lock on both the NIT and the NCAA championship games.

Gard was paddling around the pool one day late in the summer when he couldn't help noticing a shapely brunette in the company of a squat, middle-aged man. Gard ambled over just to say hello. He discovered that Salvatore and Jeanne Sollazzo had been married for a little more than a year. And Eddie Gard also discovered the bankroll he had been seeking.

Salvatore Sollazzo was born in Palermo, Sicily, on the last day of 1904. Papa Giochimo made and repaired jewelry. It was a nice enough living but nothing compared to the way a man could live in America. The Sollazzos made the voyage to Brooklyn when Salvatore was fifteen months old. Giochimo was a skilled craftsman and he worked out of his house on assignments received from large jewelry firms. It wasn't long before he was able to open his own store on Fulton Street in downtown Brooklyn. Giochimo trained his sons in the trade, and business boomed. A few years later, he moved into a bigger, fancier shop on the Lower East Side. Salvatore attended public school through the eighth grade and quit in 1919 to work for his father. Six years later, Salvatore married the daughter of an immigrant family and moved in with his in-laws. Salvatore found employment as the manager of a jewelry store and earned the princely sum of $55 a week. His joy was capped by the birth of a son in 1929. But the news wasn't so good the following year. At the age of fifty-seven, Papa Giochimo died suddenly in his sleep, leaving a house in Brooklyn and a business worth $30,000. Salvatore took over his father's shop and ran it into bankruptcy within a year.

Salvatore was only twenty-six years old but his future looked bleak. His hairline was rapidly receding, he argued a lot with his wife, and he was forced to start peddling jewelry from door to door to feed his family. Salvatore was always looking for an angle, an extra edge. He was promptly arrested for selling jewelry that wasn't his. But everybody was doing it, and the charge was dismissed. Salvatore's brittle marriage couldn't survive the hard times, and he moved back in with his mother.

Salvatore was a firm believer in luck and he knew that his own personal star would twinkle one sweet day. In the meantime, money was scarce and Salvatore was arrested again for a much more sinister crime. He was an unarmed lookout in an otherwise armed attempt to rob a jewelry firm on West Thirty-first Street. Salvatore faced a stiff seven-and-a-half–to–fifteen-year sentence. In between this last arrest and his trial, Salvatore was collared again for illegally selling jewelry. The latest charge was dismissed, but Salvatore received the minimum sentence for his part in the robbery. He served his time in Sing Sing.

Salvatore was a docile prisoner and earned a parole after five years. One of his brothers helped him to start all over by providing Salvatore with a job as a jewelry salesman. Salvatore was paid $15 a week plus a commission. He worked hard, sent money each week to his wife, and adhered to his parole regulations. By the beginning of 1940, Salvatore had enough capital to start his own business. He made wedding and birthstone rings and he named the company after his mother. On a lark, Salvatore also purchased a load of platinum and stored it in a warehouse in Brooklyn. Salvatore was a new man, his lesson learned and his life rehabilitated. Salvatore's number came in three years later when platinum was unexpectedly declared a Scarce War Material. He was suddenly a wealthy man and he lost no time in starting another company. It wasn't long before Salvatore was the country's fourth largest maker of wedding rings. He employed over eighty people and did a gross business of $1.5 million a year. But

Salvatore was still looking for an angle. He set up a complicated system of phony names, forged checks, and fictitious accounts and, from 1943 to 1947, withheld over $500,000 in taxes.

Salvatore's parole expired in December 1947 and he partied for a week in celebration. The heat was off and the wraps were off. He was strictly on the up-and-up and he set out to have a good time.

SALVATORE SOLLAZZO REMEMBERS: "I was the biggest sucker to hit Broadway in years."

He began to frequent nightclubs dressed in spiffy, custom-made suits. He got an out-of-state divorce. He bought season tickets at Yankee Stadium and the Polo Grounds. He had ringside seats for the fights at the Garden and clubhouse badges for Belmont, Jamaica, and Aqueduct. Salvatore became familiar with racketeers and touts and he gambled recklessly, often betting as much as $5,000 on a horse race or a baseball game. Salvatore was poorly informed and he bet mostly on blind impulse. He was also very gullible, and his bookies could steer him on to any sure loser he didn't pick himself. The Garden State racetrack in New Jersey was one of Salvatore's favorite haunts, and whenever he made the trip he always stopped at the Embassy nightclub in nearby Philadelphia. It was at the Embassy that he met an attractive chorus girl named Jeanne. She part-timed as a photographer's model and she was tall, dark-haired, and gorgeous. Jeanne and Salvatore were married on July 1, 1948; she was twenty-three years old and he was forty-four. The newlyweds moved into a plush apartment on Central Park West where the rent was $450 a month.

Salvatore was riding a winning streak all over town, but he could shoot nothing but snake eyes with his bookie's dice. As the owner of a ring-making business, Salvatore was entitled to 165 ounces of gold a day. Each morning, Salvatore called up a jobber to find the latest price for gold on the European black market. Then he sent an errand boy to collect his ration at a federal refinery and deliver it to the jobber. Salvatore spent an hour or two scrambling his books before he'd leave the office to attend a ball game or the races. The smuggling operation defrayed his gambling losses but Salvatore wasn't entirely satisfied. If he couldn't find himself another angle, he was now rich enough to make one.

Gard and Sollazzo had plenty to discuss. Gard was invited to visit the Sollazzos' apartment late in the summer. The two of them talked about various possibilities but were unable to come up with any definite arrangements. They were both interested in infiltrating other teams besides the Blackbirds. Gard stayed in touch with Sollazzo and continued offering his wares on the streets.

LIU opened the 1949–50 season by blowing past Virginia Tech by 20 points, Texas A & M by 14, and the University of Puerto Rico by 35. None of these games was attractive enough for Gard to sell. But on December 8, 1949, the Blackbirds were scheduled to play Kansas State University at the Garden. Even though Dolf Bigos was out with an injury, Gard found a buyer. LIU was highly favored and they led 31–25 at the half. With the game drawing to a close and the Blackbirds clinging to a 2-point lead, Gard personally took the situation in hand. Gard was normally a tenacious defender, but, within a span of less than four minutes, he allowed KSU's Ernie Barrett to score 10 consecutive points. Barrett's outburst decided the ball game and LIU went on to lose by 58 to 51. Gard and Dick Feurtado shared 9 points and $2,000. The Blackbirds rushed through their next nine ball games, beating San Francisco, the incumbent NIT champs, and a tough Bowling Green squad.

Sherman White soon emerged as LIU's latest dreadnought. Sherman averaged over 20 points a game and was nationally ranked in field-goal percentage. LIU was still a selfish ball club and not the perfect complement to Sherman's game, but the big man was there when he was needed. Leroy Smith also turned into a scoring machine and the sportswrit-

ers began to give serious consideration to the Blackbirds'
chances of winning a postseason tournament. Sherman had a
63-point performance against a solid John Marshall University team and was being touted for All-American honors.

Gard continued conferring with Sollazzo. They concluded several deals involving other local teams, yet it wasn't
until January 1950 that they reached an agreement for an LIU
game. The final terms were ratified in a room at the King
Edward Hotel on West Forty-fourth Street with Bigos, Gard,
and Sollazzo in attendance. The first LIU game that Sollazzo
bought was played against North Carolina State at the Garden on January 17, 1950. The Blackbirds were the favorites
but State won, 55–52. Sollazzo won $6,000 betting with his
bookie and, minus the payoffs, he showed a net profit of
$3,000.

It was during the North Carolina State game that Sherman
White finally became suspicious. There were just too many
mistakes and too many short circuits. Sherman cornered
Bigos, Feurtado, and Gard in the locker room and bitterly
reproached them for their haphazard play. The three players
denied Sherman's charges. "We're doing the best we can,"
they said. "Why don't you leave us alone?" Sherman was
afraid his teammates might think he had a swelled head so he
let the matter drop. He hoped he hadn't offended them. But
Sherman's teammates were thrown into a tizzy, and Gard
called for a meeting with Sollazzo. They met in the gambler's
apartment. It was Gard's opinion that the entire operation
would be jeopardized unless Sherman was cut in. "He's
getting too good," Gard added. "If Sherman's not with us, he
can turn a game around all by himself." Sollazzo agreed, and
Gard was dispatched to invite Sherman to a dinner party.

After practice a few days later, Gard took Sherman aside
and candidly revealed the full particulars of the Blackbirds'
coterie of dumpers. "Why don't you come on in with us?"
Gard suggested. "It's a wonderful chance for you to make
some money. You want good clothes, don't you? You got a
girl and you want to marry her, right? Don't be a sucker.
Everybody else is making money out of this thing. Why not

you? Nobody's asking you to deliberately lose a ball game. Come on. Everybody's doing it. Everybody's always been doing it." Gard went on and on, telling Sherman of all the wonderful things he'd be able to buy. "It's easy, Sherman. Would I give you a bum steer?" It sounded good and Sherman agreed to meet the boss, the man Gard called "the big cheese."

The park was right across the street. There was an awning to keep the rain off the sidewalk and a smiling doorman in a uniform. Sherman was impressed. "Good evening, Mr. Logan," the doorman said. Sherman followed Gard into the elevator. "Who's Mr. Logan?" Sherman asked. "It's me," Gard said. "It's an alias." A black maid greeted them at the door and ushered them into the apartment. She also called Gard "Mr. Logan." Sherman couldn't look her in the eyes. Sollazzo appeared in a monogrammed smoking jacket.

"Come in, Sherman," he said, and they shook hands. "I'd like you to meet my wife."

Jeanne was wearing a seductive dress. Sherman was very impressed. Mr. Sollazzo was obviously a rich and important man. All throughout dinner, Sherman couldn't help being flattered by the gambler's fawning attentions. The meal was sumptuous and exotic, but Sollazzo's sales pitch was pretty much the same as Gard's.

"You don't have to lose," Sollazzo said. "All you have to do is shave the points. It's easy enough and I'll give you a thousand dollars a game. In cash. Everybody's doing it." Sherman let himself be persuaded. No specific games were mentioned that evening and Sherman was simply instructed to keep in touch with Gard.

The Blackbirds rolled over their next five opponents before losing a close decision to Duquesne. The Duquesne game marked LIU's only honest loss of the entire season. It was while the Blackbirds were practicing for their very next ball game that Gard gave everybody the word that the fix was in.

"Cincinnati at the Garden," Gard said. "We can't win by more than seven."

Sherman was nervous. He didn't know how to go about shaving points. But Gard just laughed and told Sherman to keep an eye on the scoreboard. The Blackbirds were putrid against Cincinnati. They were so worried about getting too far ahead that they lost all control and got destroyed, 83–65. After the game, Sollazzo tried to do some shaving of his own. He contended that the score was so lopsided the Blackbirds really didn't earn their money. But Gard insisted, and Sollazzo eventually coughed up the rest of the money. The day after the game, Gard met Sherman in the school cafeteria and handed him $1,000 in cash. Sherman ran back to his room at the Y, tucked the money in an envelope, and taped it to the back of a dresser drawer.

LIU clobbered its last two opponents and finished the regular season with a record of 19 and 4. It was no surprise to anyone when the Blackbirds were selected to play in the NIT. LIU's first-round opponent was a lowly regarded Syracuse team, but, once again, Eddie Gard gave his teammates the magic money word. LIU was bombed by Syracuse, 80–52, and their season came crashing to a close.

It wasn't two weeks after the Blackbirds committed hara-kiri that Nat Holman's Beavers chewed themselves into the history books.

The College of the City of New York was a
subway school in the middle of Harlem. It had
no dormitories, no rolling meadows, and no tuition. The
cement campus was sliced by several busy city streets, and
there were cockroaches in every building. In the late 1940s,
CCNY was nothing less than the world's third largest university and it had a reputation to match. A City College grad
could get a job anywhere in New York.

CCNY's 34,000 students were mostly of immigrant stock:
the children of peddlers and servants, of washerwomen and
pants pressers, of garment workers and streetcar conductors.
They were the grandchildren of peasants and slaves. For
most of the students, CCNY reflected the glory of a country
that provided a no-cost, guaranteed future solely on the basis
of merit. Each student needed a high school average of
eighty-one to get into City College and a ravenous intellect to
stay there. They screamed at each other in graffiti:

COMMUNISM WILL SAVE THE WORLD

VEGETARIANS ARE FRUITS

SOCIALISTS EAT SHIT

GUNS FOR THE ARABS, SNEAKERS FOR THE JEWS

They were the activists, the freethinkers, the artists, the
scholars, the engineers, the social workers, and the rabble of
their generation. But they were also basketball freaks. The
CCNY faculty traditionally included Nobel prize winners
and famous professional geniuses, yet Nat's boys were the
darlings of the campus.

Whenever the Beavers played at home, the students

would pack the matchbox Wingate Gymnasium and bellow their famous cheer until the visiting team's basket began to shake:

> "Allegaroo   garoo   gaRAH!
> Allegaroo   garoo   gaRAH!
> Eee-YAH!   Eee-YAH!
> SIS!   BOOM!   BAH!"

Should a call go against their beloved Beavers, the students would point at the unfortunate official and chant, "Evil! Evil! Evil!" Not that Nat's boys needed the extra help.

The trademarks of a City College basketball team were discipline, courage, persistence, and unquestioning obedience. When Nat blew his whistle during a scrimmage, the terrified players would freeze while they waited for the wrath to descend on whoever was out of sync. Nat pushed his players to their limits. He taught them, he bullied them, and occasionally he played the harpy. But he let them share his dream. Together they would seek the perfect play, the faultless ball game.

ONE OF NAT'S BOYS REMEMBERS: "There was no satisfying Nat. He undermined our confidence by riding us for all our mistakes. He never gave us any credit when we played well. He cursed us. He screamed. He scapegoated like crazy. He didn't even know our names. Some of the guys hated the air he breathed."

ANOTHER ONE OF NAT'S BOYS REMEMBERS: "Nat was a great coach. Maybe even the greatest. Basketball is the kind of sport that demands great personal sacrifice and some of the players just couldn't reach down as far as Nat could. Nat never pushed us any harder than he pushed himself. All of his teachings were moral. I know a lot of guys hated him, but it's the easiest thing in the world to criticize a man's personality."

Nat's boys were the team to beat in New York throughout the 1930s. From 1931 to 1934 the Beavers lost a grand total of one game. Nat's genius was unquestioned, and his grand style was proverbial. He often introduced himself as "the great Nat Holman." Nat was constantly outvoted at coaches' conventions, even when his suggestions were eminently sound. His colleagues jested that the one sure way to have a proposal defeated was to have Nat espouse it. But Nat couldn't care less what his Lilliputian contemporaries mumbled about him behind his back.

The Beavers reached another peak just before the war when both the '40–'41 and '41–'42 squads qualified for the NIT. The best either team could manage was a third-place finish. Somebody noticed that CCNY had never won a post-season championship. Nat's critics suddenly came pouring out of the woodwork claiming he couldn't win a big ball game. Then the war brought the draft, and everybody shivered for the duration. Nat didn't have another winning season until '45–'46, but by then the roost was getting crowded. There were other teams and other coaches sharing the spotlight. LIU, NYU, and St. John's passed out expensive basketball scholarships like they were cigars. Clair Bee, Howard Cann, and Frank McGuire began to be quoted in the newspapers almost as much as Nat. Rules were bent and envelopes were stuffed with money. Only Nat Holman remained chaste.

At CCNY there never was any such thing as an athletic scholarship. Every ballplayer had to meet and maintain the same stringent academic standards as the rest of the students. Nat's boys were paid a buck a game for meal money. They were treated to orange halves at halftime. And they nodded over their books on the A train just like their classmates. It was little wonder that New York's top schoolboy talent began to shun CCNY. They could get their fill of money, women, leisure time, and Mickey Mouse courses at a hundred other universities. "Basketball bums," Nat sneered. "Who needs them?" To be sure, there were those who did come to City College to learn the game from the Master. But many of them didn't have much choice. Howard Cann was effectively prohibited from recruiting blacks because NYU was the Garden's host team for the lucrative dates with the lily-white likes of Kentucky, Georgia, and Duke.

Other schools had other reasons, but it was a tradition at CCNY that the basketball team was always open to blacks. Sonny Jameson and Joe Galiber had even been named captain. LIU was the only other school in the area that made a habit of seeking black ballplayers. Other minorities were also excluded. St. John's was reluctant to extend basketball scholarships to Jews once Hy Gotkin and Harry Boykoff graduated. Fordham and St. Francis were Catholic schools playing predominantly small-time schedules, and the entrance requirements at Columbia were even more forbidding than those at CCNY. It was no accident that the overwhelming majority of Nat's boys were either Jews or blacks.

If a ballplayer had the grades, City College wasn't all that bad a second choice. CCNY was an interesting place to be. It was also a community and it took care of its own. An athlete's education was well protected at CCNY. If he chanced to come up lame sometime in his varsity career, there was no scholarship for an unscrupulous coach to rescind. By the same token, an athlete had similar insurance should he decide to quit playing for whatever reason. In addition the Beavers played in the Garden as much as any other school and both Sonny Hirshberg and Red Holzman had graduated into the NBA. Nat also liked to boast about the five members of his '41–'42 team who had gone on to be doctors.

When the war ended, the Beavers' roster was saturated with returning GI's. Nat insisted on the same blind obedience from them as he did from green-eared freshmen. The '45–'46 team was 14 and 4. Some of the veterans agonized under Nat's verbal lashings. They threatened mutiny more than once. Nat's boys were 16 and 6 in the '46–'47 season. The players and the coach locked horns in public. There were disagreements on the bench. The war-worn players wanted to have fun playing basketball. They wanted to run free and uncontrolled, not along Nat Holman's dotted lines. And Nat was man enough to sniff the wind. "What the heck," he said. "Sooner or later, you've got to go along with the times and give the game back to the boys." The '47–'48 Beavers suddenly had an 18 and 3 campaign. They qualified for the Olympic playoffs and the NIT, but were an early loser in both tournaments. Help was on the way. Nat's once and future "Cinderella Team" was being put together by Sam Winograd and Bobby Sand.

Sam Winograd was a star on CCNY's outstanding '33–'34 squad. Concurrent with his varsity career, Winograd moonlighted as a professional for $20 a game. He graduated from City, earned a law degree from NYU, and joined the CCNY faculty in 1945. Winograd coached baseball and worked in the evening sessions office. Four years later, he was the athletic director. Sam Winograd's hands were always clean but he was well acquainted with the underside of sports. Winograd spent his summers at Young's Gap Hotel in Parksville, New York, where he not only ran the betting pool but distributed the winnings. It was alleged that Winograd had intimate connections with a certain strong-arm man who worked for a loan shark; and with a successful Philadelphia bookmaker. One of Winograd's delegated duties as athletic director was to oversee the purchasing of all the department's sporting goods. Orders of that size were usually put out for competitive bids and were ultimately transacted with at least a 40 percent discount. Winograd bought all of the department's merchandise at Circle Equipment, a firm owned by a friend and neighbor of his. CCNY always paid the full list price. Winograd never accepted a penny from his friend, but every so often he would be presented with a golf bag or a new set of clubs.

ONE OF NAT'S BOYS REMEMBERS: "Sam Winograd was nobody's fool. He told us to stay away from the LIU players. He was forever warning us about gamblers. He made an issue out of it."

Bobby Sand played for City College from 1936 to 1938. He wasn't blessed with an abundance of talent, but he always hustled and followed Nat's orders to the letter. By the time Sand was a senior, he was coaching the third team. Sand was a brilliant student, a Phi Beta Kappa. He was quiet, efficient, and unobtrusive. He was invited to become the Master's apprentice. By 1945 Sand was Nat's entire staff. Sand coached the freshman team, handled the bulk of the recruiting, scouted future opponents, and did all of the paperwork. Sand's wife had a chronic heart ailment and his daughter had tuberculosis. They both spent most of the winter in Florida, leaving Sand with a lot of free time during the basketball season.

CCNY's gym would be made available to high school teams during vacation periods when the city's public schools were closed. Sand would often arrange for two schools to scrimmage each other, and the coaches were grateful for the extra practice time. Sand was there to observe the workouts and to open the pool once the scrimmages were over. Sand got to know all the players and to introduce them to the wonders of CCNY. Bobby Sand was always there. He was the first and most intimate contact with any aspiring City College hoopster. First Sand convinced the player and then he convinced his parents. Sand filed the admission papers. He counseled the players and suggested the proper courses. He coached them as freshmen and gently prepared them for Nat.

Everybody loved Bobby Sand. He was a little gremlin of a man whose round face was always twinkling with good humor. His smile shone a light on his soul, and his intellect was just as scintillating. Sand was perpetually devising new and better offenses for the Beavers. His views on a variety of basketball complexities were sought by such prestigious journals as *Scholastic Coach* and *Sport Magazine*. But Sand was pinned beneath Nat's throne. Nat steadfastly refused to let Sand write anything for publication. "I'm the big shot here," Nat would say. "Lou Little at Columbia doesn't let his staff write articles, so why should I?"

But Nat Holman was never totally sufficient. He was a notoriously bad bench coach. Nat would fume and linger over a player's mistake until he often lost sight of the ball game. It was Sand who made most of the substitutions. Whenever Sand's maneuverings failed to salvage a ball game, Nat felt free to curse him out in front of the team. Yet Sand spurned attractive offers to become the head coach at a variety of fancy universities. Sand was the whipping boy and the infantry, but he was also the heir apparent.

ONE OF NAT'S BOYS REMEMBERS: "You had to like Bobby. He was a mother hen to us. But he owed his first allegiance to Holman. Bobby followed Nat blindly. Bobby was kind and loving, but he made decisions for people and sometimes he damaged them."

The official apparatus for luring athletes into CCNY was the Student Athletic Guidance Council (SAG). It had been set up in 1945 and refined a year later by Winograd. SAG was totally financed through the Athletic Department's budget. The payroll list included three of New York's finest high school coaches: Dave Tobey of Clinton High School in the Bronx, Bill Speigel of Franklin High School in Manhattan, and Max Hodesblatt of Jefferson High School in Brooklyn. "Remember your alma mater," was the call to arms. CCNY grads all over the city scouted the bushes, canvassed other coaches, and submitted written recommendations to Winograd. Even the school yards and the YMCA's were covered. SAG also secured certain administrative channels to facilitate "unusual" registration matters.

But the teams were never quite good enough. Nat Holman would never retire without at least one collegiate championship. A great CCNY team would also mean a promotion for Winograd. A hundred eyes sifted games and practice sessions. A thousand questions were asked. LIU's tryouts were scrutinized. And SAG came up with four of the finest basketball prospects in the country: Floyd Layne, Ed Warner, Alvin Roth, and Ed Roman.

When "Clyde" Frazier was interested only in intercepting cookies, the fastest hands in captivity belonged to Floyd Layne. Floyd was 6 feet 4 inches and 170 pounds. His body was lithe and defiant, and his taut cheekbones bespoke his Caribbean ancestry. Floyd moved sinuously and flawlessly up and down a basketball court—popping a set shot, knifing a pass to a cutting teammate, holding fast the reins of the team's offense. Floyd played with no wasted motion, with a quiet brilliance, and with great dignity.

Floyd was born in Brooklyn and was moved to the Bronx as an eight-year-old when his father left home. His mother remarried when Floyd was twelve. The emotional turmoil unsettled Floyd and kept him in constant trouble in school. But his mother was a strong-willed woman and she insisted that he be held accountable for his whereabouts and his doings. Floyd finally calmed down when he reached junior high school—when he learned how to play basketball. Floyd discovered he had the body and the heart of an athlete, and the game quickly became a religion.

He went on to attend Clinton High School where he met his buddy Ed Warner. Floyd later transferred to Franklin High School, but the two friends played on the same team in the Harlem YMCA. At Franklin, Floyd became an All-City performer in his senior year. The scholarship offers came fast and furious, and the rhinestone wheel began to spin. Even though his high school average was a mere 70.5, Floyd always wanted to play basketball for CCNY. Two of his friends, Sonny Jameson and Joe Galiber, were already there. His coach at Franklin, Bill Spiegel, was one of Nat's boys.

"I wanted CCNY," Floyd said, "because of the sound curriculum, the educational standards, and coach Nat Holman." Floyd was scouted by Sand and told that CCNY "would wink its eye at the academic standings of the basketball players." Floyd was enrolled as a "special student" in a night course during the summer of 1948. His scholastic showing was deemed good enough to warrant his admission as a matriculated student in September 1948.

When Earl Monroe was nothing but a grain of sand, Ed Warner was rolling, juking, triple-pumping, and shooting bank shots from all over the court. Warner was 6 feet 3½ inches and a hard 190 pounds. He was neither a great leaper nor a great shooter but he used his body well and he thought like a passer.

Warner's mother died of pneumonia when he was five, and his father was killed in an accident not long afterward. Ed was reared by a succession of aunts, great-aunts, and grandparents. He sang in the choir at St. Phillip's church and he called his elders "sir" and "ma'am." But Ed Warner was an orphan in the hard-time streets of Harlem. He was always serious and somber beyond his years. While in junior high school, Ed was considered "mentally dull" and his reading scores were more than two years behind his peers. He managed nevertheless to gain admittance into one of New York's most highly respected academic institutions, De Witt Clinton High School. His coach was Nat April, one of Nat's boys. Ed was an All-City center as a junior and an All-American as a senior. He was inspected by the ubiquitous Bobby Sand, who seconded everything his coach told him about CCNY and about Nat Holman. Sand also dangled the prospect of CCNY's being the team to represent America in the 1952 Olympics.

Ed Warner hesitated. He had graduated with an average of just over seventy-one and he was 827th in a class of 942. But CCNY was right in the neighborhood, and his pal Floyd was planning to go there. Ed consented and Sand had him register as another "special student." Ed's fees were paid by a mysterious loan from a mysterious student fund. In September 1948, Ed Warner also became a Beaver in good standing.

When Ernie DiGregorio was still throwing behind-the-back passes to his teddy bear, the best-passing chubbo in the game was Alvin "Fats" Roth. Al was 6 feet 4 inches and a puffy 210 pounds. He couldn't shoot and he couldn't run, but he was steady, heady, and a pinpoint passer.

Al had been brought up in a strictly kosher home. His father earned an honest subsistence by driving a soda truck. Al was a private young man and he always preferred listening to talking. Al attended Erasmus Hall High School in Brooklyn and in the spring of 1948 he led the team to a city championship. The seventeen-year-old was suddenly bedazzled with dozens of scholarship offers. He had his heart set on an out-of-town school, but, in immigrant families, sons didn't leave home until they were married. Al quickly narrowed his choices down to NYU and CCNY. Bobby Sand was around and about, warmly extolling Nat and the virtues. A student with a high school average of 75 could qualify for CCNY by acing a brain-boiling entrance examination, but Al's grades came out to only 70.4. And if Al had to stay in New York, he could at least go to a school that had a greenly growing campus. Al chose NYU. He went so far as to pay his fees and pick up his registration card.

But Sand never gave up; he simply shifted into overdrive. Al didn't know which way to fall. Nor was there any chance his parents could ever understand his predicament. Al was cast to his own resources. Sand was always there, giving off such good vibes. . . . CCNY started classes a week earlier than NYU, so Al changed his mind and tried for City. His records were altered and his high school average boosted to 75.5. Al scored an 89 on the entrance test and gained acceptance into CCNY in September 1948.

ONE OF NAT'S BOYS EXPLAINS: "Forging transcripts was a widely accepted practice at City. It wasn't done only for the basketball players. If a teacher had a niece or a nephew who couldn't get into City because of low grades, he could always find somebody to do him a favor. It was no big deal. Everybody was doing it. When the Board of Higher Education investigated the matter several years later, they had to shove the whole thing under a rug. The official word was that there were too many people involved for them to determine exactly who did the forgery. All I know is that Nat had nothing to do with it. Nat would never sully his morals by concerning himself with such mundane matters. All Nat wanted was ballplayers. He didn't care how he got them."

When Wes Unseld was destroying a piece of furniture a week, the most devastating picks in the game were being set by Ed Roman. Ed was 6 feet 6 inches and 240 pounds. He was broad-beamed and thin-shouldered, and even as a kid he was always bumping into things. Because of his shape, Ed answered to "The Goose." But he was a powerful student and incredibly quick to master anything that attracted his intellect. He loved to read and spend most of his time by himself. Ed's dream was to become a research scientist.

Ed was a latecomer to athletics. He wasn't introduced to basketball until the coach at Taft High School spotted him ambling through the hallways in his sophomore year. Ed was large and self-conscious, and it was explained that basketball would do wonders for him. Taft's star player was Irwin Dambrot, a great jump shooter and scorer. During Ed's sophomore year, he was a full-time scrub, but he studied the game and practiced nine hours a day. Dambrot broke his wrist the following season, and Ed was led out of the laboratory and into the center-jump circle. Ed responded by breaking all of Dambrot's scoring records. Ed showed a pair of dancer's feet and an uncanny one-hand shot that he flicked right off the top of his forehead. He was All-City in his junior year and All-American as a senior.

Everybody was after Ed. Even St. John's was willing to open up its pearly gates for him. But Ed decided to accept a package deal from the University of Cincinnati that included equal provisions for his brother. Each of the Roman boys received tuition, board, a job, $50 a month for expenses, and the use of a car. They attended classes at Cincinnati for two days before the omnipresent Bobby Sand appeared. City's dream team desperately needed a good big man, and Ed Roman was the best around. Sand brought another pitch with him. He promised admission to City for Ed's brother and a job for his father. "You have a better average than I did when I entered City," Sand added. "I made Phi Beta Kappa and you can too. If you do I'll promise you this: I will personally buy your PBK key for you." Ed was impressed. When he told the Cincinnati people the bad news, they raised the ante in an effort to keep him there. But in September 1948, Ed Roman enrolled at CCNY.

Bobby Sand guided the '48–'49 freshman team to an 11–3 record. He psyched them, he hosed them, and he gave them what he thought they needed. Sand pushed Warner, he encouraged Layne, he tried getting next to Roth, and he sympathized with Roman. Sand had them for only a year so he constantly clucked over them. He shielded them from Nat's withering ego while at the same time he conditioned them to Nat's patterns, drills, and demanding expectations. The freshmen stretched out comfortably under Sand's gentle prodding. They played none of their games in the Garden and were free to have a good time. But if the frosh had fun playing ball, the '48–'49 varsity season was fraught with tension. Nat had given the game back to the boys but he held on to the whistle.

The highlight of the varsity season was supposed to be a glorious West Coast swing that the team took around mid-season. The Beavers started off in fine fashion by defeating a previously unbeaten Stanford team. Nat was so overjoyed that he promised his boys a night on the town once they reached San Francisco. But then the Beavers suffered an unexpected loss to the University of San Francisco, and all vows were canceled. "Give them a buck apiece," Nat fumed. "Tell them to get a malted and a sandwich and go to bed." A few days later, Nat was given a dinner in Los Angeles. Several noteworthy CCNY grads showed up to pay him homage. Eddie Cantor entertained them and Nat made an appropriately humble speech. But the team sat sullenly through the standing ovation, staring at their plates and picking at their food.

There was also another thread of concern that nearly unraveled the varsity season: several of the ballplayers were in league with gamblers, and the bookies knew their every move. One night the varsity was playing in Buffalo. Their pregame meal happened to include some tainted barley soup and all of them wound up with dysentery. Within an hour the news was flashing through the streets of New York. The point spread plummeted and there were fix rumors.

ONE OF NAT'S BOYS REMEMBERS: "We were all chugalugging Kaopectate. The only one who escaped was Nat, because he never ate with the team. When the game started, we were afraid to spread our legs for fear we'd shit in our pants. Don't ask me how, but we won the game by a bundle."

The Beavers had a very close shave later in the season in a game played against Syracuse in the Garden. The district attorney got a tip about the game and there were droves of detectives at courtside. Their obvious mission was to ask questions in the locker room after the game was bagged. The players were afraid of the law but they were terrified of the mob, so they went ahead and bent the score. But late in the game, an unsuspecting substitute scored 10 straight points to lift the Beavers up over the point spread. Doomsday was miraculously averted. The fixers showed innocent palms to the gamblers, and the detectives suddenly had no questions to ask. The benchwarmer, however, was immediately asked by his teammates if he wanted to be put on the payroll. The Beavers finished the season with a mark of 17 and 8.

By the spring of 1949, Al Roth had seen enough and attempted to escape. Al asked Howard Cann if NYU was still interested in tendering a scholarship. Cann was glad to oblige. "All we need," the coach said, "are the transcripts covering your course work at City." When Al arrived at the

CCNY registrar's office, he discovered that his records had disappeared. Al was summoned to a meeting with Nat and Winograd. Nat smiled and made sweet overtures. Al was assured that he was being counted on to do great things. He was reminded that CCNY graduates always got superior job opportunities. Al Roth was eighteen. He wasn't strong enough to resist the pressure and he promised to stay put. "Good," Nat said. "You won't regret it." Then Nat and Winograd vacated the city for the summer, leaving several minor tasks for Bobby Sand to handle.

Ed Roman had to be made to see that laboratory courses conflicted with basketball practice. Sand had little trouble. Then Ed Warner needed a summer job. Sand couldn't get Warner a cushy resort job but he landed him a spot in the garment district. It was hard work but it counted as a big favor.

The summer was a hot one in New York. The Dodgers lost another World Series to the Yankees. There was a water shortage and a polio epidemic.

In the fall of 1949, the wondrous City freshman became sophomores, and their protective umbrella fell away. They were introduced to their new varsity teammates, to Nat Holman, and to the Garden. There was no longer any room in their lives for fun.

Norm Mager was the oldest of the '49–'50 Beavers. He was 6 feet 5 inches and a bony 160 pounds. He had been pilfered by Bobby Sand from the LIU meat market. Mager was too frail to be anything more than a shooter, but he was a great one. He was the Beavers' sixth man, the one who came off the bench and made the offense explode. Every player on the team had a carefully defined role, and Mager was the Zone Buster. Mager was also the Beavers' contact with one Eli Kaye (né Klukofsky), a front man for the mob.

ONE OF NAT'S BOYS REMEMBERS: "Norm was Nat's scapegoat that year and he hated Nat with a passion. Norm wanted to provoke Nat into a fistfight. Norm would have dumped for nothing."

Another varsity holdover was Irwin Dambrot, a co-captain, a senior, and a starting forward. Dambrot was 6 feet 5 inches and 175 pounds. Whether he was playing basketball or just talking, Dambrot was fired with enthusiastic persistence. His teammates called him "The Kid," until he got married and became "The Man."

The other co-captain, Joe Galiber, was the incumbent varsity center. Galiber was 6 feet 4½ inches and 180 pounds, a hustler and a constant man in motion. But Galiber had a bad back that prevented him from setting picks and screens. Dambrot needed a pick for his shot, and Ed Warner could get a step on anybody with a brush screen. Before the season began, Ed Roman replaced Galiber in the Beavers' starting lineup. Ed Warner was penciled into a starting spot at forward, Al Roth became a fixture at one guard, and Floyd Layne was eased into the other backcourt position.

The other members of the team were

Herb Cohen	5 feet 11½ inches	150 pounds
Mike Witlin	5 feet 11 inches	165 pounds
Whitey Levey	6 feet 3 inches	185 pounds
Arnold Smith	6 feet 2 inches	165 pounds
Ron Nadell	6 feet 0 inches	175 pounds
Artie Glass	6 feet 1 inch	180 pounds
Leroy Watkins	6 feet 7 inches	200 pounds
Ed Chenetz	6 feet 4 inches	220 pounds
Larry Meyer	5 feet 8 inches	155 pounds

The team rehearsed for six weeks before the season opened. Nat's practice sessions were models of efficiency and seriousness. They began at 4:00 sharp, and for the next three hours every minute was accounted for. Nat retained his belief in drilling and redrilling his team. He hopped on every mistake. The players spent most of their time standing around listening to Nat's corrections, and cringing. Going to practice was like going to the dentist. Nat used only the first ten men in practice; the third team was forced to learn by osmosis. As much as some of the ballplayers detested Nat, they were still young men living in a chimerical environment that tended to stifle their emotional growth. Some of them desperately needed a behavioral model. Several players tried to emulate Nat's style of dress; some of them loved him. But Nat remained aloof and unconcerned. He called Floyd Layne "Eddie," and Ed Roman "Big Boy."

ONE OF NAT'S BOYS REMEMBERS: "Nat was a narcissistic bastard. As a person, he typified everything that was

wrong with big-time college basketball. He was very de-
structive to the sense of community that existed at City
College. He had no business being there."

Twice a week, Nat would leave practice at six o'clock to
look after his "social commitments," and Sand would take
over. The assistant coach tried hard to loosen up the time.
Sand laid down his whistle and let all of them play. The sophs
always murdered the lettermen, so there was never any hos-
tility generated among the players.

The Beavers inaugurated the '49–'50 season by annihilating
Queens College by 46 points and Lafayette by 32. After only
two games, the sportswriters were heralding the team as one
of the best in the country. They made their share of sophomore mistakes, but they were brilliant. The Beavers ran their
share of set plays, yet sometimes the spirit got into them and
they free-lanced. It was usually Roth with his finger on the
team's trigger. The ball would zip into the pivot and back out
again. The players would cut and pick and move with a
shared intelligence. The ball wouldn't touch the floor until an
easy shot was uncovered; and Warner could always invent
one whenever they got stuck. They were intelligent enough to
let the flow decide who would do the scoring. They were the
best shooting team in the country and they played like blood
relatives.

ONE OF NAT'S BOYS REMEMBERS: "We were a great ball
club. If we were playing today, we'd still be great."

It's true that the "Cinderella Team" was on the smallish
side, but Roman, Layne, Dambrot, Roth, and Warner had all
played center in high school and knew how to box out. Since
they were virtually the same size, they could also play an
aggressive, switching, man-to-man defense. They were especially adept at helping out, at clogging the middle against a

big man. The Beavers were highly intelligent players and they felt capable of coaching themselves. Sometimes, during ball games, Al Roth overruled the substitutions sent in from the bench. Nat fussed a bit, but he didn't care as long as he was the one who got the credit.

The third game of the season was scheduled at the Garden on December 8, 1949, and the Beavers followed their usual day-of-the-game procedure. The players were excused from classes in time to make a 4:00 shooting practice at the Garden. Then they ate dinner as a unit and checked into a nearby hotel. While the players rested, Bobby Sand stood guard in the corridor. At 7:00 Sand waked the players and ushered them into the locker room. The Garden's capacity was 18,490 and it was always SRO for college games. Before they played, the players had enough time to sell their complimentary tickets for $10 each. The Beavers' opponent was a short, poor-shooting squad from Southern Methodist University. CCNY was favored by 13 points, but Eli Kaye asked Mager if any of his teammates were interested in doing business. Mager rounded up Dambrot, Roman, and Roth at $1,000 a head, and City was supposed to beat the SMU Mustangs by a maximum of 7 points. Herb Cohen was a sub and was promised only $500.

> ONE OF NAT'S BOYS EXPLAINS: "I hate to say it, but shaving points was a time-honored tradition at City. The choice was to go along with everybody else or to tell the authorities. Most of us were very broke and very naïve. We were this and we were that. . . . But in our hearts we knew it was wrong."

It was hard to keep the fix a secret. SMU had only one good player, a pivot man named Jack Brown. The Mustangs' primary claim to fame was the presence on the roster of Doak Walker, the All-American football player. As small as City was, they towered over the visitors. Jack Brown had an off night, and SMU was horrendous. Yet with four minutes left in the first half, the Beavers led by only 29–26. An irate bettor couldn't take any more and he singlehandedly stormed the City bench. "You guys are dumping!" he screamed. Mason Benson was out for the season with an injury and he sat on the bench with his ankle in a cast. But Benson was sufficiently insulted to shuffle into the stands after the fan. Benson finally cornered his prey in the lobby behind a refreshment stand. The bettor grabbed a mustard wand and waved it in self-defense while the 6-foot-5-inch Benson prepared to beat him into jelly. The situation was tense until the hot-dog vendor stepped in. "Mason," he said, "what do you need this aggravation for?"

The action was certainly less exciting out on the basketball court. The Beavers practically sat on the floor, but they couldn't help overwhelming the hapless Mustangs.

CCNY (67)	G	F	P	SMU (53)	G	F	P
Dambrot	7	0	14	Brown	5	3	13
Nadell	1	1	3	Wilson	0	0	0
Warner	8	2	18	Lutz	4	0	8
Galiber	0	0	0	Haynes	0	0	0
Roman	4	0	8	Mitchell	4	1	9
Mager	0	0	0	Holm	2	0	4
Roth	3	1	7	Salmon	2	1	5
Layne	4	1	9	Wheeler	0	0	0
Smith	0	0	0	Freeman	5	2	12
Witlin	2	0	4	Owen	1	0	2
Cohen	1	2	4		23	7	53
	30	7	67				

In the second game of the doubleheader, the Blackbirds took their dive against Kansas State.

Later that evening, Eli Kaye was indignant when Mager asked him for the payoff. "What are you, crazy?" the gambler said. "How the hell can you ask for the money when you went over the spread? I took a beating and you guys ain't getting a dime." The ballplayers were upset but they readily acknowledged the justice of Kaye's argument. They agreed to try again at a later date.

The Beavers dulled Kings Point, 82–28, and routed Brooklyn College, 71–44. Then a highly disciplined Oklahoma team handed City its first setback of the season by the score of 67–63. Nat didn't like losing, especially to another old-timer like Oklahoma coach Bruce Drake, and he let his players feel the hot breath of his anger. The CCNY students and faculty were also upset by the loss. "Win!" said the student body. "Win!" said the professors. Some of the players had difficulty living with the pressure.

Without a basketball in his hands, Eddie Roman appeared to be just another big, ungainly kid. Eddie was the youngest, most sensitive member of the team. Whenever anything went wrong, Eddie complained to his brother, who relayed the message to Bobby Sand. There were intrigues within intrigues, but the open line of communication kept Eddie relatively secure. Yet Eddie was perpetually on the verge of quitting the team. Eddie was bitter because he couldn't register for the science courses he longed to take. Nor had the job for his father ever materialized. In fact, the only promise Sand had made good on was a part-time job for Eddie in his free hours. Eddie worked ten hours a week in the athletic department. Things were brought to a head one day, when Sam Winograd buttonholed Eddie and charged that he wasn't putting in his minimum hours; that Eddie was shortchanging the department. "Just for that," Winograd said, "I'm going to cut *down* on your hours." There was a noisy scene and Eddie threatened to quit. Nothing Bobby Sand could do would mollify Eddie, and Nat finally had to be called in. Nat delivered a monologue in accents unfamiliar, and flavored with dozens of aphorisms. "The only thing that counts," Nat said, "is how much money you have in your safe-deposit box."

Eddie stayed. He was already on the dean's list and taking aim at a golden scholar's key. Once Eddie got down to the nub, the thought of actually leaving City and starting again someplace else was more frightening than appealing.

On December 27, 1949, the Beavers matched their 6–1 record against UCLA in a ball game played at the Garden. The Beavers were 5-point favorites, but Eli Kaye and Norm Mager cooked up another deal to replace the abortive SMU fix. As before, Mager, Roman, Roth, and Dambrot were promised $1,000 each and Cohen would get $500. The Beavers started the game in sloppy fashion, but they soon rallied to an early 30–22 lead. Then the fixers took over, and City led by only 32–30 at the half. Nat drew diagrams and gave the team holy hell during the intermission. The Beavers trailed meekly throughout the second half and lost the game, 60–53. The combination of Mager, Dambrot, Roth, and Cohen shot 6 for 19 from the field and 0 for 3 from the foul line. Eddie Roman led the Beavers with 22 points, but he was only 8 for 23 from the floor. After the game, Mager had no trouble collecting the money from Kaye.

The next ballplayer who threatened to transfer out of City was Al Roth. Bobby Sand once again worked around the clock but another meeting with Nat finally had to be arranged. "Stay at City," Nat told Roth. "You'll get a well-respected degree. Then when you have money you can tell them all to go to hell." Al Roth's eyes were sea-gray and steady at the helm, but he also was too frightened and too weak to actually leave.

The Beavers started to sputter at midseason. They struggled to a 54–52 decision over St. John's. They blew past three of the weaker teams on their schedule, Loyola (Illinois), West Virginia, and Muhlenberg. Then, after the semester break, the Beavers held on to beat a tough Boston College team, 64–56, but Bobby Sand was disturbed by the Beavers' performance. After the game, Sand accused a bewildered Ed Warner of deliberately mishandling the ball. Sand told both Winograd and Nat that "something was wrong," but they brushed him off. "Take it easy," said Winograd. "Quiet down," said Nat. And the matter was dropped.

The Beavers moved on to destroy Princeton and St. Francis. Their record was now 12 and 2, but their success tasted sour, and the tension continued to build. Norm Mager's anger was coming closer and closer to the surface, and Bobby Sand was worried sick. Sand went so far as to ask Mager's father to remove his son from the team. "Norm's going psycho," said Sand. But Mager was only a few months away from graduation and he was also hoping for a shot at the pros. Mager stayed.

The Beavers suffered their third loss of the season to Canisius by 53 to 49. A few days later, the Beavers were preparing to entertain Niagara at the Garden. City had been installed as a 10-point favorite, and Eli Kaye asked Mager if the boys wanted another try at the "easy" money. Roth and Cohen agreed to go along with Mager, but Roman and Dambrot both backed out. They were still trembling with shame for what they had already done. Because of the realignment, Cohen's share was increased to $1,000, and Mager and Roth received an additional bonus of $250 each. The Beavers played a wild, inept ball game against Niagara. Mager, Roth, and Cohen shot a collective 3 for 13 from the field. Dambrot and Roman were clean, but Irwin shot 2 for 14 from the floor, and Eddie was 9 for 33. Niagara won, 68–61, with Roman leading all scorers with 23 points.

A few days later, the CCNY entourage left for a short road trip. The players were glad to escape the Garden and the city. They were further delighted when they learned that Nat was taking two days off to tend to a speaking engagement. Bobby Sand took advantage of the opportunity to tinker with the team's offense. He instituted a pattern-style attack identical to the one used by the University of San Francisco Dons. The Beavers and the Dons had very similar personnel: left-handed jump shooters, smarts in the backcourt, and mobile,

Above: *Nat Holman wearing Original Celtic green on the streets of New York's Lower East Side.* (Wide World Photos)

Above left: *Clair Bee was a basketball scholar who helped nurture a mutant flock of Blackbirds.* (Wide World Photos)

Left: *Adolph Rupp's imperious knowledge of the game sparked the University of Kentucky to three NCAA championships.* (Wide World Photos)

Sherman White was fast, strong, fluent, and deadly—the greatest player of his generation. (Wide World Photos)

A detective leads Sherman White through felony court after the LIU All-American admitted conspiring with gamblers to rig basketball games. (UPI Photo)

Barely eight days later, CCNY beat Bradley again for the NCAA championship. Nat and his boys posed with dignitaries and a trophy. Bobby Sand has a bright smile and a hand on Ed Roman's shoulder. Despite their remarkable achievement several players are abnormally pensive. (UPI Photo)

Top opposite: *Nat Holman plots a winning play for his '49–'50 Beavers. The players are* (front row) *Norm Mager, Joe Galiber, Irwin Dambrot, Mike Witlin, Ed Roman;* (back row) *Ed Warner, Al Roth, Whitey Levey, and Herb Cohen.* (UPI Photo)

Bottom opposite: *In March 1950, the Beavers beat Bradley to win the NIT in Madison Square Garden. Coach Nat Holman rides the shoulders of Leroy Watkins and Floyd Layne and reaches for the sky.* (Wide World Photos)

On February 18, 1951, Ed Roman was arrested at Grand Central Station and taken to the Elizabeth Street station house for questioning. Nat Holman waited up all night for a phone call that never came. (UPI Photo)

Ed Warner was named the Most Valuable Player in the 1950 NCAA championship tournament. Al Roth provided the Beavers with quiet leadership in the backcourt. (Wide World Photos)

Floyd Layne escaped detection for five days. After he was finally arrested, the district attorney's detectives fought over the right to escort Layne past the photographers. (UPI Photo)

Connie "Crazy Shots" Schaff, NYU's leading scorer, confessed to offering bribes to several of his teammates. (UPI Photo)

Bradley's Gene Melchiorre was a hard-driving 5-foot-9-inch dynamo who often took his opponent into the pivot. (Wide World Photos)

husky centers. The more deliberate tempo cut down sharply on the Beavers' turnovers while increasing the players' endurance.

When Nat returned and discovered what had transpired behind his back, he was surprisingly amenable. The two consecutive losses had jolted him, and he was ready to try anything so long as it bore his name. City's record was now 14–4, and the sportswriters were starting to turn against them. The experts now called the team "a flash in the pan" and charged that the players were "no good in the clutch." In addition to adopting Sand's innovation, Nat took the additional step of castigating the team in public. The players gritted their teeth. Their hatred grew so intense they began rumoring among themselves that Nat Holman was involved with gamblers. "When Nat wears his brown suit," they said, "then you know he's doing business." The gossip was malicious and unfounded and was a measure of the players' bitter frustrations. But Nat made another move that was to bear a much more positive result. He switched Roman to forward and moved Warner into the pivot. Roman now had room for his one-hander and Warner was free to roam a mere three fakes from the hoop.

The Beavers brought their record to 16–4 by beating St. Joseph's and Fordham. They lost to Syracuse on the road, 83–74, and they closed out the regular season by squeaking past Manhattan and NYU. Despite all of their problems, the Beavers logged an impressive 17 and 4 season, and Nat immediately began to lobby for a bid from the NIT. The field was quickly filled with some of the top-ranked teams in the country: San Francisco, Kentucky, LIU, Syracuse, Duquesne, Bradley, and St. John's. The Beavers were the twelfth and last team selected.

City was paired against San Francisco in the opening round of the tournament. Eli Kaye lost no time in contacting Norm Mager and doubling the pot. "Two grand for each of you," Kaye said. "What have you got to lose? If you ain't shaving points, the other guy is. What are you going to do? Piss against the wind? Two thousand dollars apiece." Mager called a meeting to discuss the gambler's latest offer. "Hey," Mager said. "What do you think?" But Roman and Dambrot were still bleeding from the SMU and the UCLA debacles. "Not now," they counseled. "We've come too far." Their teammates agreed to turn Kaye down, but all throughout the tournament they had to peel the gambler off their backs.

The Dons were a veteran ball club whose success revolved around their All-American, Don Lofgran. The Dons had beaten the Beavers twice in '48–'49 and had captured the NIT championship a year before. But the Beavers knew the intricacies of their offense. Throughout the game, the Beavers taunted the Dons. "Move here," they said. "Now you're supposed to move over there." Ed Warner drove at will through the Don's defense and City won easily, 65–46.

CCNY (65)				USF (46)			
	G	F	P		G	F	P
Dambrot	2	1	5	Hickey	1	1	3
Mager	3	2	8	Hanley	0	0	0
Galiber	0	0	0	Giesen	1	1	3
Warner	8	10	26	McNamee	2	4	8
Smith	1	0	2	Metikosh	1	0	2
Roman	3	1	7	Lofgran	5	5	15
Watkins	0	0	0	Sobek	0	0	0
Roth	0	0	0	Herrerias	0	1	1
Cohen	2	0	4	Guidice	0	0	0
Witlin	0	0	0	Lavin	2	0	4
Layne	4	1	9	Kuzara	4	2	10
Nadell	1	2	4	Wong	0	0	0
	24	17	65		16	14	46

The sportswriters screamed their acclaim. Marriages were canceled, vacations were postponed, and honeymoons were spent at the Garden. An entire city suspended its disbelief and scratched the rash of anticipation. The Beavers were launched on a crusade. It was the ninety-seven-pound weaklings against a universe full of Black Barts. It was Snow White against Oil Can Harry. It was the poor against the rich.

Next in line for the Beavers were the awesome Kentucky Wildcats. Kentucky couldn't compare with the incredible Groza-Beard machines of recent memory, but they were still 25–4 and ranked third in the nation. The ball club was moved by Bill Spivey, a 7-foot All-American with enormous bulk and an unstoppable hook shot. Through the years, the University of Kentucky has produced 24 All-Americans, 7 Olympic Team members, and 26 pros, but the star of the Wildcats was always coach Adolph Rupp. "I know I have plenty of enemies," says Rupp, "but I'd rather be the most hated winning coach in the country than the most popular losing one." During his forty-two-year reign, Rupp's Wildcats won 24 Southeastern Conference crowns, 4 NCAA titles, 1 NIT championship, and 82 percent of their ball games. "The secret of my success is easy," says Rupp. "It's good coaching."

Adolph Rupp came from a family of German immigrants who settled in the plains of southeastern Kansas on a homestead grant from the federal government. Papa Rupp had five boys, 160 acres, and a girl. In 1907, when Adolph was six, the area experienced the first year of a three-year drought. Adolph was nine when the rains came back. He was nine and a half when his father died. The only chance Adolph had was to grow up tough, resourceful, and independent. He pitched the neighbors' wheat, went to a one-room school, and worked in a grocery store seven miles from the farm. Young Adolph also read several books on how to get rich. In his free time, he swam, fished, and played basketball. Adolph nailed a barrel-stave hoop to the barn and scored his first lay-ups with a gunny sack filled with grain.

He grew to a slender 6 feet 1 inch and he had no trouble making the Halstead High School basketball team. In Adolph's senior year, the coach of the team abruptly left to join World War I. The players decided to elect one of their number "coach" and finish out the season. Adolph quickly sidled up to the lowliest scrub on the team. "If you vote for me," Adolph said, "I'll make sure you'll start next game." Adolph was elected in a landslide. He had learned to measure his life in achievements.

From high school, Adolph passed on to the University of Kansas. He didn't play much but the Jayhawks were the national champions in 1923. Forrest "Phog" Allen was the coach and his buddy James Naismith showed up to grace the team's official portrait. Adolph learned all the basketball he could from both of them. Under the impression that he would be coaching basketball, Adolph accepted a teaching position in Marshalltown, Iowa. Adolph wound up tutoring the wrestling team. After two years, he shipped out to Freeport High School in Illinois. Over the next four years, Adolph's basketball teams won 67 and lost only 14. Then in 1930, the basketball coach at the University of Kentucky suddenly resigned his position in a squabble over money. Adolph took the next train down to Lexington to become one of seventy applicants for the job.

ADOLPH RUPP REMEMBERS: "Bear in mind that where Memorial Coliseum now stands, there were a bunch of little Negro one- and two-room shacks. Bear in mind that I got a cab from the Southern Depot to Alumni Gym, and we went through an awful area of town. They took me to eat at the university cafeteria and out the third-floor window I could see some more of those little Negro shacks. I said, 'Good gawd almighty, what kind of place is this here Kentucky?' "

At UK, the primary indoor sport was women's basketball. The men's team had had a brief moment of glory in 1921 when they beat Georgia, 20–19, on a free throw after the final buzzer to win the Southern Intercollegiate Basketball Tournament. Since then, the men's team had been moribund. For $2,800, the men's basketball coach was also expected to help chaperon the women's team and to assist with the football team. Adolph hesitated when he was offered the job but eventually decided to take it. In 1931 the first edition of Rupp's Wildcats was 15–3. One of the losses still rankles the Baron.

ADOLPH RUPP REMEMBERS: "We won our first ten games in a row before losing at Georgia and Clemson. Then we won the rest of the way until the finals of the Southern Conference tournament in Atlanta. I'll always think that game should've gone into overtime. For some reason, they let the clock keep running on us. Bozo Berger of Maryland got the center tip and let one fly from the middle of the floor right after time should have run out. It went in and they beat us 29–27. We got back to Lexington about seven-thirty by train that night. There were several thousand people at the station to meet us, and we walked from there to Alumni Gym for a big celebration, and everybody wound up dancing. Then I went home, took a shower, and went to bed. That's how we celebrated in those days. Take a shower and go to bed."

The Kentuckians loved Adolph's success and they adored his blustering bravado. "Some of my boys used to present me with a bottle of good ol' Kentucky whiskey at Thanksgiving or Christmas," Rupp says. "They knew how fond I am of the bottle and they figure it would elevate their status on the team. And I'll be damned if they weren't right." Rupp also loved to see his name in print. He was once asked by a sportswriter what he would do to improve the game. "Well," said Rupp, "I'd put the center jump back and take off the backboards and the net. I'd raise the hoop five feet and leave it there all by itself." One of Rupp's players asked him if he was serious about his suggestions. "Hell, no," said Rupp. "But I'll say anything for a column." The sheer power of the Baron's personality rapidly propelled the game of basketball throughout the state. It wasn't long before basketball was Kentucky's official sport.

The smallest basketball court in the country is inside the

furnace building of the St. Alphonsus Grade School in St. Joseph, Kentucky. The court measures 20 feet long and 10 feet wide. The players have to shoot between the steam pipes that pass overhead 7 feet above the floor.

Joe Hall was Rupp's assistant at UK and later the Baron's successor. "People throughout Kentucky really care about their basketball," says Hall. "Businessmen tell me that business goes up or down depending on whether or not the Wildcats win."

Joe Begley runs a general store in the mountains of eastern Kentucky. In the 1930s he played on a high school team that qualified for the state tournament. "If a lump of coal ain't Jesus Christ," says Begley, "then a basketball is."

By the spring of 1950, Adolph Rupp was a living legend, a wealthy man with large financial interests in cattle, land, and tobacco. He was the only other coach in the land with an ego that could compete with Nat Holman's. Needless to say, the two men were not overly fond of each other. "Our boys are under constant and absolutely complete supervision while they're on the road," said Rupp. "Especially in New York." With his usual unflappable arrogance, Rupp didn't even bother to have the Beavers scouted. Nat, on the other hand, approached the game as if it were a life-and-death situation.

Nat had a little-used sub named Leroy Watkins replace Eddie Roman in the Beavers' starting lineup. Watkins beat Spivey to the tap and the Beavers went straight for Kentucky's throat. Instead of continuing the slowdown tactics that had roasted the Dons, the Beavers reverted to early season form. Roman checked in for Watkins and climbed back into the pivot, Warner returned to forward, and the Beavers came out running and gunning. The strategy seemed to backfire when Spivey stuffed Roman's first three shots, but Nat was quick to switch Eddie back to forward. Roman responded with four consecutive one-handers, and the rout was under way. The Beavers ran like greyhounds and Spivey never had a chance to set up. The big man picked up his fourth personal foul during the first half and the Beavers closed out the Wildcats' season with an 89–50 pasting.

CCNY (89)	G	F	P	KENTUCKY (50)	G	F	P
Dambrot	9	2	20	Line	2	1	5
Warner	10	6	26	Linville	5	3	13
Watkins	1	0	2	Hirsch	1	0	2
Roman	8	1	17	Morgan	0	0	0
Mager	2	2	6	Spivey	4	7	15
Roth	3	3	9	Watson	1	0	2
Cohen	0	1	1	Pearson	3	1	7
Witlin	0	1	1	Townes	0	0	0
Smith	0	0	0	Barnstable	3	0	6
Layne	1	1	3	Whitaker	0	0	0
Nadell	2	0	4				
Glass	0	0	0		19	12	50
	36	17	89				

Nat was so overjoyed with the victory that he treated the team to a Broadway show. "Good gawd almighty," said Adolph Rupp. "I just sent my poor boys back home to Lexington with a tin cup." On the day following the game, the Kentucky state legislature passed a resolution calling for the capitol building's flag to be flown at half-mast.

The Beavers' next opponent was Duquesne, the sixth best team in the country. The Dukes were led by Chuck Cooper, who was one year away from being the first black ever to play in the NBA. The Beavers had an understandable letdown after their scintillating showing against Kentucky. But City had too much firepower from too many positions to have any serious difficulty with Duquesne. Roman, Dambrot, and Roth sparked the Beavers to an early 32–23 lead before Duquesne spurted to close the gap to 2 points. Quick baskets by Warner, Layne, and Roman doused the Duquesne rally, and the Beavers coasted to an easy 62–52 triumph.

CCNY (62)				DUQUESNE (52)			
	G	F	P		G	F	P
Dambrot	4	2	10	Dahler	3	3	9
Mager	0	1	1	Goldberg	0	0	0
Warner	5	9	19	Farrell	3	3	9
Cohen	0	0	0	Manning	1	1	3
Roman	7	1	15	Cooper	4	1	9
Roth	1	2	4	Horne	0	1	1
Layne	4	4	12	Skendrovich	0	1	1
Nadell	0	1	1	Cerra	4	3	11
				Dougherty	2	3	7
	21	20	62	Pacacha	1	0	2
					18	16	52

The Beavers had miraculously made it into the finals. CCNY students, graduates, and faculty members danced through the streets shouting a new defiant chant:

"Who owns New York?

Who owns New York?

ALLEGAROO OWNS NEW YORK!!"

The other NIT survivor was Bradley University. The Braves were 29–3 on the season and ranked number one in the country. Nat literally coached himself into a fever preparing for the championship game. He showed up at the Garden with a temperature of 103°, and his doctor insisted upon sitting on the bench beside him. Floyd Layne was the Beavers' best defensive player and he was given the task of controlling Bradley's heart, soul, and motorman, Gene Melchiorre. The Beavers also returned to their running game, but they started out by throwing passes into the seats and flubbing a suspicious variety of easy shots. The bettors began to get nervous. The Braves couldn't miss and All-American Paul Unruh controlled the backboards. With six minutes left in the first half, Bradley led 29–18. Nat sent Norm Mager into the game to try and settle things down. Mager passed up several shots and concentrated instead on working the ball to his teammates. His presence and experience soothed the Beavers, and CCNY fought to a 30–27 deficit at the intermission.

The second half was a fast-paced battle of nerves. There were six ties and seven lead changes in the first ten minutes. Melchiorre fouled out with 8:10 left in the game but the Braves went to Unruh and hung tough. The Beavers were trailing 56–55 with less than five minutes to go when Ed Warner suddenly blitzed the Braves with a dazzling array of spectacular shots. The exhausted Braves couldn't keep up and they collapsed in a hurry. A driving lay-up by Warner gave City a 4-point lead with two minutes left. The Beavers pulled the game out of the woods on Roman's tap-in, two free throws by Warner, and one by Joe Galiber. The final score was 69–61.

CCNY (69)	G	F	P	BRADLEY (61)	G	F	P
Dambrot	10	3	23	Grover	3	0	6
Warner	6	4	16	Preece	2	0	4
Roman	9	1	19	Unruh	7	1	15
Galiber	0	1	1	Schlictman	1	0	2
Roth	0	0	0	Chianakas	0	0	0
Cohen	0	0	0	Behnke	6	3	15
Mager	2	0	4	Kelley	0	2	2
Layne	2	2	6	Mann	4	0	8
				Melchiorre	2	5	9
	29	11	69		25	11	61

The Beavers were carried off the floor on the shoulders of their delirious fans. Ed Warner was named the tournament's Most Valuable Player. The Garden was a bedlam of celebration. The players laughed and screamed with hilarious abandon. But as soon as the team entered the locker room, their joy was suddenly snuffed.

ONE OF NAT'S BOYS REMEMBERS: "Nat was walking from reporter to reporter with his arm around Warner. Then Nat started sucking up to the rest of us. It was disgusting."

Nat had no special reward or ceremony planned and he was one of the first to leave. The players were perfunctorily handed their meal money and sent on their way. Sand and Winograd huddled for a moment, trying to salvage the situation. They finally offered to take those players who had not already left out to dinner at Mamma Leone's. But the dinner was a heavy, sullen affair. All of them knew it was an afterthought.

Most of the credit for the "Cinderella Team's glorious victory" was generously ladled out to Nat. "There are many of the opinion," said a *New York Times* editorial, "that the work of Nat Holman in the recent NIT ranks as his top achievement in coaching." There were spontaneous rallies on the CCNY campus, and a few days later the Beavers were invited into the NCAA tournament. The NCAA championship was also decided at the Garden and ticket scalpers came out of retirement. It was New Year's Eve every time the Beavers played.

The Beavers defeated Ohio State in the first round of the NCAA playoffs primarily on the basis of an acute scouting report turned in by Bobby Sand. The Buckeyes played a bruising zone defense anchored by Dick Schnittker, a 6-foot-5-inch, 205-pound All-American. Sand knew that the Beavers would never be able to drive to the basket so he advised Nat to start Mager in the backcourt instead of Roth. Floyd Layne was the only City player who still used a two-hand set shot and he started at the other guard. The long-range bombing of Mager and Layne was the difference in the ball game. The Beavers led all the way and hung on by their teeth to post a 56–55 victory and advance to the quarterfinals.

Two nights later, the Beavers got 51 points from their frontcourt of Roman, Warner, and Dambrot, and rolled to a 78–73 win over North Carolina State. In the NCAA's Western Regionals, the Bradley Braves beat Kansas, UCLA, and Baylor to set the table for a delicious rematch of the NIT title game. The Braves were thirsty for revenge. The Beavers were seeking to accomplish the unduplicated feat of winning both the NIT and the NCAA championships in the same season. Nat Holman was reaching for justification and for sainthood.

The Braves had already played thirty-six games over the course of the season and their coach, Forrest Anderson, opened the game with a surprise zone defense. His athletes were simply too tired to play man-to-man for forty minutes. The unexpected move stymied the Beavers for a while. The score was tied six times and there were nine early lead changes before the Beavers found the range. City put together two separate strings of 5 unanswered points and led 39–32 at the half. Just before the buzzer, Norm Mager was sent sprawling to the floor from a head-on collision with Bradley's Aaron Preece. Mager required five stitches in his head before reappearing for the second half.

It looked like the Beavers were in firm control of the ball game. Roth was moving the ball extremely well and they were finding nothing but good shots. The third quarter featured more of the same. The Beavers continued to shred Bradley's zone and led 58–47. Then, with nine minutes left in the game, the Braves switched to a man-to-man, and Gene Melchiorre turned into a buzz saw. With two minutes to go, the Beavers' lead was sliced to 66–61 and the crowd was on its feet. Anderson substituted two fast scrubs for two tall starters, and the Braves launched a full-court press. Melchiorre stole the ball and dribbled ahead of the field for an easy lay-up. City led 66–63. Norm Mager was fouled and sank his free throw to stretch the Beavers' lead to 4. Two seconds later, Floyd Layne made a steal and fed Dambrot for a basket that made the score 69–63. There were only fifty-seven seconds left. Bradley's Joe Stowell was fouled and made the score 69–64. Then Melchiorre tried to bust the ball game by himself. Within the next seventeen seconds, Melchiorre made two more steals and two more baskets to slice City's edge to 69–68.

There were only forty seconds left in the game, and Nat ordered his boys to freeze the ball. Nat clapped his hands but nobody heard him. He stomped his feet but nobody saw him. The clock ticked down while Roth and Layne tried to keep the ball out of Bradley's reach. Then Melchiorre struck again. He swiped one more pass and headed downcourt for pay dirt. Irwin Dambrot had a slight angle and he set off in desperate pursuit. Dambrot caught Melchiorre at the basket, and there was a jarring collision. No foul was called, and Dambrot popped up with the ball. Dambrot looked upcourt to see Mager standing by himself under the Beavers' basket. Dambrot threw a perfect pass and Mager's lay-up was the final score in a history-making 71–68 victory for Nat's boys.

CCNY (71)				BRADLEY (68)			
	G	F	P		G	F	P
Dambrot	7	1	15	Grover	0	2	2
Roman	6	0	12	Schlictman	0	0	0
Warner	4	6	14	Unruh	4	0	8
Roth	2	1	5	Behnke	3	3	9
Mager	4	6	14	Kelley	0	0	0
Galiber	0	0	0	Mann	2	5	9
Layne	3	5	11	Preece	6	0	12
Nadell	0	0	0	Melchiorre	7	2	16
				Chianakas	5	1	11
	26	19	71	Stowell	0	1	1
					27	14	68

His bandage stained with blood, Norm Mager was carried off the court on the jubilant shoulders of his teammates. The courtside consensus was that Mager would definitely get the MVP award, but it was voted instead to Dambrot.

The Beavers' Cinderella story flooded the front pages of America's newspapers. *The New York Times* called their double victory "a vindication of the democratic process."

At eleven o'clock the very next morning, some 2,000 students came pouring out of CCNY's School of Business on Lexington Avenue and Twenty-third Street. They paraded up Fifth Avenue, stopped traffic in Times Square, and swarmed into the subways. The boisterous, cavorting business majors reached the main campus at noon and immediately created a disturbance that couldn't be ignored. Another 4,500 students streamed out of their classrooms and mobbed the campus quadrangle. They shouted cheers and waved spontaneous banners. Their usually staid professors were eager to join the conga lines and the snake dances. A platform was hastily erected and a microphone connected. A hoary professor puffed furiously on his pipe and made an announcement. "There will be no action taken against any student who cuts his afternoon classes," he said. "This is the greatest thing to ever happen in the one-hundred-and-two-year history of this venerable institution." The players were introduced to madly adoring cheers. Students clambered up trees to gain better vantage points. Then CCNY president Harry Wright was moved to make a speech. "This is one of the proudest days of my life," he said. "This team came here to study, not to play basketball. I am proud of the team and what it has done for the college. I want to emphasize that the players have been given no scholarships to play ball. They are not imported mercenaries. I am particularly proud of their high scholastic ratings." The president added that last night's hero, Norm Mager, could not attend the rally because he was taking a midterm examination. Then Professor J. Bailey Harvey concluded the demonstration by grabbing a baton and leading the students in all of the college songs.

A few days later, the CCNY alumni gave the Beavers a

formal dinner at the Waldorf. Nat played buddy-buddy with his boys and presented the team with commemorative fountain pens while most of them spat curses at his back. Adolph Rupp had been a co-coach of the 1948 Olympic basketball team, and Nat dreamed of riding his supersophs into a gold medal in the 1952 Games. Nat said he was planning to postpone his retirement for two more years, and the players moaned so loudly that even the alumni were startled. But the Beavers were the darlings of the nation and there was precious little time for brooding over crimes real or imagined.

Manhattan Borough President Robert F. Wagner convened a fancy ceremony and presented the team with engraved scrolls. As a special honor, Nat was sworn in as Honorary Deputy Commissioner. In order to legalize his latest title, "Mister Basketball" had to pay a registry fee of six cents.

Then Howard Hobson of Yale announced another laurel for the Beavers. Hobson was president of a committee that would choose a basketball team to represent the United States in the 1951 Pan American Games. Hobson said that seven City players and their coach would be asked to provide the backbone of the team. The offer created a hubbub on the City campus, and a faculty board was asked to investigate the invitation. But Ned Irish wanted to make sure that the Beavers stayed home, because the Pan American Games were scheduled for Brazil in February and March, at the same time that the Garden would be hosting the next NIT. Even before the Double Championship, the Beavers' huge student body and numerous alumni could always be counted on for large blocks of tickets. In May, Irish rode up to Harlem to make a special presentation on behalf of the Garden. Irish talked about how much the Garden had done for City College. He reminded the faculty board that City's take from college basketball at the Garden amounted to over $50,000 a year. Irish pointed out that all of the Beavers' Double Championship games were in fact played at the Garden. A few days later, President Harry Wright publicly announced that Howard Hobson's flattering offer had to be refused.

"The Pan American Games will be played while school is in session," Wright said. "The players simply cannot afford to miss that much class time."

There were several other strange fruits, nuts, and berries for the Beavers to sample. In the spring of 1950, the National Basketball Association was only a year old. It had teams in Anderson, Waterloo, Tri-Cities, and Sheboygan, and its financial outlook was bleary. The pros simply couldn't compete with the colleges. But a secret deal was worked out between a sportswriter named Max Kase and the Commissioner of the NBA, Maurice Podoloff. After the City supersophs were graduated in 1952, they would be granted a franchise in the NBA. The new franchise would be owned and operated by the players and it would be situated in either Chicago or Brooklyn.

In June 1950, the Beavers were asked to participate in still another surefire money-making scheme. Les Nichols's official title at CCNY was Assistant to the President, but he was also a professional public relations man. Nichols knew that the citizens of South America were clamoring to see black men play basketball. It was no secret that Abe Saperstein's Harlem Globetrotters were making a fortune on their comic tours south of the border. Nichols had contacted a Brazilian promoter named Joachim Almeida about a basketball tour for the LIU Blackbirds. But there were complications with the LIU bigwigs, so Nichols turned the idea over to CCNY. Almeida would guarantee expenses and another $2,500, and the college could bargain for a percentage of the gate.

Nat was completely behind the plan. Irwin Dambrot, Joe Galiber, and Norm Mager were the only players Nat had lost to graduation. Nat wanted the returning lettermen to make the trip along with the new freshman team. The preseasoning would be invaluable. "But," said Nat, "who's going to go with the team and coach them?" Winograd had his summer sinecure at Young's Gap Hotel, and Nat owned a boys' camp in Elizaville, New York.

That left Bobby Sand. The tentative plans were to leave in August and return in mid-September. The players would get daily expense money for their food, laundry, and sightseeing. A faculty committee was appointed to draw up a preliminary agreement. But the ballplayers were also discussing terms. The trip would curtail their resort earnings, and they were very unhappy. At the players' initiative, a formula was reached whereby they would each get $300 over and above their expenses. The proposal was accepted on the condition that the players sign affidavits declaring their willingness to take the trip. The next step was to find a mechanism to preserve the players' amateur standing. It was decided that Bobby Sand would be allowed to take his wife, and the players would split a "coach's salary" of $2,250. The college stood to make several thousand dollars, and all parties seemed to be well satisfied. Then the Brazilian promoter reminded everyone that the squad must contain at least one black player: either Ed Warner or Floyd Layne. Less than a week later, Layne suffered an injury while playing baseball and had to be scratched from consideration. Suddenly, it was Ed Warner or no trip.

Because of the Beavers' sudden eminence, Sand had been able to get Warner a resort job for the summer of 1950. Ed was working as a waiter at Klein's Hillside. On June 21, Bobby Sand and Les Nichols conferred in the City College cafeteria with some of the ballplayers. They all pooled their thoughts, and Sand penned a letter to Warner. The letter stated that Warner owed it to his teammates to sign the enclosed affidavit and join them on the junket. The players would personally chip in to make up any moneys Warner would lose by forfeiting his summer job. Nichols made certain that the letter also included some unofficial pressure from the college administration. Warner received the packet a few days later. He had no desire and no intention to spend his precious summer vacation running around South America. But he yielded to his teammates' plaintive urgings and signed the affidavit. On July 14, Sam Winograd dropped in at Klein's Hillside to keep tabs on Warner. In the course of their conversation, Winograd asked Warner if he was really planning to go on the trip. "No," said Warner. "I don't care what the letter says." "What letter?" asked Winograd. Warner was more than relieved to turn the letter over to Winograd.

Winograd immediately called Nat and read the letter over the phone. Nat was furious and wanted to fire Sand on the spot. But Winograd reminded Nat that such an action would be certain to arouse bad publicity. Nat and Winograd finally agreed to take the letter to Dr. Frank Lloyd, their chairman and superior. There was a lengthy conference, and several days later Winograd secured the letter in a safe-deposit box.

Without Warner or Layne the deal was dead. But an alternate scheme was hatched in which Bobby Sand would tour Brazil with an all-Jewish ball club. Instead of CCNY filling its coffers, the golden percentage would be paid to the United States Committee for Sports in Israel. The team included Eddie Roman, Al Roth, Herb Cohen, and Ron Nadell from City College; Ed Goldberg from Duquesne; and Eddie Gard from LIU.

An hour after the team landed in Brazil, they played and beat a team of local talent. The club went undefeated in a five-game whirlwind tour. Eddie Roman was a sensation. He scored a total of 80 points, and the Brazilian newspapers called him "The Human Point-Maker." Eddie was asked to become a Brazilian citizen and play for a team out of Rio de Janeiro called the Carioca All-Stars. Strangely enough, Eddie Gard made no attempt to solicit either Roman or Roth for the Sollazzo All-Stars.

7

By July 1950, Salvatore Sollazzo was already wading in problems. The Internal Revenue Service was sniffing around his tax returns, and Sollazzo had no acceptable explanations. Sollazzo was also losing money on the horses and on the currently unfixable game of baseball. His income from the illegal sale of gold remained hefty, but the overseas demand was slackening. To make things worse, Sollazzo's basketball interests were nearly defunct. In certain circles, LIU was well known as a dump team, and several bookies were nosing it about that they would no longer be accepting bets against the Blackbirds. Sollazzo desperately needed to buy himself another edge, another sure thing. Time was starting to close in around Sollazzo's neck. And if Sollazzo fell, so would Eddie Gard.

Even though the Blackbirds were a potentially bad risk, Gard wanted to keep his finger in their pie. The '49–'50 season had used the last of Gard's basketball eligibility, and one of his biggest summertime chores was maintaining a hold on his two surviving fix-mates, Adolf Bigos and Sherman White. Bigos was easy to find. He was working in his father's grocery store in Perth Amboy. But Gard had to sprint to catch Sherman White. Sherman's summer was a rerun. He went to school and played basketball in the Catskills on weekends. It seemed to be a good system for Sherman: he had a B average and an All-American rating. Sherman saw a great deal of Eddie Gard that summer. Every so often, Gard would slip Sherman $50 to keep him on the line. Sometimes, Sollazzo would even drop by to say hello.

Gard also sought out Ed Warner at Klein's Hillside, bringing the news that Roth and Roman were point shavers.

Warner twitched with surprise but held on to his cool, and the matter was left hanging.

One of Gard's oldest friends, Sol Levy, was another appointment on Eddie's summer calendar. Levy had been Gard's basketball coach at the East Brooklyn YMHA. Levy was forty-one years old, the director of a summer resort, and a referee in the National Basketball Association. One day in early July, Gard arrived at Levy's hotel with Jeanne and Salvatore Sollazzo in tow. "Sol," said Gard, "good to see you. I'd like you to meet a friend of mine." Eddie bit down on a smile. He had chosen Sollazzo's alias by himself. "Sol Levy . . ." Eddie said. "This is Mr. Tarto."

The two men shook hands and exchanged pleasantries. "I'd like to arrange for my wife to stay here for the summer," Sollazzo said. "Do you think you could help me with the details?" Levy was happy to oblige. He booked Jeanne through Labor Day and Sollazzo on weekends.

On Saturdays and Sundays, from one end of the summer to the other, Eddie Gard chauffeured Sollazzo's Cadillac on a Catskill shuttle. They saw as many ball games as possible, and they tried to drum up some business. Sol Levy habitually picked up some exercise and some extra change by officiating the resort games, and he periodically bumped into Gard and "Mr. Tarto." Sollazzo treated Levy and his wife to drinks and sandwiches on several occasions. The gambler usually dominated the conversation by blabbing about his extensive betting. But Levy's salary from the NBA was a paltry $3,000 a year, and he was impressed with Sollazzo's obvious familiarity with large sums of money. Sollazzo and Gard decided to try and work on Levy, but the gambler laid low while Eddie toured South America.

Almost as soon as Gard returned from Brazil, he had another parley with Ed Warner. Gard talked about all the money that CCNY made on the ballplayers' backs. Gard cited chapter, verse, and bottom line. It didn't seem fair that the players should go unrewarded. "Besides," said Gard, "everybody's doing it." Ed Warner, from the flimflamming streets of Harlem, never had any difficulty recognizing a hustle. They were soon talking business. It was agreed that the cooperation of Floyd Layne was essential to the success of their operation. Gard made himself invisible while Warner popped the question. Floyd turned his buddy down in no uncertain terms.

On Labor Day, Sollazzo used his Cadillac to help the Levys move their belongings back to the city. Within the following two weeks, Jeanne called several times to ask Sol and his wife over for cocktails. But the Levys had trouble finding a baby-sitter and they reluctantly refused the invitations. Gard's husbandry was growing plenty of interesting contacts but precious few contracts, and Sollazzo wasn't sure if he could survive until the harvest.

School started in late September with Eddie Gard still several light-years away from graduation. But he enrolled once again at LIU and registered himself into every one of Sherman White's courses. Then on October 15, college basketball teams all across the country started practicing, and the new season was only six weeks away. Before the first whistle blew, the sportswriters were already touting the Blackbirds as championship contenders. They knew that Clair Bee certainly had the material. Bee had recruited Hal Uplinger from California and 7-foot Ray Felix from Queens. Leroy Smith and Adolf Bigos were both coming back, and no one dared to estimate the boundaries of Sherman White's irresistible talent. Sherman's last collegiate season was expected to be a record-setter.

Even before the season began, there were active rumors that the New York Knicks were especially anxious to sign Sherman. There were also third-party feelers from the Harlem Globetrotters. Despite his glowing prospects, Sherman remained uneasy and confused about his future. The Knicks were a notoriously selfish ball club, and Sherman had a feeling he'd be unhappy playing with them. The Globies sounded like fun, but deep in his heart Sherman was a homebody. All he wanted was to play pro ball for a while, raise a family, and coach a high school team somewhere in New Jersey.

Eddie Gard hawked all of the Blackbirds' practice sessions. He was amazed at the improvement in Leroy Smith. Gard began to think that maybe Sherman and Bigos couldn't control a ball game by themselves. The task of recruiting Smith fell to Sherman. Smith was flattered that he was considered worthy of joining this exclusive confederacy and agreed to juggle scores for only $500 a game.

As the college season drew near, Gard and Warner continued to pepper Layne with arguments and inducements, and the "Tartos" kept after Sol Levy. On a Friday night in mid-October, the Levys had a baby-sitter as well as tickets to see Ezio Pinza in *South Pacific.* After the show, they finally made it over to the Sollazzos' for drinks. Eddie Gard was also there, accompanied by Jeanne's sister. The evening was a pleasant one, with no talk of either basketball or betting. Sol Levy enjoyed himself so much that he felt obligated to ask the Sollazzos over to his place the following week.

The second get-together was once again casual and innocent. But the pro season opened a full three weeks before the colleges, and Sollazzo decided to start leaning on Levy. Gard invited Levy and his wife to a big shindig that Sollazzo was throwing at the George Washington Hotel. During the course of the festivities, Sollazzo wandered over to Levy. "Eddie tells me you're working the Knicks' game at the Garden tomorrow night," Sollazzo said. "I've got a big bet on the game. If I win, I'll take good care of you." They were both a bit sociable from their drinks and Levy didn't take Sollazzo very seriously.

Then over the next few days, Gard burned up the telephone wires calling Levy. "Tarto's losing a bundle," Gard said. "He wants you to help him out." Levy kept refusing, but he did accept another invitation to a party at the Hotel New

101

Yorker. With Gard at his side, Sollazzo was quick to corner Levy. "If I had all your games," Sollazzo blurted, "I really would take care of you."

"Sol," Gard chimed. "Don't be stupid. There's a lot in this for you." Levy couldn't hold out much longer. He eventually agreed to conspire with Sollazzo for $1,000 a game. Then, on the brink of the college season, Floyd Layne also yielded. Sollazzo was elated. He began to think that he might even win the million dollars he needed to pay his back taxes.

As LIU prepared to inaugurate the '50–'51 season, Sollazzo came up with an intriguing notion. What if the Blackbirds went over the point spread instead of under it? The switch would certainly befuddle the bookies and convince them that the Blackbirds' games were honest. But Gard said it was hard enough to win a ball game played on the level. Point shaving was much safer. The Blackbirds' opening game was played against Kansas State on December 2 at the Garden. The morning line had the Blackbirds favored by 8 points. When rumors of the fix hit the streets, the spread fell to 6. And when Sollazzo tried to bet $7,500 on Kansas State, his bookie would only give him 4 points.

The Blackbirds were in firm control throughout the ball game. They led by 7 with less than two minutes to go and they clung to a 60–59 win. Sherman and Bigos got $1,000 each and Smith got $500.

SHERMAN WHITE REMEMBERS: "It was a new season, but we had the same old trouble of trying to keep the points down without being passed at the finish. I had a so-so game with only 15 points. The Kansas State game convinced me, though, that the best way to do the job was to let my man score. It was difficult for me to cheat on my shots like the rest of the guys were doing. Anyway, I was supposed to be the big scorer on the team, and it wouldn't look good unless I got my 20 points a night."

The Beavers punched into the season by flooring St. Francis, 81–62, and Queens, 61–53. Despite Gard's opinion to the contrary, Sollazzo was still persuaded he could get ballplayers to exceed the spread. At Sollazzo's insistence, a deal was concluded with Warner and Layne. For $500 apiece, they would attempt to go over the points against Brigham Young at the Garden. Warner and Layne did their best, but Roman and Roth had suspiciously poor games, and the Beavers won by only 71–69. The ball game cost Sollazzo a total of $6,000, and Eddie Gard arranged a meeting between the gambler and Al Roth.

Once they were face to face, Sollazzo wasted little time in presenting his spiel, but Roth had his own terms in mind. Roth promised to get Roman involved and said that the two of them would work for Sollazzo only if they could play underneath the point spread. They also demanded wages of either $1,000 or $1,500, depending upon how large a bet Sollazzo could get down. The thought of "having" the Double-Championship Beavers burned a hole in Sollazzo's pocket. "Listen," Sollazzo said. "Let me give you a couple of bucks to celebrate our mutual good fortune. Let's call it a bonus for signing. Or a gratuity." On December 4, Roman and Roth played well above par in a 59–43 victory over Washington State at the Garden. After the game, Gard handed Roth $1,000 to split with Roman. "I'll be in touch," said Gard.

The next order of business for Sollazzo and Gard was an LIU-Denver game on December 7 at the Garden. By this time, the wary bookies were giving a maximum of only 3 points to any money bet against the Blackbirds. Eddie Gard showed up in the locker room before the game to turn the players on to the fix, and LIU won in double overtime, 58–56.

SHERMAN WHITE REMEMBERS: "We seemed able to control the game much better. We could now shave as close as we wanted without blowing the game. I guess we were getting to be better dumpers."

LIU (58)				DENVER (56)			
	G	F	P		G	F	P
Roges	3	5	11	Griffin	0	3	3
Belopolsky	0	1	1	McGaughey	0	0	0
Murtha	1	0	2	Ryen	8	3	19
Bigos	2	2	6	Hicks	0	0	0
Alpert	0	0	0	Toft	5	3	13
White	6	10	22	Gray	2	1	5
Felix	0	0	0	Hughes	0	0	0
Uplinger	2	3	7	Howell	0	0	0
Smith	4	1	9	Johnson	3	2	8
				Knickrehn	4	0	8
	18	22	58		22	12	56

On December 9, City College played the Missouri Tigers at the Garden. Missouri's center, Joe Stauffer, was only 6 feet 3 inches, and Eddie Roman had always cooked him to a turn whenever they played against each other in the Catskills. The early line had the Beavers favored by 14 points. Roman, Roth, Warner, and Layne were promised $1,500 each to duck under the spread. By the time Sollazzo contacted his bookies, the spread was down to 6. Sollazzo had to spend the whole day getting $7,500 bet against the Beavers.

The game started with the Beavers banana-peeling their way up and down the court. They shot with reckless imagination and they threw passes into the seats. When Eddie Roman found himself free in the corner for an easy one-hander, his shot hit the side of the backboard. Joe Stauffer looked like an All-American. Early in the first half, the Tigers went on a 17–0 tear that ripped the ball game wide open. "Nat," said Bobby Sand. "Get them out of there. Put in the second team." But Nat waved Sand into silence. At halftime, the Beavers had only 5 field goals and trailed 31–14. Nat roasted the team with purple exorcisms but the second half was more of the same. "Let's go into a press," said Sand. "No," said Nat. "It's too early." The starters played most of the way, and the

Beavers were embarrassed by Missouri, 54–37. Roman, Roth, Warner, and Layne worked in concert to shoot 18 percent from the floor. Floyd Layne took his money and bought his mother a washing machine. Then he rolled the rest in a handkerchief and buried it in a flowerpot.

CCNY (37)	G	F	P	MISSOURI (54)	G	F	P
Warner	3	5	11	Witt	2	1	5
Nadell	2	3	7	Landolt	4	0	8
Smith	0	1	1	Loomis	0	0	0
Gold	0	0	0	Heineman	8	3	19
Roman	3	1	7	Rubin	0	1	1
Chenetz	0	0	0	Clark	0	0	0
Roth	1	1	3	Stauffer	5	5	15
Hill	1	0	2	Gosen	0	0	0
Layne	2	2	6	Lafferty	0	6	6
				Zimmerman	0	0	0
	12	13	37	Dippold	0	0	0
				Adams	0	0	0
				Hamilton	0	0	0
				Schaeffer	0	0	0
					19	16	54

After the game, Bobby Sand was informed by his friends that several bookies had refused to handle the contest. In the Garden's main lobby, all the guys in the fat suits and the Havana cigars were talking nothing but "fix." Sand telephoned the information to Frank Thornton, a member of CCNY's Intercollegiate Athletics Committee, who agreed to undertake an investigation. Thornton went first to Frank Lloyd, Sam Winograd, and Nat Holman. He was told there was no chance in the world that a City College ballplayer would ever do such a thing. "Unless you have hard evidence," they said, "we can't do a thing." The door was closed on Thornton's foot. But the authorities at City College certainly weren't the only ones who didn't want to hear bad news.

Charlie McNeil is a big-time professional gambler and a cohort of television personality Nick "The Greek." During the '49–'50 season, McNeil discovered that a certain basketball referee in a major college conference was being fixed like a broken clock. The commissioner of the conference was a man of righteous wrath who believed in only the loftiest clichés about sports. The commissioner cut short McNeil's report. "I can't even conceive of the possibility of an amateur sportsman being corrupt," the commissioner said. "And I won't listen to any such accusation from a man who makes his living in so despicable a way as you." The result was that the referee went on fixing ball games. But McNeil kept plugging away. Eventually he encountered an aide who was less rigid and more realistic.

"You keep the referees' assignments secret, don't you?" McNeil asked.

"Of course," the aide said.

"Well," said McNeil, "I'll make you a deal. You keep the assignment under your hat, and I'll come to you the day before the game and tell you where he's working. I'll also tell you within a few points how his game is going to come out."

It was easy for McNeil to figure out which conference game was attracting an unusually large number of bets and which way the bets were lying. McNeil's predictions were correct in every detail, and the information was passed along. The stodgy conference commissioner solved the problem by simply letting the referee's contract lapse at the end of the season. The shady referee was promptly hired by another conference and was still in circulation.

The betting public's rabid interest in point spreads was encouraged and catered to by all the New York papers. The *Post*, for example, would regularly send sportswriter Sid Friedlander up to Buffalo or Boston to scout any college team that was headed for the Garden. Friedlander's only responsibility on these trips was to compose a point spread that would be printed in the sports section.

IKE GELLIS EXPLAINS: "I've been sports editor here at the *Post* for a long time and I've always felt that printing the point spread was a service for our readers. We provided a line for the bettor to compare with the one quoted by his local bookie. We also reported suspect games, off-the-board lines, and fluctuating spreads to the coaches. All of the newspapers did the same thing."

Sollazzo "had" more teams than just CCNY and LIU. But as 1950 rolled to a conclusion, the gambler was ahead by only a couple of thousand dollars. Sollazzo always tailored his basketball bets to Eddie Gard's specifications and had no idea he was being fooled. To a certain extent, Gard was using Sollazzo's money to manipulate point spreads all over the city. Gard was making his own private wagers and feeding Sollazzo counterfeit information of other fixes. In order to square his accounts, Sollazzo believed he needed to purchase the services of another ball club.

The Oklahoma Sooners came into town for a December 21 date with CCNY. Sollazzo entertained several members of the Oklahoma team at his apartment the night before the game, but his money hook failed to attract a nibble. The Sooners edged the Beavers, 48–43, and after the game, the gambler tried again. He hosted another bash with the same guest list and the same discouraging results. Sollazzo's necessity was increasingly acute, but there were certain players even he didn't want. One of them was Connie Schaff from NYU.

Connie Schaff was a hoary nineteen years old when he graduated from Seward Park High School on the Lower East Side. Connie's grades were barely passing, and he lived to play hooky and basketball. Connie was a fine ballplayer and a very inventive shooter. His joy was taking weird shots from improbable angles. Connie was scouted by a friend of Howard Cann's. At an alumnus's expense, Connie was forwarded to the Brooklyn Academy so that his high school transcript might receive a transfusion of easy A's and B's. It was while Connie attended the prep school that he started palling around with a classmate and teammate named Eddie Gard. Connie took four subjects at the Academy, earning three D's and one F. Connie and Eddie worked together during the summer waiting on tables at Grossinger's. Connie's grades were still comatose, but NYU signed him to a basketball scholarship in the fall of 1949. His first semester at his new school was a familiar disaster, and Connie was placed on probation. He was reinstated just in time for the '50–'51 season. NYU's athletic department arranged for special tutors, and Connie never lost a ball game to scholastic ineligibility.

Connie began the season on the bench, and the Violets struggled out of the gate. Then more and more of Connie's moon shots began making soft landings through the hoop, and NYU started winning. Connie became a starter in mid-December, and the sportswriters dubbed him "Crazy Shot Schaff." Connie loved his new nickname, but his teammates continued to call him just plain "Crazy." Connie was smart enough, however, to know what was going on with Eddie Gard, the Beavers, and the Blackbirds. Connie suggested to his friend that he would like to be cut into the action, but Sollazzo nixed any possibility of a deal. The gambler didn't think that Connie was a good enough player to deliver. Connie was never the kind of person who surrendered to circumstances, so he tried getting his NYU teammates to join him. Connie even introduced a few of them to Sollazzo. "Nothing doing," said his teammates. Then Connie began calling Sollazzo on a regular basis, begging for a chance to dump. "Nothing doing," said the gambler. Sollazzo kept Schaff at a tolerable distance by providing some free entertainment and an occasional sawbuck. The handouts were also designed to keep Connie's mouth shut.

Throughout the fall and winter of 1950, Connie's play showed a steady improvement, and the Violets were on their way to a surprising 12–4 season. Connie kept pestering Sollazzo, but he also took the opportunity of peddling his wares elsewhere. By Christmas Eve, the Violets' leading scorer was "Crazy Shot" himself. Connie camped beside the telephone and waited for a call from Santa Claus.

The Blackbirds, meanwhile, were destroying Georgetown, Cortland State, and UCLA to remain undefeated. Sherman White passed the Christmas vacation back home in Englewood and soon filled the house with the holiday spirit. As a Christmas present to his parents, Sherman paid up the mortgage and financed some urgently needed repairs. Sherman's old playground chums were also delighted to see him, and he continued spreading the good cheer. Sherman bought them meals and he bought them suits.

> FLETCHER JOHNSON REMEMBERS: "Sherman had money from wherever, and he insisted on sharing it with us. He wouldn't talk about where it came from but you could tell he wasn't doing anything he thought was wrong."

On Christmas Night, the Blackbirds were 3-point favorites to beat Idaho at the Garden. Sollazzo pledged a reward of $2,500 to be divvied up among Sherman, Bigos, and Smith if the team went under the spread. The bookies were so leery of LIU that Sollazzo had to call everyone he knew to get $2,000 down on Idaho to win. The Blackbirds prevailed, 59–57, and Idaho covered; but with the bookies' vigorish and the players' payroll, Sollazzo was minus more than $500. No matter how many winners he bought, Sollazzo couldn't break even.

After the Blackbirds' narrow victory, Sherman treated his buddies to a Christmas out on the town. A couple of LIU hangers-on also hooked a ride, and the caravan stopped to water at Birdland, where the fabulous Sarah Vaughan was singing the blues. "It's on me," Sherman announced. "For everybody. For all of my friends."

Fletcher Johnson pulled his friend aside. "What are you doing, Sherman?" he asked. "Hey, man. That's a lot of money."

"Don't worry about it," Sherman smiled. "I can take care of it."

It wasn't until just before the New Year that Sherman was forced to have second thoughts about his recent good fortune. Sherman's father was his number-one fan. He had been rejoicing in his son's progress ever since junior high school and he knew every one of Sherman's moves. But he was disturbed by what he was seeing, and when they could sneak away, he sat Sherman down for a chat.

"Sherman," he said quietly. "What's the matter, son? You don't seem to be playing like you used to. Is something wrong?"

Sherman looked away in sudden shame. Then he shook his head and mumbled, "No." It marked the first time in his life that he had ever lied to his father.

There was another doubleheader at the Garden on December 28. As usual, the morning papers printed special boxes framing the day's point spreads. CCNY was favored by 9 over Arizona, and LIU by 11 over Western Kentucky. Sollazzo pledged a $5,000 pot to Roman, Roth, Warner, and Layne. The gambler had to move fast to get $6,000 down on Arizona, and he was only quoted a 6-point line. The Beavers lost the game, 41–38, and Sollazzo made a profit of about $900.

For the second game, Sollazzo induced the LIU conspirators to take the Blackbirds over the spread. The gambler had no problem betting $10,000 on LIU minus the original 11 points. If the Blackbirds won by 12 or more, Sollazzo would clean up. LIU sat on a comfortable 20-point lead throughout most of the game, but they went into a tailspin in the waning moments and won by only 77–70. Sollazzo was furious and refused to shell out any money to the players. He was positive that the Blackbirds were double-crossing him and doing business with another gambler.

If Sollazzo was angry, there were plenty of bookies who were ready to kill. Crooked games are anathema to an honest, workaday bookie. They prevent him from evening out his bets and make him vulnerable to a big loss should the "wrong" team win. A bookmaker would much rather work on commission and never lose money. The New York bookies were in a bind and were forced to make a move. They couldn't refuse action on LIU and CCNY for long and hope to keep their customers: The suckers also bet on hockey and the horses and would soon be betting on baseball. Some of the bookies banded together to place a $50 limit on any bets against either CCNY or LIU. Several of them pooled $5,000 and hired a private detective to try and run down all the specifics of the fixed ball games.

IKE GELLIS REMEMBERS: "If the bookies were aware of the monkey business, so were the sportswriters. All of the New York basketball writers had contacts with bookies. A lot of them played the ponies. Any sportswriter worth his salt had to know what was going on."

In 1950, Max Kase was the sports editor of the *New York Journal-American*. Kase wasn't much of a basketball fan, and some of his associates swear that he never saw a college game in his life. But his staff was beginning to turn in sarcastic stories whenever the stench at the Garden became unavoidable. Before the year was out, Kase took it upon himself to try and turn over a few headlines. He began dropping into gambling joints and sports hangouts. He asked discreet questions and kept his eyes and ears alive. Then, with a handful of facts to justify all the rumors, Kase turned several of the newspaper's best crime reporters loose on the story.

It was a busy time for everybody. Salvatore Sollazzo paid homage to the New Year by throwing an extravagant party at the Latin Quarter. Some of the country's finest collegiate basketball talent was in attendance. There were photographs taken. A very busy time.

From December 28 to 31, the American Communist Party held a secret convention in New York. In Detroit, Joe Louis knocked out Freddie Beshore at 2:48 of the fourth round. North of Seoul, an artillery barrage by the Chinese Reds broke a New Year's Eve calm on the Korean battlefield. Michigan upset California in the Rose Bowl. "Our democratic institutions are sound and strong," said President Truman in his State of the Union Address. "Our country is in a healthy condition." On January 1, 1951, Miss Erma Leach ended a 152-day session atop a 60-foot flagpole in San Francisco, winning $7,500, a mink coat, and a Cadillac. Miss Leach, a shapely blonde, was sponsored by a used-car dealer. And it was business as usual at the Garden.

At the turn of the year, the Beavers were only 5 and 3. Bobby Sand was distressed, and Nat Holman was outraged. But whatever their current failures and whatever abuse they received from other quarters, the City College students and alumni continued to clasp the Beavers to their bosom. "Allegaroo" still owned New York. A capacity crowd witnessed a New Year's Day twin bill at the Garden. The lineup matched CCNY against St. John's, and NYU against Cornell. The Beavers lost the first game, 47–44, with Roman, Roth, Warner, and Layne each receiving another $250 "tip" from Sollazzo. The gambler managed to scrounge up a few thousand on the game but he was still losing money.

The long-awaited Christmas present that finally tumbled down Connie Schaff's chimney was a trio of gamblers fronted by Jackie Goldsmith, the Blackbirds' old "Brownsville Bomber." During their negotiations, Schaff informed Goldsmith that he was also representing another teammate, and their price was $1,500 each. Goldsmith consulted his cronies, and the deal was consummated. The maturing Violets were favored by 4 over a veteran Cornell team, but Schaff instrumented a mild upset, and the Big Red emerged triumphant, 69–56. Goldsmith began to hedge when Schaff appeared for his $3,000. Goldsmith's excuse was that the afternoon game time prevented his organization from betting as much as they had planned. Schaff was given $1,900 to split with his phantom teammate.

LIU ripped South Carolina, 84–58, to run their record to 8–0. The Blackbirds were nationally ranked, and Clair Bee had every reason to be satisfied with himself. Bee always claimed credit for "creating" the basketball powerhouse that had allowed LIU to grow and prosper. The school's enrollment had tripled since Bee joined the faculty, and his salary was now $12,000 a year. Like Nat Holman, Bee also had a financial interest in a summer camp. After practice one day in early January, Bee called Sherman into his office to offer his prize pupil some advice. There was fresh news that the Knicks were preparing a long-term contract for Sherman's signature, and the Blackbirds looked like a cinch for both the NIT and the NCAA.

"Isn't it wonderful?" Bee said. "Everything is happening even better than we'd hoped."

Sherman didn't answer. He sat with his elbows resting on his knees, his shoulders hunched, and his hands clasped between his legs. Sherman thought about the fraternity of basketball players. He thought about the lie he had told to his father's face. Sherman stared at a spot on the floor and numbly nodded his head.

"Don't make a mistake now," Bee warned. "If the referee calls a foul on you that you don't like, take it. Don't say a word. Only a couple more weeks and you'll be done. You're still not the best player you could be, but you're the best there ever was."

Sherman remained mute and Bee interpreted his nodding as understanding and assent. When Bee was finished, Sherman raced out of the office, chased by his own footsteps and haunted by his own shadow.

On the morning of January 4, the newspapers announced the Blackbirds as 7-point favorites over Bowling Green. Because of the $10,000 Sollazzo lost on the LIU–Western Kentucky game, he was able to get a large bet down on the Falcons +7. Sollazzo was horrified when Sherman and Leroy Smith sparked the Blackbirds to an early 20-point lead. The Blackbirds had fun for three quarters before they remembered the task at hand. Then Sherman proceeded to kick the ball out of bounds and Smith shot two air balls from the foul line. Their performance was so transparent that the fans began to jeer and shout insults. "Hey, Smitty," yelled one leather-lung. "What's the points tonight? Huh, ya bum?" The Blackbirds won the game, 69–63, and Sollazzo's bets were good.

Two days later, Clair Bee received an anonymous letter accusing White, Bigos, and Smith of being a party to a fix. Bee brought the charge to the players, who made vehement denials. But the letter scared them straight. The LIU coterie met and decided to be done with dumping, fixing, and shaving points. Gard communicated their resolution to Sollazzo, and the gambler pleaded for the players to change their minds. "No more," said Sherman. "No more deals." But it was already too late. Max Kase's investigation began to churn up some incriminating connections.

Eddie Gard loved to talk in codes, but he was always careless and overt in his movements. It wasn't too hard to spot him as a bagman. Kase had Gard's name within a week. Then on January 10, Kase contacted Manhattan district attorney Frank Hogan to say that Eddie Gard was worth watching. Hogan was already involved with the Junius Kellogg case and he was extremely interested in the news. In return for the tip, Kase was granted exclusive rights to the scoop whenever the story broke. The D.A. put a tail on Gard and a tap on his phone.

The day after Kase spoke to Hogan, there was another brace of ball games at the Garden. In the first contest, the Beavers went against Boston College. CCNY opened as a 13-point favorite, but by the time Sollazzo started his inquiries, the spread dropped to 7. It was also announced that Ed Warner had a bad knee and wouldn't be able to play. The more Sollazzo kept losing, the more he tried to prime the pump. Sollazzo said he'd give Warner $500 anyway, and he promised $1,500 each to Roman, Roth, and Layne. But the heat was on, and Sollazzo was lucky to get $2,500 bet on Boston College. Once again, the gambler was a certain loser even before the first dribble. The Beavers shot poorly and they trailed by 6 at the half. Nat had a fit during the intermission and rained maledictions on the players' heads. Al Roth and Ed Warner were twenty-one years old, Eddie Roman and Floyd Layne were only twenty. They were all young enough to be intimidated and sometimes frightened by Nat. The players went out for the second half and they played with a common purpose. Nat had stoked them. And if they could hate again, they could also love again. They suddenly forgot about their private lives and moved about the court with a shared consciousness. Everything clicked back into place. The Beavers rallied to take a 4-point lead with only minutes remaining in the game.

ONE OF NAT'S BOYS REMEMBERS: "We were still the champs. No matter what."

Boston College outscored the Beavers 9–1 down the stretch to win the game, 63–59. When the players cornered Gard later that evening, he handed them each an envelope and then split. Al Roth received $1,400 in cash, but the rest of the envelopes were empty. There were arguments, feuds, and poison blood. Over the next few weeks, more than half of Eddie Gard's telephone conversations dealt with the $2,100 Sollazzo still owed the Beavers. The players didn't like being stiffed. They were disillusioned and confused. They finally decided to play to win for the rest of the season.

The second half of the January 11 doubleheader matched St. John's against the top-ranked team in the country, the undefeated Bradley Braves. By the end of the third quarter, Gene Melchiorre, Aaron Preece, Billy Mann, and Bud Grover had all fouled out and the Braves were upset, 68–59. "To put it bluntly," said *The New York Times*, "St. John's played basketball while Bradley concentrated on other things."

A BOOKIE REMEMBERS: "It was a crazy time. There were players dumping, coaches dumping, and referees dumping. But there was one college game that really stood out. One of the refs was doing business, and all game long he didn't even make one call. The other official was running around like a lunatic trying to cover the whole court. The Garden went bananas. Every guy there was screaming at the guy standing next to him."

A few days later, there was an NBA game played in Fort Wayne, Indiana. One of the players from the visiting team hailed from the Lower East Side. As the teams warmed up, the player was startled to see Eddie Gard sitting in the front row. They greeted each other politely. The player also paid his respects to another familiar face, referee Sol Levy. The player scored 14 points in the first quarter, and his team broke out on top. But, early in the second period, before his coach had a chance to lift him, the player was fouled out of the ball game. "Sol," he said. "What the fuck are you doing to me?" A pair of plainclothes detectives overheard every word.

The Blackbirds ran their unbeaten string to 10 with wins over St. Louis, 74–62, and Ithaca, 79–45. LIU-Duquesne and Manhattan–De Paul were in the Garden's spotlight on January 16—the night that Junius Kellogg refused to fall. Duquesne was a 6-point favorite and Sollazzo somehow wasn't convinced that the Blackbirds were finished doing business. He bet a huge wad on the Dukes with the points. White, Smith, and Bigos amassed a total of 64 points, and the Blackbirds trounced Duquesne, 84–52. The second game wasn't much better for Sollazzo. Gard had informed him that Junius Kellogg would be leading the Jaspers down the drain, and Sollazzo bet another load on De Paul with 2 points. When Manhattan won, 62–59, Sollazzo was into his bookies for

$75,000 on basketball alone. Sollazzo spent the next few weeks smuggling gold as fast as he could and trying to pick his own winners.

The Manhattan College betting scandal broke into the news on January 18. When Jackie Goldsmith read the papers, he immediately tore up his address book and began blackmailing one of his gambling associates. Nat Holman reacted by summoning his boys to a meeting.

ED WARNER REMEMBERS: "Nat explained to us that we should keep clean. He told us to stay away from gamblers, to keep our noses clean, and to keep our records clean. He said if we were ever approached by gamblers to report it to the authorities."

The Blackbirds were 16–0 and ranked in the top 10 when the first tremors rocked the front pages. The team was preparing to depart on a lengthy road trip, and Sherman was palpitating with anxiety. Some of his friends showed him the newspaper stories and jokingly asked if he was involved. Sherman swore to his innocence, but there was a bleeding ulcer inside his soul. The road trip was a catastrophe. LIU whipped San Francisco before losing to California, 69–67.

On January 29, the public was still reeling from the dump revelations. Even the most casual fan lived in fear of tomorrow's headlines. But the Blackbirds lost their second game in succession, 62–61, to Arizona in Tucson, and Clair Bee couldn't contain himself. "I hate to say it," Bee said, "but we lost to Arizona simply because the referees wanted us to lose. They took the game away from us. There's no doubt in my mind that their actions were deliberate." The Blackbirds closed out their western swing by losing to Kansas State, 85–65, and St. Louis, 62–57.

SHERMAN WHITE REMEMBERS: "Maybe there was some kind of psychological letdown. We were glad to be rid of the dirty work, but we couldn't shake the feeling that something awful was going to happen."

117

8

The City College fixers sighed with deliverance once they were out of Sollazzo's clutches. The Beavers beat John Carroll University, 79–67; Lawrence Tech, 68–66; Holy Cross, 73–63; and Loyola of Chicago, 69–61. But then the Manhattan College arrests frosted their sleep with nightmares, and for weeks they were worried and skittish. Frank Hogan squeezed the scandals hard, and his office began issuing daily press releases. But there was no connection reported between the Manhattan crew and the Sollazzo-Gard axis. In their youthful naïveté, the City fixers began to think that maybe they had been exempted from their fate. Perhaps they had been given a second chance. After all, they were the "Cinderella Team." They made a habit of defying the odds and the gods. Lessons were learned and solemn vows were sworn. The Beavers' flurry of victories boosted their record to a respectable 10–5. They began pointing to the NIT. Then the team lost two clutch ball games: 63–61 to Fordham, and 67–64 to Canisius. CCNY was now 10–7: Nat began to fume and Ned Irish began to twitch.

On Saturday night, February 17, Nat and his boys girded for a ball game they had to win. The Beavers were playing Josh Cody's tenacious Temple Owls down in Philadelphia. Cody was a wizard of zones, and the Owls played defense like spiders. The Temple student body engulfed the court and shook the visitors' basket. They screamed and they hooted the school cheer. But the Beavers were oblivious. They concentrated on the flow of the ball game, and CCNY de-horned the Owls, 95–71. They had once again persevered in a pressure situation. The team boarded the train and headed back to New York with light hearts. They laughed and joked like college kids out on a lark. They were only a month away from the Garden's glamorous NIT. Another championship would be atonement enough, and they had almost four weeks to tune their game. After the NIT, there would be the NCAA postseason festival in Minneapolis, the U.S. Olympic team in Helsinki in 1952, then the pros: the Golden Cinderella Brooklyn Beavers. They'd all be rich.

Even Eddie Roman was in a jolly mood. He was headed out to Brooklyn for the wedding of his closest friend. His whole family would be there. Most of the other ballplayers also had parties waiting for them back in New York. "Allegaroo!" they shouted. "Garoo garah!"

Nat Holman sat alone in the rear of the car with his reading light switched off. It was after midnight. Nat had been coaching basketball for thirty-three of his fifty-six years. He was weary and he longed for nothing more than a good night's sleep. As the train eased out of Camden, a stranger sat down beside Nat. "Mr. Nat Holman?" the man said. "I recognize you from the newspapers." Nat thought the man was an autograph seeker until he flashed a badge. "I'm from the district attorney's office," the man said. "There's another detective here with me. The D.A. wants to talk to some of your players. . . ."

Nat was stunned into silence. The detective flipped open his notebook. "Edward Roman," the detective said. "Alvin Roth and Edward Warner."

"My God," Nat gasped. "What for? What did they do?"

"I really can't go into the details," the detective said. "But the D.A. thinks they might be involved with gamblers."

Nat was dumbstruck.

"We don't want a scene," the detective continued. "When the train gets into Penn Station, the D.A. wants you to take the team aside and talk to them. Tell them to cooperate."

Nat nodded weakly and the man vanished. Nat sat for a lonely moment in the darkness. What could he possibly tell them? Then Nat had an aide summon the members of the team one at a time. Nat told his boys to wait for him on the platform when they reached New York, he had something important to say to them.

The train whistled into Penn Station at 1:15 A.M. Even at that hour, the depot was a bedlam of madly scurrying people: businessmen, redcaps, hookers, vacationers, winos, detectives, and reporters. And right outside the steaming train, a group of young giants huddled around a proud, silver-haired man. Four detectives advanced to seal off the perimeter, and Nat cleared his throat. He was mindful that the temper of the time viewed the Fifth Amendment as the last resort for scoundrels and thieves.

Nat pointed to the detectives. "These men," he said, "want to take some of you boys over to the district attorney's office. But I want you to know this, that I'm talking to you as if you were my own brothers. And I'm telling you to go with them. Go without fear. Tell them everything they want to know. If your consciences are clean, you'll be all right and you won't get into trouble. If not, then I'm sorry for you. If there is a mess, the sooner they clean it up the better."

Nat instructed Eddie Roman to call him after the D.A. was through. He told Bobby Sand to telephone the players' parents and inform them that their sons were being detained by the police. Then Nat turned to the detective. "Can I go along with them?" he asked.

"No," said the detective. "The D.A. doesn't want it done that way." Nat watched while Roman, Roth, and Warner were handcuffed and led off to jail.

At the same time, in various parts of the city, detectives were also rounding up Salvatore Sollazzo, Eddie Gard, and Connie Schaff.

It was 2:30 when Bobby Sand made the painful phone calls. Eddie Roman's family was still wide awake. They were afraid that Eddie had been in a train wreck. "The sword has fallen," Bobby said. The parents wept and so did Bobby.

Floyd Layne rode the subway back home to the Bronx, shivering through his heavy winter coat, his life in the grip of a secret miracle.

Roman, Roth, and Warner were booked at the Elizabeth Street precinct on the Lower East Side. Then, in the company of several detectives and a growing army of reporters, the players were walked the few blocks to the Centre Street Station. The troop was hounded by a Sunday morning crowd of strollers. The players were fingerprinted and mugged. An attendant relieved them of the zipper bags holding the wet uniforms they had worn against Temple. The three young men were then separated and questioned late into the night.

"I stayed awake until dawn," Nat said. "But Eddie never called."

The evidence that Hogan had was not the sort that leads to convictions. He had recordings of conversations between Gard and several of the players haggling about the money due for the Boston College game. There were opaque references to "squaring things with the uptown girls" (the CCNY players), and to meetings between "that girl Sally" (Sollazzo) and "that girl with the big nose" (Roman). Hogan's detectives had also observed a long, intense conversation between Sollazzo and Roman one Sunday afternoon in a bar on East Fifty-ninth Street. The interrogation was orchestrated by Hogan with the assistance of Vincent O'Connor and Vincent Scotti.

Carmen Miranda's hats were the rage of the silver screen, but the Miranda decision was legality of the future. The policemen made the players listen to recordings of their own telephone discussions. They told the young men stories designed to illustrate the D.A.'s omniscience: they told them that the Bradley Braves were dumping and that gamblers had broken Gene Melchiorre's knuckles. They told each player that his two teammates had already confessed.

Eddie Roman was the first to give. He tearfully admitted to his numerous crimes against society. The others quickly followed suit, with the notable exception of Sollazzo, who steadfastly maintained his innocence. Toward noon on Sunday, Hogan had sufficient solid evidence to have everybody arrested. Bail was set at $10,000 for Schaff, and $15,000 each for Roman, Roth, and Warner. Hogan conferred with agents from the IRS, the Immigration department, and the Treasury Department, and Sollazzo was hauled before Chief Magistrate John M. Murtagh. The judge excoriated the gambler as one who "appears to have corrupted these young men and brought disgrace on a great institution." His Honor was a CCNY alumnus, and Sollazzo was held without bail. Eddie Gard made it known that he would cooperate freely with the D.A. and asked to be held in protective custody. Bail was posted for the others, and they were released on Sunday afternoon, just in time to read Max Kase's sensational story in the *Journal-American*.

Enterprising reporters found Eddie Roman's parents hysterical, locked inside their bedroom. "I have nothing to say," Eddie told them. "Nothing." The unanimous opinion from Eddie's in-laws, uncles, and aunts was, "He's a good boy." The detectives also made an appearance. They were zealous in tracking down the remnants of the bribe money since, according to the law, everything they recovered went into the Police Pension Fund. Eddie handed them the $2,500 he had left from his share. Several days later, Eddie's brother walked into Hogan's office with an additional $500.

Ed Warner led Hogan's detectives to $3,050 that he had secreted in a shoe box in the basement of an aunt's house. But the distraught aunt refused to speak to the reporters. "I don't want anybody in here," she shrilled through the closed door. "I don't want any people. I don't want Eddie. I don't ever want to see him again." Another of Ed's aunts ushered the press into her living room and showed them a tableful of Ed's trophies and citations. "They gave him all that," she cried. "Now they say he did all those terrible things. How can it be? . . . But just tell me where they've got him. I've got to see him." The verdict on the streets of Harlem was also merciful. "Ed was a hero," reported his friends and neighbors. "Whenever he walked by, people would always stop and stare. If Ed took the money, then he must have needed it."

Al Roth's mother was glad to have her son home. "It's good," she said, "that there's no more basketball. He was working so hard and getting so tired. It was too much. But I was very proud of him." Al had deposited his share of the bribe money in his mother's bank account. His mother met detectives at the bank on Monday morning and handed them $5,060. When Al was badgered by the reporters, he immediately spilled his guilt onto the front pages. "I know I did a wrong thing," Al said. "Nobody will ever know how sorry I am. Why did I do it? I guess I did it because I wanted to be grown up. I mean, I was sick and tired of asking my father for money all the time. Whenever I needed a suit or something I always had to go to him. I wanted to be able to do things myself. You know, like a grown-up. My father works hard. He's been driving a soda truck for twenty-five years. I knew he didn't have too much money to give me."

Neither Connie Schaff nor Eddie Gard had any secret hiding places. Most of their dumping dollars were already spent.

The reporters needed a scorecard to sort the Sunday morning traffic that flowed through Hogan's headquarters. But the contingent from St. John's University was the most prominent: Several ballplayers shepherded by a big-shot lawyer named Henry Urgetta, and a slew of priests.

AN EX-DUMPER REMEMBERS: "I played for St. John's around that time, and a lot of the guys on the team were involved with Sollazzo and Gard. We were no different from anybody else. Some of the guys were sleeping with Sollazzo's wife."

But Urgetta wouldn't permit the D.A.'s men to question the players in private, individual quarters. Hogan was forced to build his own case and the D.A. had nothing but wiretaps and rumors—nothing but inadmissible evidence. Hogan was also being compelled by a variety of forces to limit the scope of his investigations. The D.A. had several recordings of conversations between certain St. John's players and Eddie Gard. In those days, the recordings were made on brittle celluloid platters. While one of the St. John's boys was being questioned, "an appointed official of the City of New York" burst into the room and accidentally knocked the platter to the floor, shattering it into splinters.

A LAWYER REMEMBERS: "Frank Hogan was a decent man and a devout Catholic. He couldn't help breaking the Manhattan College story, but several of the other local Catholic universities got off very lightly. A lot of guys lost a lot of sleep until the statute of limitations ran out on them."

A photograph found its way into Monday morning's newspapers. It was taken at Sollazzo's gala New Year's Eve party and it showed a St. John's player yoo-hooing with Eddie Gard and Jeanne Sollazzo. Urgetta and the player were immediately called downtown for a fifteen-minute interview. The player's father was a policeman who had been killed in the line of duty in 1945. "I am convinced," said Hogan, "that this boy is absolutely innocent of any wrongdoing. He told us of his social relationship with Sollazzo, and it was one to which any boy of his age would have been attracted because of the good times and because of his own relationship with Eddie Gard. The boy told us of an offer that Sollazzo made to him at the party and that he refused and left the premises shortly thereafter. It is significant that the young man never saw Sollazzo again after the party." Hogan added that the player confessed to taking money from gamblers whenever he played well, just as other players from other colleges often accepted envelopes from rich alumni. Regrettable, but certainly not criminal. "Everything we have heard about the young man," the D.A. continued, " is entirely to his credit. I have no reason to disbelieve his story." The press let the matter drop into oblivion.

Monday morning, February 19, marked a weekly luncheon of the Metropolitan Basketball Writers Association at Mamma Leone's. Nat took the opportunity to announce that Roman, Roth, and Warner were indefinitely suspended from the school. Nat added that CCNY would honor its legal commitment to play three more games in the Garden. But the college was reserving judgment about scheduling any more games there in the future. Several other coaches also addressed the gathering.

"Everybody seems to be talking about bringing the game back to the campus," said Howard Cann. "But the way things are, you could play in the attic or the cellar, and the gamblers would still be operating. I guess that from now on coaches will have to start sacrificing talent for character."

"I'm very disappointed in Eddie Gard," said Clair Bee. "But the rest of my boys are innocent. I swear it on the heads of my children."

Nat returned to the CCNY campus later that afternoon to face 3,000 students gathered in the Great Hall in a "show of confidence rally" for the twelve players remaining on the team. Nat voiced his disappointment and amazement at the involvement of Roman, Roth, and Warner. "I was close to those boys," Nat said. "And I repeatedly told them that if they wanted to dance they would have to pay the piper." Nat then named Floyd Layne as one of the Beavers' new co-captains. The team was due to play Lafayette at the Garden on Thursday, and the students were urged to attend the game. They were asked to "stand by their team and counteract the jeers and hoots of needlers." A petition was circulated demanding the readmission of the guilty players. The twelve surviving players were introduced to resounding "Allegaroos" and a standing ovation. One of the newspapers erroneously reported that Floyd Layne took the microphone to announce that he would take over the broken ball club and provide leadership for the rest of the season. But Floyd didn't dare to say a word.

It didn't take the politicians long to dance their way out to center stage. Two New York State legislators introduced a bill to increase the penalty for bribing athletes. Governor Thomas Dewey supported the measure, and the current penalty of one to five years was doubled. A congressman from New York asked the House to set up a committee to look into the scandal. Senator Estes Kefauver of Tennessee, a man with presidential ambitions, replied that his Senate Crime Commission had been probing the basketball fix "for some time." Frank Hogan laughed when he read the senator's latest bulletin. "It's a surprise to me," the D.A. said.

The basketball scandals were also dragged into the international arena. Arthur Daley of *The New York Times* said that the United States could cure many of its ills by exporting the game of basketball to Russia. But the Soviet Union wanted no part of American sports. According to *Soviet Sport*, "Student sports in the United States are used as a means of training young boys in the spirit of militarism. Most large American colleges are now directed by former generals and admirals who are primarily interested in educating the future soldiers of America's aggressive armies. New games played in American colleges include races run backwards and wrestling in pits filled with rotten fish."

In an issue of *The Sporting News* placed in the mail three days after the CCNY arrests, Sherman White was named Player of the Year in college basketball. Sherman was averaging 27.7 points per game and he needed only 77 more to set an all-time collegiate scoring record. The Blackbirds had rebounded from their shaky road trip by winning their next four games. They were currently 20–4 and ranked sixteenth in the country. Sherman was walking out of school after his last class on Tuesday, when a detective put a hand on his shoulder. Sherman knew who it was without looking. It was almost a relief to have it over with. The detective who chauffeured Sherman to the Elizabeth Street precinct was very sympathetic. "We all gamble," the detective said.

"I know," Sherman moaned. "But no one gambled for higher stakes than me."

Sherman, Dolf, and Leroy were subjected for ten hours to the identical methods used so successfully on their CCNY counterparts. Recordings were played, tales of police power were retold, and false confessions were placed in front of the young men. Assistant D.A. Scotti grilled Sherman in a harsh and abrasive manner and Sherman resisted. Then Hogan, the master of the soft sell, took over. The D.A. was a rabid sports fan. He reminisced with Sherman about great games and great players. It wasn't long before both the prisoner and his accuser were crying their way through all the details of Sherman's participation in the scandal. Sherman meekly led the detectives to a $5,500 cache taped to the back of a dresser drawer in his room at the Y.

Adolf Bigos telephoned his mother and told her to conduct the detectives up to the attic. From the lining of a sports coat, the policemen recovered $5,000 in crisp bills. They also found $1,030 in a shoe in Leroy Smith's room at the Y, and another $900 in a safe-deposit box registered in the name of Leroy's brother. Bail was set at $15,000 and the ex-ballplayers were permitted to go home.

SHERMAN WHITE REMEMBERS: "I'll never forget those days. I didn't go back to school at all. I just sat at home by myself in my room, looking at all the pictures and trophies I'd collected since I was a kid. It was hell. I finally made myself call Clair Bee. I told him there was no use saying I was sorry, but I wanted him to know that I *was* sorry and that I hated doing what I did to him. I guess I didn't make much sense. Bee was as nice as could be, but there wasn't much to say except I'd made a terrible mistake. The only good thing was that my family stood by me."

If Sherman's father was loyal, he was also heartbroken. "It would have been different," he said, "if Sherman was raised on the streets. But Sherman had to go to college to learn something he was never taught at home."

On Wednesday morning, the trustees of Long Island University announced the suspension of White, Bigos, Smith, and the school's entire intercollegiate sports program. Several of the trustees favored following CCNY's example: finishing out the season at the Garden, honoring their contractual obligations, and sucking out every last dollar. But the majority of the board voted to "withdraw from the whole mess entirely and get away from the Garden and its atmosphere of corruption." They also forbade LIU's intramural athletes to play basketball in the Catskills.

There was another doubleheader scheduled for the Garden on Thursday, February 22, and the canceled LIU-Cincinnati game was replaced by a CCNY–St. John's frosh contest. The featured game had the Beavers playing Lafayette. Only 7,500 fans showed up, and 3,500 of them were City College students. In the locker room before the game, Nat tried to motivate his boys. "Everybody thinks this is a patched-up team," Nat said. "Let's show them we're not." The defending NIT and NCAA champs started Herb Cohen and Ronnie Nadell at the guards, Herb Holmstrom and Arnie Smith at the forwards, and Floyd Layne at center.

"I was numb," Floyd recalls. "I didn't feel a thing. I don't remember the game at all."

Floyd scored 19 points and the Beavers won, 67–48. After the game, the City students roared out of the Garden and deluged Times Square. They formed a ring around the Times Building and barricaded the streets with their bodies. But the police at the scene were remarkably indulgent. Traffic was rerouted, the impromptu rally burned out after forty-five minutes, and the students were gently herded into the subway. "That kind of spirit is exceedingly commendable," commented CCNY president Harry Wright. "We all enjoyed it."

Reasons were sought to explain the situation, and everybody took a shot at apportioning the blame. A *New York Times* editorial, written like a knotted snake, pointed at the universities: "Too many of our colleges, nationwide, have, themselves, chased the easy buck (just as these basketball players did) or passed it on. Proselytizing of good players, the soft campus job for the star who can produce on the court; the building up by dubious means of a 'name' team for the aggrandizement of the college, the unearned passing mark on the report card, the glorification of a game and the devaluation of principle through failing to put first things first—these are the crimes that finally beget crimes."

A coaches' organization seconded the motion: "We believe the recent gambling exposé has grown out of a laxity on the part of college administrators to actively uphold the standards which would discourage such practices. Entirely too much emphasis has been placed by the schools on income and on winning the game."

The *New York Post* announced it would no longer be printing daily point spreads. The newspaper simultaneously launched a poll, asking their readers "How Would You Deal with the Players Who Sold Out?" Hogan moved quietly and squashed the offensive survey.

The blame began to settle on two fronts: Madison Square Garden and the Borscht Belt. The Bradley Braves voted 11–0 to reject any invitation to play in the upcoming NIT. Madison Square Garden, Inc., debated whether or not to close its facility to college basketball. But roundball doubleheaders generated almost as much revenue as the rodeo and the circus, and the discussion was very brief.

Phog Allen of Kansas jumped to defend the hinterlands: "Out here in the Midwest these scandalous conditions, of course, do not exist. But in the East, the boys, particularly those who participate in the resort hotel leagues during the summer months, are thrown into an environment which cannot help but breed the evil which more and more is coming to light."

Newspaper columnists all over the country joined the attack. The resort teams were "subterfuges for professionalism." In the Catskills, "the seeds are planted by the wily fixers for future harvests." The "softening up process" begins in the Jewish Alps. Milton Kutscher fronted a group of hotel owners who called a press conference to announce that corruption was not confined to any one geographical area.

One day in early February, a man named Saul Chabot had delivered to Pier 90 a 1950 two-door Buick that he was planning to take with him to France on the *Queen Elizabeth*. That afternoon, a pier checker began to prepare the car for loading. When he tried to empty the gas tank he discovered that the rear end was riding so low on its springs he couldn't get at the drain valve. He immediately notified a customs inspector. In a specially built compartment located under the rear bumper the inspector found eighty-two packages containing nearly $200,000 worth of gold bullion. The serial numbers had been obliterated in an operation personally supervised by Salvatore Sollazzo, but the authorities still traced the gold back to him.

On Saturday, February 24, the federal government filed a lien against Sollazzo for unpaid income taxes totaling $1,128,493.57. The books of both of his ring-making companies were seized: one was mortgaged to pay off the IRS, the other was auctioned to pay Sollazzo's legal fees. Sollazzo rested in the Tombs while awaiting trial on thirty charges of offending the peace and dignity of the people of the State of New York. He faced a total of sixty-five years in jail and additional fines up to $130,000. The Immigration office was also preparing an order to deport him to Italy.

In addition to his legal difficulties, Sollazzo's bookies were suddenly left with flashpaper IOU's. Sollazzo laughed at the threatening messages they sent him. Salvatore Sollazzo was an authentic celebrity. Jeanne was attractive enough to fetch at least one picture a week in the newspapers. "I'm innocent," Sollazzo insisted. He was defiant at the arraignment, and detectives caught him trying to smuggle notes to his business associates through his wife. One of his lawyers noted that the news of the scandal had pushed the Korean War over to page two, but Sollazzo's attempt to get his trial moved out of New York was unsuccessful. Acting on the advice of their attorneys, everybody except Eddie Gard pleaded not guilty, and the cases were all remanded to the courts.

The country was sweating out an epidemic of brain fever. Joe McCarthy terrified millions when he waved a sheet of blank paper in front of a television camera. "Here's my proof," the senator said. "Over one hundred Reds, pinkos, and fellow travelers in the top echelon of the State Department." Senator Kefauver remained in public view by conducting daily interviews with Mafia chieftains, bookmakers, and call girls. Paranoia was big at both the box office and the voting machines. Even the New York Police Department was simmering with scandal.

There was news of forgotten indictments and strange irregularities. When several reporters began digging into the basketball fixes they came upon some interesting bones. The new reports were that the NYPD had "suppressed" forty recordings of telephone conversations made before and after the '49–'50 season that detailed a "gigantic fix involving players from every big-time college in and around New York." The publication of the data would undoubtedly result in the demise of the entire sport of college basketball. Educational institutions would be ruined, lives would be blighted. And political careers would eclipse one another.

William P. O'Brien was the police commissioner in 1950, and it was alleged that he "failed to use the information on orders from a higher authority." There were rumors of religious pressures. O'Brien answered the charges with a categorical denial, and the current commissioner ordered an investigation into the existence and/or whereabouts of the recordings. When a "double-checking" of the police files failed to reveal any such recordings, the matter was forgotten along with yesterday's ball scores.

But the guilty players were relentlessly marched across the front pages, and the basketball scandals became America's favorite soap opera. The newspapers printed outrageous lies every day. The ballplayers were falsely accused of galli-vanting with girls at the Copa. The newspapers strongly hinted at continuing illicit behavior.

ONE OF NAT'S BOYS REMEMBERS: "It was just to sell news-papers. The newspapers knew that the scandal was partly their own responsibility. With their point spreads and their paper bets they helped make gambling a way of life in New York City. Some of the sportswriters were very close to us. They trusted us and when everything finally blew open, they felt betrayed and carried on a personal vendetta. Sid Friedlander was a City grad. We gave him a gold tie clasp when we won the NIT. Virtually all of the arrested players were either black or Jews. And almost all of the New York sportswriters were Jewish. They were in a position to help us, but they turned their backs and stepped us into the mud."

IKE GELLIS REPLIES: "I want to puke. That kind of crap doesn't even deserve an answer."

If the kings were lepers, if the champs were chumps, the dumpers were still coming out of the woodwork. Eddie Gard kept warbling, and two more arrests were made on Monday, February 27. The first involved Natie Miller, a senior and a dumper at LIU in '48–'49 when Sherman White was yet an unsuspecting sophomore. Then at 3:00 P.M., as he was leaving his last class of the day, Floyd Layne was finally collared by the law. "It was definitely a relief," said Floyd. He was immediately whisked down to the D.A.'s office. At 3:30, officials of the college announced the cancellation of CCNY's two remaining games at the Garden. Floyd made a full con-fession shortly before 4:00. His flowerpot was dug up and weeded of $2,890 in bribe money. Floyd's bail was set at $15,000 and a home owned by a relative was posted as se-curity.

FLOYD LAYNE REMEMBERS: "The five-block walk from the subway station to my house seemed like a thousand miles. I was sure that people were staring down at me from every window in every building I passed."

After Floyd was arrested, Nat called together the remaining members of the varsity and the entire freshman team. The meeting was held in Nat's office on the second floor of Lewisohn Stadium. Hiding in the bathroom, at Nat's connivance, was a reporter from the *Post*. Nat's critics had been resurrected when the scandal broke and "Mr. Basketball" felt the need to defend himself. The main charge was that Nat had failed to protect his boys; that he should have let them know about their imminent arrest in time for them to get off the train before it reached New York. Nat's detractors claimed that the CCNY players should have been given the opportunity to get a lawyer like the St. John's kids. With the reporter's ear at the keyhole, Nat reminded his players how many times both he and Winograd had warned them about gamblers. Nat's virtue was rinsed and drip-dried in the next day's newspapers.

Not long after Floyd's arrest, the Board of Higher Education announced the establishment of a three-man committee "to investigate every phase of this matter, to ascertain cause and to study the problem created by increased emphasis on intercollegiate basketball, to consider administrative changes and changes in athletic practices." Heads would roll at CCNY. Veteran faculty members smiled knowingly at Bobby Sand and clucked with anticipated sympathy.

Farther uptown, Floyd Layne and Eddie Roman had a somber, stillborn reunion. "It's all over," said Eddie. "We'll never get another chance. We might as well go down to the docks and start looking for work."

If there were those who rejoiced at the scandals, at the vipers in the Big Apple, there were also poets and righteous men who sang in the wilderness. Jimmy Cannon was the star of the *Post*'s sports department and his eloquent sorrow was almost a balm: "The tall children of basketball have been consumed by the slot machine racket of sports. They are amateurs exploited by a commercial alliance of culture and commerce. . . . It is not because I am a sports writer that I have compassion for the arrested players. They have forfeited honor at an age when the dream of life should be beautiful. We should weep when we come upon a boy who has been fleeced of principles before he is a man. What made them special has destroyed them. Their youth has been slain. The assassin of youth is the most repulsive of criminals."

Dr. Ordway Tead was the chairman of the Board of Higher Education: "These students did a terrible thing. But the hardened men who misled them are more guilty than these youths. They are all under suspension from school, and my personal opinion is that after a year's suspension they should be given another chance—for the Christian attribute of forgiveness should continue to be a part of our civilization."

And down in Lexington, Kentucky, Adolph Rupp grabbed at another chance to get his name in the papers. "Gamblers," chortled the Baron, "couldn't get at my boys with a ten-foot pole."

On March 2, the National Collegiate Athletic Association made its voice heard. The NCAA's august Council spoke on behalf of 292 subscribing schools ranging from the University of Alabama to Youngstown College, from Princeton to Rose Poly, and from Brooklyn College to Buena Vista University. The NCAA was the last bastion of amateurism, and the bureaucracy and regulator of intercollegiate sports. The Council announced that there would never ever be another NCAA basketball championship staged at the Garden. It recommended that its entire membership boycott the joint. But the Council also allowed that its recommendation was "not binding."

Several days later, the presidents of Manhattan College, St. John's University, NYU, and CCNY issued a joint statement declaring their intentions of rescheduling their respective basketball teams at the Garden for the '51–'52 season. City College noted that its return was dependent upon the approval of the Board of Higher Education. The quartet made the undeniable point that the Garden "was not totally responsible for the present status of intercollegiate basketball in metropolitan New York." The presidents pledged in chorus to join the directors of Madison Square Garden, Inc., to insure that the scandals would have no sequel. They argued that "returning college basketball to the campus would not relieve the inherent dangers of gambling and corruption." They announced that a "top level" committee would be set up to "establish ticket prices, ticket allotments, team accommodations, and radio and TV rights." The four-part harmony concluded with a hymn: "We firmly believe that part of the process of higher education is the development of moral integrity and stature in our students."

On March 4, an ex-con named Robert Scroggins was arrested for offering a University of Southern California basketball player $1,500 to "throw" a game against UCLA. The player, Ken Flower, reported the bribe to his coach. While the USC-UCLA game was being decided, Scroggins was apprehended in his hotel room. He was indicted and returned to the county jail in default of $50,000 bail. Two weeks later, the thirty-one-year-old Scroggins pleaded innocent by virtue of temporary insanity.

On March 26, three more CCNY players were arrested: Irwin Dambrot, Norm Mager, and Herb Cohen. Bail was set at $1,000 each. There was weeping and wailing at Passover seders all over Flatbush, Canarsie, and the Lower East Side. But Lent was also lean in the spring of 1951. Later that same day, Hank Poppe and John Byrnes pleaded not guilty to charges of trying to bribe Junius Kellogg and conspiring with gamblers to deliberately lose ball games.

On the very next evening, March 27, there was to be an amateur basketball tournament in Hoboken, New Jersey. The participating teams were named after sporting-goods emporiums, athletic clubs, bars, and furniture stores, and sometimes the players were named after colors. The tournament's organizers had advertised that one of the teams would include Sherman White, Eddie Roman, Ed Warner, and Floyd Layne; and the first game was a sellout.

The ballplayers found their lives welded together with a common guilt, and they all needed the affirmation of something positive in their lives. They were thoroughbreds trained to perform and they desperately required the release of playing basketball. But only Sherman and Eddie actually showed up for the game. They were both nervous as they trotted onto the court and they tried to shake the vitality back into their legs. For Sherman and Eddie, the game marked the first time in weeks they had worn a uniform. The team glided through a lay-up drill, and both Sherman and Eddie took extra care with their shots, knowing that a miss would bring a snicker from the crowd. But the pregame drills were suddenly halted, and the tournament director ordered Sherman and Eddie off the court. In the eyes of the law, the players were still free and innocent, so the game was delayed while they appealed the decision. Their request was denied to scattered applause and the game began without them. After they got dressed, Sherman and Eddie huddled in the stands and watched their friends playing basketball.

Floyd Layne wasn't in Hoboken that night, but not because he didn't have the inclination. Floyd was always a fighter and a battler who played from buzzer to buzzer. He was much too proud to hide. Bobby Sand got Floyd a job in the garment center, and Floyd exhibited his face in public every day. Maybe some people would make wisecracks. Maybe some would hold him in disgrace. But Floyd knew that he was chastened. He knew the look on his mother's face. Floyd resolved never to do another dishonest thing in his life. His love was his ballast and his pride was his purifying fire. Floyd needed them both in full measure to survive.

A few weeks later, Abe Saperstein contacted Floyd about the possibility of touring with the Harlem Globetrotters. At Saperstein's expense, Floyd flew out to St. Louis for a workout and a talk. Floyd was never out of shape and he played brilliantly. But Saperstein was cautious and wanted to test the public's reaction by having Floyd play with a farm team, the Kansas City Stars. "No," said Floyd. "I'm not going to play in a tank town just because of what I've done."

The basketball scandals hung around like smoke after a fire. The glossy magazines competed for profiles, advice, and confessions from the participants. Bobby Sand had several articles accepted by *Scholastic Coach*. But Nat Holman wasn't interested in the theory and practice of the fast-break offense. Nat had more grandiose opinions to express.

"I think it is obvious that there is a general relaxation of morals in the country," Nat said in an issue of *Sport*. "Brought on by the war hysteria, by the military draft, and by boys being at loose ends. . . . There has been recruiting without conscience. Boys have been bought, subsidized, catered to, and pampered. A coach tries to train his boys, to motivate them and inspire them to play the game for the joy of honest competition. Then they turn around and sell out. I felt I had control of my boys. I spoke to them often of the shady deals that would be thrust at them. I warned them to be careful. But the easy money was a great temptation. The rumors about dumps had been prevalent for some time, but I swore my boys would be immune. They were good boys and they had been warned. I couldn't be suspicious of my boys. When they made bad moves, I saw them as technical errors. . . . I always kept moving my boys in and out of a ball game. I'm known as a strict disciplinarian, and when a player goofs off on the court, out he comes. It would seem that such a practice would kill any attempts to dump a game, but I had seven of them against me. My first seven men were all in on the fix. I was strapped."

Nat went on to propose "the elimination of the point spread." He also added to the growing attack against resort basketball. "The hotel teams," Nat said, "are schools of crime. . . . And since playing for these hotel teams may have a bad influence on the boys, we at CCNY have decided not to allow their participation. We feel our basketball players represent CCNY throughout the year, not only on the basketball court but everywhere. If they want to represent someone else, they'll have to seek our permission. I've told the boys that if they disobey this new regulation, they'll be dropped from the squad." And Nat scoffed at premature reports of his retirement. "I wouldn't leave at a time like this," said Nat. "I think the college needs me now more than ever."

. . . ARRESTED . . . 3/30/51 . . . LOUIS LIPMAN . . . IN VIOLATION OF NYC PENAL CODE #302 . . . BRIBERY . . . FOR LIU-DUQUESNE AT MSG . . . 1/1/49 . . . RELEASED ON PAYMENT OF $1,000 BAIL . . .

With the arrests, the families of the accused usually contacted a lawyer friend or relative to arrange for bail. Most of the players had different lawyers handling the preliminaries, but some shared the same one.

ONE OF THE PLAYERS REMEMBERS: "People were using us right and left. One of my lawyers stole eighteen hundred dollars from me. He was a friend of the family. He wanted me to pay his fee as well as a fee for some of the work he had done for a teammate. The lawyer said something about my teammate not having any money and that we'd never get ourselves a top-flight lawyer unless there was money around. I gave him a total of thirty-six hundred dollars and I never knew what became of the money. When I asked the lawyer about it afterwards, he told me to ask my teammate. . . . The lawyer stole it from me, pure and simple. Everybody was dumping on us."

The CCNY alumni finally got together and persuaded Jacob Grumet to act as legal counsel for all the City College kids. Grumet was a former Assistant D.A. under both Thomas E. Dewey and Frank Hogan, and a former General Sessions judge. Grumet was a CCNY grad, class of 1919, and everybody called him "Judge." He announced that he was accepting the case for nothing. " This task," said Grumet, "is one of the saddest assignments I have ever undertaken." Grumet gave the players some familiar advice. "Cooperate," said the Judge. "Tell the authorities everything they want to know." Hogan indicated that the grand jury presentation would regard the entire case as one and that he was expecting multiple indictments.

There were causes and remedies advocated on street corners all over the city. Some suggested that intercollegiate basketball be suspended for a few years. One irate letter writer blamed the scandals on parks, sliding ponds, and sandboxes: "Sturdy teenagers scorn snow shoveling and lawn mowing. They would rather pester front doors like well-clad beggars asking for money to buy uniforms and athletic paraphernalia.

Soft-hearted adults provide a surplus of public recreational facilities, and the kids grow up thinking that everything coming their way—including bribes—should be accepted as their due." On March 10, even J. Edgar Hoover got into the act. Hoover scored the "hypocrisy and sham" of intercollegiate athletic codes. "In the name of victory," the G-man said, "college officials will go out and consummate very atrocious crimes." Hoover added that certain college fraternities are sadistic. But there were also serious attempts to salvage the situation.

Bobby Sand proposed a radical change in the shape of the game. Sand charged first that the colleges and the promoters are always resistant to new ideas. He pointed to the battle that raged over the widening of the 3-second zone. Sand's alteration called for restructuring a ball game into three 15-minute periods. The game would start and proceed as before until one team won two "sets." Total points scored and point differentials would be rendered unimportant. If a team won the first "set" by one point or by 100, it would still have to win another. Sand also suggested amending the rule that disqualifies a player on the accumulation of five personal fouls: when a player reaches his limit of fouls, he would be disqualified for only a period of 3 minutes, during which a substitution could be made. Sand argued that the hypothetical changes would prevent a dishonest referee from controlling a ball game. Sand's innovations were ridiculed for "breaking the continuity of tradition."

. . . ARRESTED . . . 4/13/51 . . . RICHARD FEURTADO . . . IN VIOLATION OF NYC PENAL CODE #302 . . . BRIBERY . . . RELEASED ON PAYMENT OF $1,000 BAIL. . . .

For a black man, the garment center provided a steady, subsistence wage and a lifetime of drudgery. Floyd Layne hated working there almost as much as he hated being inquisitioned by the grand jury. The courtroom guards would fight among themselves to escort the defendants and perhaps get their pictures in the newspaper. Floyd tried to accept each new setback and each new humiliation. He digested his experiences slowly and he forced his life to continue. Floyd finally quit his job in the garment center and began working as a shipping clerk. He was always a good worker, but sometimes the weight of his punctured dreams hung heavily around his neck. When Floyd was a student at CCNY, he had worked part-time at the Forest Neighborhood House, a community center just two blocks from his home. Floyd would coach the little kids and the big ones. He would officiate at ball games, break up fights, and remember everybody's name. Floyd loved working with kids. In the wake of his crime, he labored instead with packages, letters, and brown manila envelopes.

Both Floyd and Eddie Roman received an unbidden blessing when they were asked to represent the Immaculate Conception Roman Catholic Church in an amateur tournament held in the Bronx. The church's tiny gym was bulging with four hundred people, and the players didn't know what to expect. Floyd hit the first shot of the game, a two-hander from the corner. Then Eddie popped in a one-hander. And, each time, the players were engulfed by an outpouring of applause, forgiveness, and love. "It was one of the nicest things that ever happened to me," said Floyd.

On April 28, Eli Klukofsky AKA Eli Kaye was arrested—the gambler who had worked the Beavers in their Double Championship season. Several of Kaye's relatives were bookies and they were detained for questioning when they arrived to arrange Kaye's bail. The men kept talking until they mentioned the name of a college in New England. "Eli was doing business with a couple of guys on the team," the bookies said. Their inquisitor happened to be an alumnus of the very same school. "My God," he said. Then he threw up his hands, sent Kaye and his relatives home, and buried the testimony he had just received.

Clair Bee took every opportunity to confess his own culpability. "Confidence in college basketball is shattered," said Bee in the *Saturday Evening Post*, "and the fault is partly mine. I was a 'win-em-all' coach who helped to create the emotional climate that led to the worst scandal in the history of sports." But Bee also denied having made cash subsidies to his players. "I considered them loans," he said, "to be repaid at a later date." Bee lamented the crimes of his players. "I used to go to church with Bigos," Bee said, "and I cried with him at his father's funeral. I had so much faith in Gard that I told the other players to look to him for leadership. Feurtado and Lipman were frequent guests in my home. Natie Miller had a shoulder that he had banged up in the war. He had more guts and spirit than any other player I've ever coached. . . . Even White and Smith spent time at my home. I ate with them in a kitchen when they were refused service in a restaurant in Oklahoma. My relationship with my players did not end on the court. But there was one false note in the environment I tried to cultivate. We were playing basketball for money and some boys followed the college's example."

Ever the scholar, Clair Bee detailed an ideal budget for a university's varsity basketball program:

Equipment	$2,000
Medical care	1,500
Laundry	500
Office supplies and part-time personnel	750
A student aide to handle publicity	500
Meals after games	800
Expenses for one 2-day road trip a year	1,000
Other traveling expenses	3,000
Guarantees for visiting teams	5,000
Referees' fees	750
Rental for gymnasium	1,000

The total expenditure of $16,800 would be financed by adding a $10 athletic charge to the students' registration fees. And the public would be admitted into all college basketball games for free.

"As one who has learned through bitter experience," said Bee, "I know that having a losing team is better than having no team at all. Anything is infinitely better than waiting beside a telephone at four o'clock in the morning while kids in a police station are signing confessions that will brand them as long as they live."

There were also less specific analyses made of the situation. At a CCNY alumni dinner, President Harry Wright delivered a State of the Universe speech in which he cleverly skirted the most relevant issue, and neatly tossed the onus into a sewer. "The Western world," said Wright, "is torn by a conflict between a philosophy arising from moral relativism, which breeds totalitarianism, and a philosophy based on fundamental moral issues, which encourages the growth of freedom. Nazism was only an episode of the former philosophy which permeates the world."

ONE OF THE PLAYERS REMEMBERS: "We were burdened with so much guilt that it overwhelmed me. When I would meet some of my oldest friends I could see the hesitation on their faces, and I began to feel sorry for myself twenty-four hours a day. But I found that being sorry wasn't enough. It wasn't enough for other people, and it wasn't enough to give me any measure of peace."

From time to time, Nat Holman showed up at the Garden to see the Knicks. "The pros are always worth watching," said Nat. "They're the hope of basketball in New York." The only one of his boys who came to see Nat, who came to apologize, was Irwin Dambrot. Others felt Nat was the one who should apologize.

In early May of 1951, the Board of Higher Education finally decreed that CCNY was permanently prohibited from playing in the Garden. But the Board agreed that the cavernous 69th Regiment Armory might be leased by the college for possible games against NYU, St. John's, Fordham, and Manhattan. "These games," said a spokesman, "would pack the house."

Jack Goldsmith was arrested on May 20. He was the only player taken into custody who failed to volunteer any information or answer any questions. Goldsmith's bail was set at $50,000.

A few days later, the Eastern Collegiate Athletic Conference (a subdivision of the NCAA) made the ban on resort basketball official. The only exception to the new rule allowed a player to compete as an alumnus against his former high school team during vacation periods. The ECAC also made a statement that was in direct contradiction to what every basketball coach recognizes as common sense. "It is the opinion," said the ECAC, "that the college basketball season is already long enough, and that additional competition is not only not necessary to the normal development of players, but actually harmful to it." With this new directive in mind and Memorial Day at hand, basketball coaches began sending their players to summer camps to work as counselors. Any place with a good indoor court was sufficient. The coaches knew that the more a young player plays, the more he learns, the better he gets, and the less work for Coach.

With all the doomsday comments indiscriminately blasting the landscape, several sportswriters began to worry about the survival of the Golden Goose. They claimed that sports scandals have purgative effects. They promised that the basketball scandals will "increase vigilance, strengthen safeguards, and hold up to the public gaze discouraging examples of unfortunate young men." But the doctrine of the Fortunate Fall requires a crucifixion or two.

The grand jury hearing dragged on into the summer. Floyd Layne left his job in the mailroom after only a few weeks. He stopped by the Forest Neighborhood House to ask if his old part-time position was still available. The director of the center was George Gregory, an All-American hoopster at Columbia in 1931. Gregory hired Floyd on a full-time basis, putting him in complete control of the recreation program. And Floyd made sure to teach the kids that being a good ballplayer isn't enough.

ONE OF THE PLAYERS REMEMBERS: "I went into a relative's business, so I didn't have to worry about employment like most of the other guys. But I stayed under cover for fifteen years. I'd leave for work at six o'clock in the morning just to avoid the rush-hour crowds. Whenever I rode the subways I pulled my collar up around my face. I stayed inside the office all day. I used to cringe whenever anybody asked me if I played basketball. I told them that I wasn't who they thought I was. I told them the only sport I ever played was checkers. When an ex-teammate of mine got married I sent him a present. He returned it with a nasty note. I felt condemned by everybody. I felt like a murderer. I was resentful. I dreamed of running away to Hawaii and picking beaches for the rest of my life."

Sherman White got a job running a machine in a knitting mill. He married his high school sweetheart and awaited the trial. Eddie Roman worked in a haberdashery. But some of the "fixers" just disappeared.

A FRIEND REMEMBERS: "Ed Warner was a hard street person. He learned to live on the street when he was an adolescent and when times got tough he went back to the street. Eventually, he got into selling narcotics."

Jack Goldsmith pleaded guilty but he remained uncooperative. Assistant D.A. Vincent O'Connor said that Goldsmith was "a hardened criminal." Goldsmith's $50,000 bail was revoked and the defendant was committed to the Tombs to await sentencing. Eddie Gard pleaded innocent to two indictments charging him with accepting bribes and conspiring with other players to fix games. Gard was released pending trial with the proviso that he report to Hogan's staff every day.

On July 6, several players appeared before Judge Saul Streit to change their pleas from innocent to guilty. The defendants included Eddie Roman, Al Roth, Floyd Layne,

Norm Mager, Irwin Dambrot, Herb Cohen, Lou Lipman, Dick Feurtado, Adolf Bigos, Natie Miller, Sherman White, Leroy Smith, and Connie Schaff. Grumet had been plea-bargaining with the D.A. and making deals wherever he could. By their change of plea, the young men escaped prosecution on bribery charges that carried a maximum sentence of ten years in prison. For the lesser charge of conspiracy, they each faced jail terms of up to three years. Most of the players also announced that they would stand as witnesses against Salvatore Sollazzo. Hogan's staff was delighted with the deal. "We do not believe the public interest requires that these young men receive felony convictions," said Assistant D.A. O'Connor. "In our view, justice is adequately served by the acceptance of misdemeanor pleas from them. The trial of Sollazzo is our major objective."

On July 12, Salvatore Sollazzo pleaded guilty to charges of bribery and conspiracy. Three Negroes in Indianola, Mississippi, confessed to a murder that never occurred after heat was applied by the local police. Joe Louis won a ten-round decision over Cesar Brion in San Francisco. William Hill, Jr., died while trying to ride over Niagara Falls in a barrel. On July 18, Jacob Grumet was named as New York City's new Fire Commissioner. And on July 25, Frank Hogan's office announced that the basketball scandals had a Midwest connection.

10

Toledo University was a "flesh factory" like LIU. In 1950, TU spent $19,000 on athletic scholarships and $10,000 on what was called "student labor." Jerry Bush was Toledo's basketball coach. He was a native New Yorker who had captained the St. John's varsity in the thirties. Bush came to TU in 1947 and in his first year had a 21–5 season. The Toledo Rockets had concluded the '50–'51 season with a 22–7 record and were ranked fourteenth in the Associated Press poll. College basketball was big business in Toledo, and Bush had a reputation for winning.

Bill Walker was twenty-five and from Queens, New York. Walker's game featured fancy passing and spectacular dribbling and he had led the country in assists in '50–'51. Walker was married and the father of a one-year-old son. He was the co-captain of the team in his senior year and had graduated only six weeks before Hogan's office branded him a fixer.

Carlo Muzi was twenty-eight and a native of Akron, Ohio. Jerry Bush called Muzi "the greatest defensive guard in the nation." Muzi was the other co-captain and like Walker, a June graduate. Muzi had recently signed a contract to play for the Syracuse Nationals of the NBA.

Bob McDonald was twenty-five and also from Queens. "Bouncing Bob" was only a junior and was still enrolled in TU. He was a fine rebounder, a good student, and the captain elect of the '51–'52 team. McDonald's plans included law school and a career in Ohio.

Jack Feeman was from Akron. He was only a sophomore but he was the Rockets' leading scorer with an average of 15.6. The fingerman was Joe Massa from Brooklyn. Massa was the star of the '50–'51 freshman team and he was slated to replace Walker on the next year's varsity.

Late in October 1950, Joe Massa approached Bill Walker on the basketball court in the Toledo University field house. Walker had spent several summers sitting on a comfortable resort job in the Catskills and he knew Massa from there. "I never liked him," said Walker. "I never hung around with him."

Joe Massa brought a friend to introduce to Walker. "This is an old pal of mine," said Massa. "From back in New York. . . . Bill Walker . . . I'd like you to meet Eli Kaye. Eli knows a lot of the same people that you do." Kaye spouted his references while Walker nodded and smiled. "Let me tell you why I'm here," said the gambler. "How would you and the other members of the team like to make some easy money?" Kaye's offer called for $250 a game for every other player Walker could corral. For his troubles Walker would earn an additional $250 a game. "You're a sucker if you don't do business," Kaye prompted. "Everybody else is doing it." Walker expressed his interest and he said he would contact a few of his teammates. After Kaye left, Massa took Walker aside. "If you don't like doing business with Kaye," said the freshman, "I have plenty of other friends who'd like to meet you." Walker invited Muzi and McDonald out to his home and they discussed the situation. Muzi was willing and McDonald had to be convinced, but eventually they all agreed to throw in with Kaye.

The first game the gambler tried to arrange was Michigan at Toledo on December 6, 1950. Kaye called Walker from New York to confirm the particulars, but Walker said there was no possibility of a deal in any game involving a team from the Big Ten. "It's a traditional rivalry," said Walker. The Rockets proceeded to beat the Wolverines so badly that Michigan removed itself from Toledo's '51–'52 schedule. Three days later, Kaye called again to ask about a fix against Illinois. Once again, the gambler was turned down. The Rockets won 68–54, and Illinois also announced it wouldn't be rescheduling TU for next year.

Kaye called next to submit a bid for a December 12 game

against Denver. "We're going too good," said Walker. "No dice. In fact, we're going to beat Denver. You can bet on it." "I will," said Kaye. The Rockets prevailed, 50–44, and Kaye won a bundle. After the game, Kaye called to offer his congratulations and to report that he was mailing Walker a bonus of $200. The following morning, Walker's wife went down to the Western Union office to collect the money.

The Rockets were scheduled to play next on December 14 against the Niagara Purple Eagles. Kaye telephoned to say that this was the one game that really had to be fixed. It was Walker's last chance. Kaye didn't care if TU won or lost as long as they didn't win by more than 7 points.

BILL WALKER REMEMBERS: "I agreed to go along with Kaye and his 7-point spread because Niagara was a tough team and I figured it would be all we could do to beat them by 3 or 4. We'd beaten Michigan and Illinois easily, but that was mostly because we were up for those games and it didn't figure that we could maintain our peak for so long. It seemed as if I was going to get money for doing nothing but foxing a gambler. I was able to ring Carlo Muzi and Bob McDonald in on the deal by convincing them we wouldn't have to play less than our best. Bob more or less came along for the ride."

But the Rockets' easy road turned out to be a labyrinth. "Jumping Jack" Feeman came up with a sensational 26-point performance, and before anything could be done the Rockets blasted into a quick 20-point lead. Toledo was leading 65–46 when Feeman finally fouled out with only four minutes left in the game. Walker tried to correct the scoreboard by mishandling the ball, but two minutes later he also fouled out of the game. Carlo Muzi panicked and called a time-out. Muzi told McDonald that he was also going to foul out because the pressure was too much. "Don't do it," McDonald advised. "If we double-cross the gamblers something bad might happen to Walker." With two minutes left, the Rockets led by 11.

With one minute remaining, they led 73–65. Then Niagara converted two errant passes and a free throw to make the final score 73–70.

TOLEDO (73)	G	F	P	NIAGARA (70)	G	F	P
McDonald	4	5	13	Moran	2	0	4
Russell	5	3	13	Stanbauer	4	7	15
Feeman	11	4	26	Smyth	2	0	4
Muzi	4	2	10	Sinicola	7	6	20
Walker	3	3	9	Birch	5	6	16
Nichols	0	0	0	Bertolotti	1	1	3
Morton	0	0	0	Condara	0	1	1
Moore	1	0	2	Hutson	1	0	2
				McMahon	1	0	2
	28	17	73	Nigrelli	1	0	2
				Powers	0	1	1
					24	22	70

After the game, Kaye called Walker to say he was pleased with the results and was mailing a payment of $1,700. Walker gave Muzi and McDonald $250 each and kept the rest.

It was no secret that large numbers of gamblers frequented the Rockets' home games. During the '49–'50 season, the gamblers became so bold as to sit near the Rockets' bench and shout instructions to the players. It became necessary to have uniformed police stationed at the field house to keep known gamblers away. But the Toledo bookmakers had been warned that something was amiss in the TU-Niagara game. "Before the game," said a local bookie, "we got a telephone call from New York saying that a ton of money had been put down on Niagara." When the ripples reached the campus, the university officials acted quickly. Athletic director Barney Francis appealed to the civil authorities to help stop organized betting on TU games. As a result, numerous gambling establishments were raided and the

Rockets' games were "taken off the boards" for a few days.

In early January 1951, Joe Massa introduced Walker to another of his friends: Jack Rubinstein, a bookie bred in Brooklyn, a one-time fruit peddler and an associate of a mobster named Jack West. Walker and his mates were offered $500 each if they could control a January 11 game against Bowling Green. The Rockets had to win by 6 points or less. Walker suggested that Jack Feeman be cut in so there would be no surprises. Rubinstein checked with his associate and the deal was finalized. The day before the Bowling Green game, Eli Kaye called Walker to offer his standard package. But Walker was increasingly cautious and he didn't want to contract any more business over the telephone. "Can't do it," Walker said. "Bowling Green is a traditional rival. We're playing at home and we want to win the game badly. In fact, we're up for the game and we're going to kill them. Take it from me." The Rockets swore they played the game straight and Bowling Green won, 66–59. Rubinstein came to Walker's home the next day with $2,000. Kaye called from New York to complain that Walker's tip had cost him a fortune.

When the Manhattan College scandal broke a week later, some of Walker's unsuspecting teammates noticed his new wardrobe and began to kid him about dumping ball games. Walker went along with the gag. He appeared one afternoon at practice with a cigar box full of phony money. Walker stuffed some of the money into his shorts, some into his sneakers, and he scattered the rest around the court. Everybody had a good laugh.

A few days later, Kaye made another call and Walker said there'd be no more deals because things were "too hot." But it was already too late. Two of the Toledo players had been blatantly patronizing a bookie parlor in downtown Toledo. They had made bets on the TU-Niagara game, laying $200 each on the Purple Eagles. When their identities became known, they were kicked out and told not to return. The bookies passed the information along to the *Toledo Blade*, and the newspaper informed TU's athletic department. But Barney Francis doubted the veracity of the report. Francis thought that the bookies were spreading rumors just to get even with the university for calling the cops down on their operations. No further action was taken at the time.

Jack Rubinstein was back again on January 30 with a proposition for a game at Cincinnati against Xavier. The Rockets were 13-point favorites but they blew the game by 20. Then the CCNY and LIU scandals forced the Rockets to shutter their shop for the remainder of the season.

On July 25, when Hogan first revealed the outline of the plot, he knew only of the complicity of Kaye, Walker, McDonald, and Muzi. There was no current Ohio law that dealt with the bribery of amateur athletes. Since none of the crooked games had been played in the Garden, the players seemed to be beyond the jurisdiction of the law. But Bob McDonald was suspended by the college. And TU also announced that Muzi and Walker would be denied access to the university's job-placement services.

When Muzi, Walker, and McDonald volunteered to come to New York and submit to Hogan's questions, the Toledo papers called their gesture a noble one. But the players had been advised that Hogan could very easily have them summoned before the grand jury because of the relevancy of the evidence they commanded. The testimony given in New York by the three players implicated Massa but shielded Jack Feeman. The sophomore's part in the fix was revealed through the efforts of an intracollegiate investigatory committee headed by Asa Knowles, TU's president.

The news of the latest scandal hit the rest of the country like a left hook to the groin, but the city of Toledo was merely stung into anger. The Toledo newspapers reported "a definite undercurrent of resentment" on the local scene. The Toledan on the Street was impatient with the bad news:

"Heck, let's forget the whole thing."

"So what? They didn't throw any games. Did they?"

"Who cares how many points they win by, as long as they win."

"What's this guy Hogan trying to do? Run for president? Hasn't he got enough to clean up right in New York?"

"The fact that the players refused to fix the Michigan and Illinois games shows that they did have some spark of loyalty."

The *Toledo Times* said that the scandals were still "spawned in New York" and charged that Hogan's investigations were politically motivated. The paper suggested that Hogan was only interested in investigating independent schools. "We doubt if Hogan will ever muster the courage to stick his nose into the affairs of schools backed by powerful conference affiliations and powerful alumni groups." The newspaper specified the Big Ten as one such untouchable conference.

Other local voices branded TU's involvement "a tempest in a teapot," and everybody favored the continuation of the college's normal athletic program. "Typical of such athletes," wrote Jack Senn of the *Toledo Blade*, "Walker, Muzi, and McDonald were not hometown boys. . . . I want to emphasize that the ballplayers did not actually throw any games, and that the university was not hurt one iota in the won and loss column. . . . So, if the fixer is hurting anyone, it must be a fellow who is doing something he shouldn't be doing—betting on the outcome of a ball game."

Only Joe Knack of the *Toledo Blade* dissented from the self-righteous bleatings of his colleagues. "There'll be no more finger-pointing in the direction of New York," Knack said. "And let us not be children about this. . . . Under-the-table transactions are catching up with the colleges. Who is an easier prey than a kid who has gotten an easy buck out of a college being offered another easy buck by somebody else?"

But the trickle of protest was drowned out by the loud splashing of hands being washed. "There never was a question in my mind that my boys were absolutely clean," said Jerry Bush. "If great coaches like Clair Bee and Nat Holman could be fooled by their players, then so could I."

"Who would have ever guessed," said Barney Francis, "that a stranger could come out of New York and successfully make contact with our key players—with our most trusted boys? I only hope we don't have any trouble making up next year's basketball schedule because of all this."

Gene Melchiorre was born in Joliet, Illinois, in 1928. He was raised as a Catholic and his parents were upright, God-fearing people. Gene went to grammar school in Hollywood, Illinois, and then on to Highland Park High School. There was nothing in the seedtime of his life that held a hint of dishonor. Gene reached his mature height of 5 feet 8½ inches as a schoolboy but his chunky quickness made him an excellent basketball player. Gene graduated from high school in June 1945, undecided about his future. He attended summer classes at the University of Wisconsin, but he was tired of school and after a few weeks he quit to join the army. The war in Europe was already over and the Japanese were on the verge of capitulating. Gene spent most of his twenty-two-month tour of duty playing basketball. While he was in the service, Gene picked up a nickname, "Squeaky," and a friend, Bill Mann. The two young men played on the same team in the bellicose, combative service leagues. Mann was a fine pivot man, a year older than Gene; he hailed from Peoria. They were both honorably discharged in May 1947 and decided to continue their partnership by accepting basketball scholarships to the same college.

Melchiorre and Mann were an outstanding bargain. They were both well-seasoned ballplayers of exceptional abilities. They were also covered by the GI Bill of Rights, so whatever college they selected would gain their services without expending a pair of valuable basketball scholarships. Melchiorre and Mann were pursued by dozens of schools, including Wisconsin, Northwestern, and Bowling Green, before they landed in Peoria and signed up at Bradley University. "The school had a small enrollment," Gene explained. "So freshman were eligible to play varsity ball."

During his freshman year, Gene received the price of books and tuition from the government. The college gave him one meal a day but only during the course of the basketball season, and Gene had to wait on tables to pay for his room. But he liked Bradley. The school had a long basketball tradition with only two losing seasons in its fifty-one-year history. The president of the university, David Blair Owen, was a rabid basketball fan who often traveled with the team on road trips. Owen was also the founder and prime mover of the "Booster Club" that raised $25,000 a year to finance all of Bradley's athletic scholarships. The '47–'48 Braves were sparked by 6-foot-4-inch Paul Unruh, and the campaign marked the last one under coach Alfred Robertson. The Braves were eliminated in the first round of the NIT but they still finished with a sparkling 28–3 record.

In Gene's sophomore year, his financial situation improved considerably. He was able to earn pocket money cleaning out the washroom in the armory where the team played its home games. The '48–'49 edition of the Bradley Braves was the first to bear the imprint of Forrest Anderson. The new coach brought a 27–7 record into the semifinal round of the 1949 NIT before being upset by Loyola of Chicago. Suddenly the season was a lame duck. The last game was to be played for the tournament's third-place championship, pitting the Braves against Bowling Green on March 19.

The Braves were quartered not far from the Garden in the Paramount Hotel. The day before the game, Gene Melchiorre, Bill Mann, and the other starting guard, Mike Chianakas, were returning to their room after breakfast when a stranger accidentally bumped into Chianakas. The man was short and fat and he wore thick glasses. The ballplayers remembered where they were and they reached for their wallets.

"Hey," said the stranger. "Ain't you Mike Chianakas from Bradley?"

"Yes, sir," said the flattered player.

"Hey," said the stranger. "I'm a Greek too. My name is Nick Englises. They call me 'Nick the Greek.' How you doing?"

Before the players knew what was happening, they were escorted into Nick's room and introduced to two other men. Nick Englises was twenty-six, married, and from Brooklyn. Despite his unlikely appearance, he had played football for the University of Kentucky from 1945 to 1947. Tony Englises was twenty-five and employed as a bartender in a Times Square gin mill. The third man was Saul Feinberg, twenty six, a Harvard law student, and a part-time two-bit gambler. The ballplayers were treated to drinks and a series of amazing propositions.

"The colleges are getting rich on basketball," said Nick. "It seems to me that you guys ought to be getting something out of it. Let me tell you, it doesn't last long. Believe me. I was an athlete myself. You know all those stories they write about you in the newspapers? After you get out of school, a whole room full of headlines won't buy you a cup of coffee."

"And all those people flocking around and asking for your autograph," said Feinberg. "After you've played your last game they won't even know you."

Melchiorre, Mann, and Chianakas were bombarded with stories of college dumps going back to the early thirties. They were told of all the current Blackbirds, Beavers, Violets, Rockets, and Jaspers who were doing business. The gamblers also mentioned the names of several well-known players and teams who would never be caught.

"Most of those guys," said Nick, "are putting aside money so they can start a little business of their own once they graduate. If you boys don't do the same thing, then you're prize suckers."

"All you have to do is win by a certain amount," said Feinberg. "Or if you think you're going to lose, you can lose by a certain amount. It's easy."

"Bowling Green is a six-point favorite," said Nick. "And who the hell cares about a consolation game? Right? All you have to do is lose by at least seven points. The thing is safe, believe me. It's foolproof. Nobody knows what's going on. There's no chance of getting caught. We'll give you each five hundred dollars. You might as well make something out of it for yourselves. Five hundred bucks. What d'ya say?"

The ballplayers didn't say much but they managed to mumble their consent. After the players left the room, the gamblers called in $5,000 on Bowling Green minus 6 points. They happened to lay the bet with Eli Kaye.

Bowling Green was paced by 6-foot-11-inch All-American Chuck Share and the Falcons controlled the entire game. The contest was so loosely played that careless shooting was easily overlooked. "Both sides," said the man from the *Times*, "were wilder than the waves." Bowling Green was towing a 10-point lead into the harbor when Melchiorre canned a clutch of foul shots. Then in the last minute of play, a substitute scored a bucket that narrowed Bowling Green's final margin to 82–77.

BOWLING GREEN (82)				BRADLEY (77)			
	G	F	P		G	F	P
Otten	5	1	11	Melchiorre	2	5	9
Speicher	1	2	4	Garber	3	0	6
Weber	5	3	13	Mann	2	0	4
Joyce	3	0	6	Behnke	1	0	2
Share	6	5	17	Unruh	9	2	20
Greene	1	0	2	Humerickhouse	0	0	0
Long	3	3	9	Preece	5	4	14
Payak	7	3	17	Ricci	0	0	0
Dudley	1	1	3	Chianakas	1	0	2
				Grover	7	6	20
	32	18	82		30	17	77

After the game, Melchiorre, Mann, and Chianakas encountered Nick Englises back at the hotel. "If you hadn't made those foul shots," Nick shouted at Gene, "we would have won our bet." Melchiorre offered no defense. Nick fumed and grumbled, but he handed Mann and Chianakas $25 each. Melchiorre got nothing. A few days later, the Englises brothers tapped out for the season when another of their clients flopped in a game against Villanova, but the gamblers kept in touch.

During the summer of 1949, the three ballplayers discussed their prospects for the coming season.

GENE MELCHIORRE REMEMBERS: "None of us had any money. We justified our decision to go along with the Englises brothers by saying that the colleges were making plenty out of us. We agreed to go along with them again. We argued to ourselves that what we were doing was wrong, but not too wrong."

As the '49–'50 season got underway, Mike Chianakas lost his starting spot to Charlie Grover. Mike was also replaced by Grover in the Braves' betting ring. In honor of Melchiorre's junior year, the college gave him a free room, and the alumni began slipping envelopes under his door. On December 15, 1949, Bradley went over the points in beating TCU, 85–49, in a game played at Peoria. Nick Englises paid Melchiorre, Mann, and Grover $100 each. On December 21, the Braves were 10-point favorites for a home game scheduled against Washington State. This time, the players agreed to go under the spread, but they had to play the game straight to squeeze out a 67–59 win. Melchiorre and Mann got $600 each and Grover, who missed the game with a sprained ankle, got $300.

Then in January 1950, Eli Kaye cashed in some vouchers and assumed control of the Englises' stable. On January 12, Bradley was in New York for a game against Manhattan at the Garden. Kaye put the Englises brothers on a commission: $1,000 for every fix they could arrange. And Kaye showed up at the Braves' hotel to offer the players $500 each to dump the Manhattan game. Melchiorre was the spokesman for Mann, Grover, and another player named Aaron Preece. "Sorry," said Melchiorre. "We want to win the game and play well in the Garden because we're aiming at the NIT." "That's fine," said Kaye. "But here's a hundred bucks apiece to remember me by. Maybe we can do business later on." Hank Poppe and John Byrnes were dumping for the Jaspers, and Bradley coasted to an easy 89–67 win.

The next stop on the Braves' East Coast swing was Philadelphia for a date against St. Joseph's. Bradley was a 6-point favorite and, acting through Nick Englises, Kaye arranged for the Braves to duck under the spread. It was a routine pipe job with no complications expected until the Englises brothers got cute. After the deal was set, Nick placed a call to Jack West, the same gambler who bankrolled Joe Massa and the Toledo fixes. Jack "Zip" West had been questioned in 1947 in connection with an alleged $100,000 bribe offer to Rocky Graziano. West had a gruesome reputation for strong-arm tactics.

"Bradley's taking a dive tonight against St. Joe's," said Nick.

"Thanks for the tip," said West. "It's worth a thousand dollars in your pocket."

West bet a pile on St. Joseph's with the points and took the next train down to Philly to catch the ball game. West's wagers totaled over $5,000 and they were placed with some of the most influential bookmakers in the East. Eli Kaye couldn't help but notice. Kaye quite naturally suspected a double cross and he called Nick Englises at his hotel in Philadelphia.

"Somebody's got a line into our operation," said Kaye. "I don't know who it is but I'm going to burn him. We're going to change the plans. You tell Melchiorre that instead of losing the game, I want Bradley to win by as many points as they can."

"I'll take care of it," said Nick. "I'll have Tony relay the message to Melchiorre."

As soon as Kaye hung up, Nick called Jack West to report the switch. West was furious. He had already laid his bets on St. Joe's +6, and it was too late to shift to Bradley. "The punk," snarled West. "Nobody does that to me."

Later that evening, Nick left for Convention Hall to witness the ball game while Tony remained at the hotel. An hour before game time, two of West's goons knocked down the door and kidnapped Tony. Tony was brought to West's hotel and apprised at gunpoint of the gambler's dilemma. Tony was allowed one desperate phone call to Convention Hall to have his brother paged from the crowd of 15,000. The Braves were racing through their pregame exercises when Nick barely heard the public-address system croaking his name underneath the noise of the crowd. Nick picked up a phone at the press table.

"Nick!" Tony cried. "It's me! I've been snatched by West. You've got to do something. If Bradley doesn't go under the points he says he's going to kill me! Nick! You've got to change the deal again. If West loses his money I'm dead."

The two teams were still warming up and Nick began jumping up and down along the sideline until he arrested Melchiorre's attention. Nick winked and pointed his thumb to the ground. Melchiorre nodded and passed the word. The Braves led all the way and won by 4 points. With his bets safely accounted for, West gave Tony a drink and $1,000 and sent him running off into the night. But Eli Kaye was cleaned out, and he called to accuse Nick of double-dealing. They argued and simultaneously abrogated all connections and obligations.

The Braves finished the regular season ranked number one in the country and were ushered into the top-seeded spot in the NIT. The NCAA selection committee was already tendering an invitation to their postseason hippodrome, as the Braves tore through the early rounds. The Braves and the Beavers reached the finals and Melchiorre was swamped with offers to dump the championship game. "No deal," said Gene. The Beavers captured the NIT title, 69–61, and both teams were asked into the NCAA tourney.

The Braves' first NCAA game was played on March 21 against Kansas State in Peoria. On the morning of the game, Nick Englises introduced Melchiorre to Joe Benintende — the latest, the biggest, and the most dangerous gambler in the plot. Benintende had intimate connections with the mob and was suspected of engineering a recent gangland slaying of a Kansas City politician. Benintende promised a reward of $4,000 if Bradley won the game by less than 4 points. The Braves beat Kansas State, 59–57, and Benintende's coup netted $80,000. Bradley then defeated UCLA to qualify for the final round at the Garden. The Braves slipped by Baylor, 68–66, and braced for a rematch against the Beavers. "Ten thousand," said Benintende, "for each of you. If you go under the points." Melchiorre politely refused the offer. Maybe it wasn't too late. Maybe an NCAA championship could salve a soul already scorched with guilt. The dramatic NCAA title game came down to one play: Irwin Dambrot's block of Melchiorre's breakaway lay-up.

GENE MELCHIORRE REMEMBERS: "He definitely fouled me. The referee blew the call. There's no question about it. We should have won the game and the championship."

The Bradley bunch fixed another ball game during the '50–'51 season. Just one more game. The last one. It was Melchiorre's senior year. Once more the contacts were the Englises brothers and the banker was Jack West. On December 5, 1950, Melchiorre, Preece, Jim Kelley, and Fred Schlictman agreed to beat Oregon State by less than 10 points. Aaron Preece earned another $300 when he called New York and alerted Eli Kaye to the rigged game. The Braves had to scrape to realize a 77–74 victory. Melchiorre and Schlictman each scored 21 points and Jack West cleared $150,000. Melchiorre's share was $2,000, Preece got $1,000, while Kelley and Schlictman each received $500.

GENE MELCHIORRE REMEMBERS: "Nick Englises paid us off the next day in the Morrison Hotel in Chicago. It was the best payday we ever had and it was also the last. Englises and West kept after us, but we never did business again. For one thing, we weren't a good enough team to shave the points and still be assured of a win. It was also

162

beginning to dawn on us that the whole thing wasn't as safe as Englises had said."

The New York City basketball scandals shook Melchiorre and his friends. They were thankful there were no ties connecting them to either Eddie Gard or Salvatore Sollazzo. The Braves concluded the '50–'51 campaign with a 32–6 record, but Oklahoma A & M edged them out for the Missouri Valley Conference title, and the Braves failed to qualify for the NCAA playoffs. On the heels of the CCNY revelations, the Braves had voted unanimously to avoid the NIT, and Melchiorre's varsity career fell off a cliff. In June 1951, Melchiorre received a degree in business administration. Then, in conjunction with his old friend and ex-teammate, Bill Mann, he opened a sporting-goods store in Peoria. The two athletes were local heroes and the store did very well. Gene was thinking that he'd also have a go at the pros . . . until July 25, when Frank Hogan's detectives tapped him on the shoulder and blighted his future. Melchiorre, Mann, and Chianakas were arrested because the Bowling Green game that started it all had been played in the Garden. The Englises brothers were also busted, while Grover, Preece, and Kelley were pulled in for questioning.

GENE MELCHIORRE REMEMBERS: "I'm pretty sure Hogan would never have been able to pin anything on us if we had only kept our mouths shut. The only real evidence he had was a telephone call from Peoria to New York when Preece tipped Kaye about the Oregon State game. We talked because the detectives bluffed us into thinking they had a lot more evidence than they really had. They also told us it would be easier on us in the long run if we did talk."

Melchiorre, Mann, and Chianakas were released upon payment of $500 bail, but they hung around New York long enough to implicate their teammate Fred Schlictman. Schlictman was still an undergraduate and he was arrested at a fancy summer resort in Michigan where he was being taken care of by Bradley's president, David Blair Owen. Hogan sent several men out to Peoria to track down some of the new leads. When the detectives arrived at their hotel, they immediately called for room service. "You'll get nothing from us," they were told. "If you want to eat, you can go out and get your own food." The detectives couldn't find the time of day in Peoria and they returned to New York carrying blank notebooks and dirty laundry. A few days later, Hogan's office called Peoria "the gambling capital of the country."

Paul Unruh made a speech at a church dartball dinner in Pekin, Illinois, in which the former Bradley All-American said he had turned down an offer from an unknown man to throw a game in the 1950 NIT. Unruh said he hadn't reported the bribe to his coach because he didn't think it was important.

On August 3, Frederick A. Irving, the superintendent of the U.S. Military Academy, announced the dismissal of ninety cadets for cheating on exams. Col. Earl ("Red") Blaik, West Point's football coach, revealed that the ousters had cut his varsity squad from 45 members to 2. Blaik's son, Bob, the team's quarterback, was one of the guilty cadets.

It was falsely reported in a Peoria newspaper that in addition to Gene Melchiorre's other misdeeds, he had withheld $2,000 worth of hard-earned bribe money from his teammates. Melchiorre became the latest in a series of scapegoats. He was a pariah in Peoria.

On August 17, Frank Hogan's office procured indictments against Nick and Tony Englises, Joe Benintende, Jack West, Gene Melchiorre, Bill Mann, and Mike Chianakas. The D.A. filed no charges against Grover, Preece, Schlictman, or Kelley. Hogan announced that Benintende and West were still at large. Two days later, the National Chess Championship was won by nineteen-year-old Larry Evans, a student at CCNY. There were no spontaneous rallies in Harlem. Jack West surrendered at Hogan's office, swearing his innocence and claiming that he could not bear to stay away from his wife and three children any longer. Bail was set at $50,000.

On September 14, Melchiorre, Preece, Kelley, and

Schlictman admitted before a Peoria grand jury that they had earned $1,000 each for their work in the Bradley–Oregon State game. Kelley and Schlictman dramatically placed $1,000 in cash on the table. They asked the State Attorney to have an unnamed businessman give the money to charity. They said they had thought the money was a gift from Melchiorre. Judge Howard White freed Kelley, Schlictman, and Preece. "Among other things," said the judge, "we have found the three players have never been involved in serious trouble and have to date suffered substantial mental, physical, and financial penalty." Gene Melchiorre was indicted.

The Defense Department reported that the Korean conflict had already cost the Communists 1,346,723 casualties. The total number of American casualties was given as 90,935. On September 18, Ed Warner, Eddie Roman, Floyd Layne, Al Roth, and Herb Cohen filed applications for readmission to CCNY. President Harry Wright noted that the young men would not be sentenced for another two weeks and said that their applications were therefore premature.

Late in the afternoon of October 3, Bobby Thomson socked a three-run homer off the Dodgers' Ralph Branca, and the Giants won the National League pennant. The citizens of New York spilled beer in the streets. Joe Benintende surrendered and was held on $75,000 bail. On October 8, the Colorado State Industrial Commission ruled that Ernest E. Nemeth was in fact hired to play football for Denver University and ordered the school to pay him retroactive disability payments of $12 a week for a back injury sustained in 1950 spring practice. Joe Louis, thirty-seven, was KO'd by Rocky Marciano at 2:36 of the eighth round in a fight at Madison Square Garden.

Melchiorre, Mann, and Chianakas appeared before Judge Saul Streit in New York to plead guilty to a misdemeanor. The players faced a maximum of three years in jail, and Assistant D.A. Vincent O'Connor praised them for their cooperation. On October 19, Frank Hogan exploded another bombshell that blasted the flag on the Capitol Building in Lexington, Kentucky, right off its pole.

12

The Beards were born to be great athletes. Grandfather Marvin Beard was a track star and a baseball player at Vanderbilt University. Ralph Beard, Sr., was a professional baseball player who reached the Three-I League. Ralph Junior was born on December 2, 1927, in Hardinsburg, Kentucky, and his necessity was to be a basketball player.

"Ralph's first basket," said his mother Sue, "was his potty chair. He would throw a little rubber ball into it. When he got older, he used the cutaway part of his high chair. After that, we put up a miniature basket over his bed. Then the basket was moved into the kitchen. Finally, a regulation basket had to be tacked up outside in the yard." Ralph's parents were divorced in 1937, with his father moving to Dallas to become a golf pro. Ralph Senior later fathered Frank Beard, another golfer who would earn over a million dollars on the pro tour. But Sue Beard stayed in Hardinsburg with her two sons. She stuffed quilts and comforters in a local factory owned by a relative. The bone-cold Appalachian poverty also forced Ralph from his bed before the sun every morning to work a rural newspaper route for $2.40 a week. During the baseball, football, and basketball seasons, Ralph paid his little brother 60 cents to carry the papers to the other side of the mountain.

In 1941 Sue Beard moved to Louisville so her eldest son Ralph could attend Male High School and allow his athletic gifts to be seen in the big city. Sue got a job as a guard in an aircraft factory, and her shift changed every week. Despite the instability and the continuing indigence, her love kept her shattered family together. After a few months, Sue secured a position as a supervisor of maids for a residential hotel. She paid the rent by cleaning six apartments and two sleeping rooms daily in her spare time. Ralph no longer had a paper route, but he fired the hotel's furnace every morning before he left for school.

In high school, Ralph was a standout in basketball, football, and baseball. He grew to be 5 feet 10 inches and a rugged 176 pounds. He was quick and relentless and he loved to run. The faster the break the better. Everybody liked Ralph and the Beards' home soon became a gathering place for the high school basketball team. After a game, they would sit around a cauldron of Sue Beard's chili and go over every play. But sometimes Ralph had to borrow money to eat lunch. As a senior in 1945, Ralph led Male High School to the first statewide basketball championship in the school's history. After the season, Ralph decided he'd also be the school's first four-letter man, and he promptly won the half-mile in the Kentucky Track Championships. Ralph was recruited from head to toe. Even the Yankee colleges wanted him.

"Every boy in the state," says Adolph Rupp, "from the time he's born, lives for the day when he can play basketball at the University of Kentucky."

"I'd always read about UK," said Ralph, "and I never wanted to go anyplace else."

The summer before Ralph entered UK, he was named to a schoolboy All-Star team that represented the state of Kentucky in a series of basketball games against a similar squad from Indiana. For one fabulous week, the Kentucky team trained at the University of Western Kentucky under the guidance of coach Ed Diddle. It was Ralph's first taste of the "good life."

RALPH BEARD REMEMBERS: "We had two-a-day workouts and we swam in the pool. They let us eat as much as we wanted. I swore I was in heaven."

Ralph enrolled at UK in the fall of 1945, and as a freshman he played football, starting three games at fullback behind quarterback George Blanda. But when Ralph injured a

167

shoulder, Rupp yanked him from the football team and moved him in with the basketball players. Rupp's boys lived together in the same dorm and ate specially prepared meals. Rupp was always very conscious of the way his boys ate their meals. "If a boy is aggressive with his eating," says Rupp, "then, Lordy, he's going to be aggressive on the basketball floor." Practice sessions were conducted in silence save for an occasional tongue-lashing administered by the Baron. "Boy," he would holler, "give that ball back to someone who knows what to do with it." Rupp's Wildcats played a bruising man-to-man defense, and even their fast breaks were models of precision. Rupp was caustic, belligerent, and a winner.

BILL SPIVEY REMEMBERS: "Rupp wanted everybody to hate him and he succeeded. He called us names some of us had never heard before. Those of us who stuck it out wanted to show Rupp we were better players than he thought we were."

RALPH BEARD REMEMBERS: "Some guys said they hated Rupp, but not me. He was it as far as I was concerned. If he told me to run through a brick wall, I'd have backed up as far as it would take. I wanted to show him I was the best basketball player who ever came down the pike. To me, basketball was everything. Some people have brains, some are good-looking. I had the God-given ability to play basketball."

Adolph Rupp also wanted his players to be anonymous. "If a star has an off night," said the Baron, "then so does the whole team." But Rupp usually recruited nothing but blue-chip All-Americans. There was no doubt that Ralph Beard would be a great college player and an outstanding pro. But the Baron also had a wizard's eye for a long shot. In June 1943, when Alex Groza graduated from high school in Ohio, he was only 6 feet 5 inches and 165 pounds. Groza always dreamed of playing basketball for Ohio State but there wasn't a college in the country that thought him worthy of a scholarship offer. Groza had no choice but to join the army. His tour of duty lasted twenty-one months, and he played basketball, he grew two inches, and he gained forty-eight pounds. Rupp's secret talent spies routinely scouted the armed forces leagues, and when Groza was discharged he was recruited by UK.

ALEX GROZA REMEMBERS: "Rupp's offer was the only one I had. There was no other place to go. I received room, board, tuition, fees, books, and fifteen dollars a week. Nothing illegal. I played center then the way they play center today. I was small and I had to play away from the basket and shoot from the outside, but I also had a good hook shot. We had a center-oriented offense so I handled the ball a great deal. Rupp was a success and you had to listen to him."

The '45–'46 Wildcats were 28–2 but they lost the Southeastern Conference title to LSU, and Rupp had to settle for the NIT instead of the NCAA. The Wildcats beat Arizona and West Virginia and faced Ernie Calverley's Rhode Island team in the final game. With the score tied at 45 and only seconds left, Ralph Beard was fouled. Ralph was barely eighteen years old. There was blood streaming down his knee from a fall he had taken. His eyes locked onto the front of the rim, and as he furiously chomped on a five-package wad of gum, he sank the foul shot that won the NIT championship, 46–45.

His clutch performance made Ralph as big as Tex Ritter and Hank Williams back in Lexington. During a March of Dimes radio benefit, a listener called in with a $25 pledge if only Ralph would sing "Rock-a-Bye Baby" on the air. The attention and the adulation were certainly worth enjoying, but Ralph knew he could only be satisfied by the game. During the following summer, Ralph pestered Rupp, asking for an outline of his own deficiencies. "You need to improve your foul shooting," Rupp said. "And you have to use your left hand a little more. If you can correct these few weaknesses, you'll not only be a great basketball player, you'll be an almost perfect basketball player."

Adolph Rupp knew that his Beard-Groza Wildcats were potentially the best college team he had ever seen and he drove them hard. But the Baron moved his players with rewards as well as curses. Rupp's boys regularly received cash from either Rupp himself, or from "Boosters." The sums ranged from $10 to $50, depending on how well the players performed. On the rare occasion of a UK loss, the ballplayers were lucky to get anything to eat. Rupp always maintained that any winning coach "has to blur the line" in getting athletes, motivating them, and keeping them in school. "My intention," said the Baron, "is not merely to play basketball, but to win basketball." Sometimes Rupp's myopia caused him to stumble.

Ed Curd was Lexington's most celebrated bookmaker and his connections with the mob were common knowledge. Yet, Adolph Rupp visited Curd in his home at least twice. On one occasion, the Baron telephoned the gambler to inquire about the point spread for a Kentucky-Alabama game. Rupp was also seen having a "supper snack" with Curd at the Copacabana after a UK game at the Garden. Rupp never denied the meetings but he did swear he had never bet on any games.

In the '46–'47 season, Alex Groza became a starter and Ralph Beard became an All-American. Another fabulous sophomore named Wallace ("Wah Wah") Jones played forward. The Wildcats were 34–2 and they were called back to the Garden to defend their NIT crown. UK advanced through the preliminary rounds and faced an underdog team from Utah that was led by Jack Ferrin and Wat Misaka. Utah's deliberate style of play calmed Kentucky's whirlwind attack; the 5-foot-6-inch Misaka held Ralph to 1 point; and the Wildcats' season snapped shut with a 49–45 loss.

Adolph Rupp snarled all summer long and set his goals high for the '47–'48 season. Beard, Groza, and Jones would all be juniors, and they would be joined in the starting lineup by Kenny Rollins and Cliff Barker. Jim Line and Walter Hirsch would be coming off the bench. "I'm the greatest basketball coach in the country," Rupp always said, and he set out to prove his claim. Rupp expected at least an NCAA championship and he pined for an Olympic gold medal in London.

The '47–'48 Wildcats won the SEC and an automatic berth in the NCAA on their way to a 36–3 season. Once again, Ralph Beard was honored as an All-American. The Wildcats ripped through the NCAA's Eastern Regionals before running into Holy Cross, the defending 1947 NCAA champs. The Cross was carried by Bob Cousy and George Kaftan, but the Wildcats' Kenny Rollins held "The Cooz" to one point and UK won, 60–52. The NCAA championship game against Baylor was a 58–42 mismatch and Rupp's boys worked up more of a sweat fighting each other for the privilege of carrying the Baron off the court on their shoulders.

The Baron and "The Fab Five" were welcomed back to Lexington with a ticker-tape parade, and the mountains emptied to join in the celebration. Speeches were made. A Lexington drugstore said it would be its pleasure to supply Ralph with all the chewing gum he required. Even Ralph's addictions were All-American, and he was named the Player of the Year in College Basketball.

The Olympics were set to resume in the summer of 1948 after a twelve-year hiatus: the Games had last been staged in Berlin in 1936. The Wildcats entered the Olympic basketball trials in July, mauled their initial opponents, and squared off in the final game against the Phillips Oilers. The Oilers were sponsored and employed by Phillips Petroleum, Inc. The ballplayers had preferred company status, high salaries, and lollipop jobs. Even though they played basketball on the company's time, the Oilers were officially classified as amateurs. The star of the team was 7-foot Bob Kurland, the game's premier big man. The game was played outdoors with

171

international rules. The Baron planned to have his boys accelerate the game and have Groza run Kurland from basket to basket. But Cliff Barker broke his nose early in the first half, Kurland dominated Groza, and the Oilers won, 53–49. Ralph scored 23 points and the Oilers' coach, Bud Browning, said, "Ralph Beard is absolutely the best basketball player I ever saw."

The 1948 U.S. Olympic basketball team was comprised of the starting fives of both the Oilers and the Wildcats. Adolph Rupp was the assistant coach, and the team was expected to waltz to the gold medal. The squad landed in London and was bused to a hotel. The players flung their suitcases on their beds and ran out into the street to gawk at the sights. Ralph turned into the first drugstore he saw.

"I'd like a pack of chewing gum," Ralph said. "I chew gum all the time, except when I eat and sleep. Don't make any difference what brand you got."

"Chewing gum, sir?" said the clerk. "We haven't seen any chewing gum in England since the Yanks left after the war."

"You mean," Ralph gulped, "that you don't sell gum in England?"

"That is correct, sir."

"Somebody must be crazy," Ralph moaned. But an American company learned of the problem and shipped Ralph a dozen boxes of gum, and the gold medal was saved.

The Oilers and the Wildcats split the playing time and operated as separate units, and the Baron was subordinate to Bud Browning in title only. The United States swept through its qualifying games, beating Argentina 59–57, but winning the rest by an average of 37 points. In the championship game, the United States embarrassed France, 65–21.

When the Kentucky players got back home, the citizens of Lexington lapped bourbon off the sidewalks, and the stills were drained in the hills. The players were culture heroes. They shook hands with politicians in fat gray suits, they were poked with stuffed envelopes and prodded by stuffed dresses. Alex Groza was informed by a local liquor distributor that he could expect $50 a month until he graduated. The

172

On August 17, 1951, George Chianakas, Gene Melchiorre, and Bill Mann were booked at the Elizabeth Street station house. The charges were familiar. (Wide World Photos)

Above: *Ralph Beard was an Olympic hero, an All-American, and an NBA All-Star. His only known vice was chewing huge wads of gum.* (Wide World Photos)

Top opposite: *Adolph Rupp celebrates the University of Kentucky's second NCAA championship in 1949 with two of his boys, Alex Groza and Dale Barnstable.* (Wide World Photos)

Bottom opposite: *Barnstable, Beard, and Groza face the booking desk on October 21, 1951.* (Wide World Photos)

Top opposite: *Eddie Gard was held in protective custody at his own request.* (Wide World Photos)

Bottom opposite: *Gard's testimony quickly implicated several players and tinhorn gamblers. Gard's main connection was Salvatore Sollazzo, a jewelry manufacturer, gold smuggler, and gambler. Sollazzo hid his face under his hat during the booking procedures.* (UPI Photo)

Sollazzo's wife, Jeanne, was a one-time chorus girl who readily showed her smile to the photographers. (Wide World Photos)

Salvatore Sollazzo lost thou-sands on the very games he had fixed. For his troubles, Sollazzo also spent twelve years in prison. (WideWorld Photos)

In October 1952, Jersey City (N.J.) of the American Basketball League signed Alex Groza, Ralph Beard, and Sherman White. The players worked out eagerly, but the ABL moguls decided to fold the league rather than admit confessed "fixers." (Wide World Photos)

Opposite: *All of the court hearings were well covered by the media. Leroy Smith* (far right) *tries to shield his eyes from the cameras, and Adolf Bigos* (center) *presents a brave face. But the spotlight was always on Sherman White.* (UPI Photo)

On September 5, 1974, Floyd Layne and Nat Holman share the good news of Layne's appointment as CCNY's basketball coach. "The shortest distance between two points is a straight line, and I've traveled in a wide circle," said Layne. "But I finally got back home." (Wide World Photos)

Baron himself blessed the transaction. UK increased Rupp's basketball budget to nearly $200,000 and the Baron was made into a corn-pone genius and a national celebrity.

For the '48–'49 season, Rupp wanted the only possible encore: both the NCAA and the NIT crowns. He knew that his chances were excellent. Dale Barnstable replaced Rollins in the Wildcats' backcourt and Jim Line was instant points off the bench. Ralph Beard, Alex Groza, and "Wah Wah" Jones were seniors whose fantastic talents were peaking. Rupp's boys were the most powerful team in the land.

In early December 1948, after an easy victory at the Garden, Ralph Beard received a visitor in his hotel room. "Hey," said the squat, bespectacled young man at the door. "Remember me? I'm Nick the Greek. I played varsity football at UK a couple of years back. You were on the frosh."

"Sure," said Ralph. "Nick Englises. Come in."

"That was a great game you guys just played," said Nick. "You were really good."

"Thanks," Ralph flushed.

"Here," said Nick. "This is for you." It was a $20 bill. But fans and alumni were always pressing the players with $5 and $10 gifts. Ralph assumed that Englises had won a few bucks on the ball game. Ralph folded the bill into his pocket.

"Thanks," he said.

The Englises brothers and their sidekick, Saul Feinberg, were still working for Eli Kaye at the time. They had a lot of territory to cover and a lot of teams to supervise, so they threw in $100 a week and hired a pair of legs named Nathan "Lovey" Brown to travel with the Wildcats and present the hard sell. On December 18, 1948, the Wildcats returned to the Garden to play St. John's. Nick and Tony Englises, Nat Brown, Saul Feinberg, and Eli Kaye showed up at the hotel and hustled, swarmed, and jived all over Beard, Groza, and Barnstable. But the players resisted. Ralph had a bad ankle and wasn't even supposed to play. In the end, the three players agreed to accept $100 each if they could beat St. John's by more than the point spread allowed.

DALE BARNSTABLE REMEMBERS: "Those guys were smooth talkers. They should have been salesmen. They took us out for a stroll, treated us to a meal, and before we knew anything, we were right in the middle of it. They said we didn't have to dump the game. They said nobody would get hurt except other gamblers. They said everybody was doing it. And they asked what was wrong with winning a game by as many points as we could. We just didn't think. But if somebody who suspected what was going on at the Garden had warned us that things like that were against the law, we'd never have done it."

Before the game, Rupp ordered the team doctor to administer a shot of Novocain to Ralph's sprained ankle. Then Ralph and his two accomplices played the game at full throttle, and the Wildcats decimated St. John's, 57–30. They collected their payoff from Nat Brown after the game.

The UK triumvirate made two more command performances during the '48–'49 season. On January 22, 1949, the Wildcats beat De Paul, 56–45, in Chicago. Nine days later, they defeated Vanderbilt, 72–50, in Nashville. Beard, Groza, and Barnstable were richer by $300 each. As far as they were concerned, nothing sinister, immoral, or even unusual had taken place. Then in early February, the Wildcats played Tennessee at Alumni Gymnasium. Nick and Tony Englises journeyed to Lexington to watch the game. Feinberg and Brown also converged on the players—and for the first time, Beard, Groza, and Barnstable agreed to go under the points. The Wildcats won by 71–56, and each player collected $500. Nobody seemed to be the wiser.

But the Lexington bookies were pointing a crooked finger at the game. There had been too much out-of-town money bet on Tennessee, and they convened a caucus. A few days later, a headline in the *Courier-Journal* announced their decision: BOOKIES GIVE UP NET PLAY. The local sharpies would no longer be taking bets on any college basketball game. It was thought to be a foolish move. But the Lexington bettors continued gambling on high school basketball and the bookies' handle suffered no noticeable decline.

The Wildcats concluded the '48–'49 season at 29–1 and with a number-one ranking in the AP poll. The All-American team included Tony Lavelli of Yale, Vince Boryla of Denver, Ed Macauley of St. Louis, and Beard, Groza, and Jones from Kentucky. Once again, Ralph was named the Player of the Year and the Wildcats were asked into the NIT.

UK was the tournament's top-seeded team, which meant that their first opponent was the NIT's sixteenth and last seed, Loyola of Chicago. The Wildcats were installed as 12-point favorites. It was a close ball game, primarily because Alex Groza made little attempt to defense Loyola's pivot man, Jack Kerris. Orthodox strategy called for Groza to spot himself either in front of, or alongside of, Kerris. But Groza played behind his man and backed away from Kerris's hook shots. Groza was 0 for 3 from the floor in the first half, Beard scored only 2 points, and Loyola led 32–31 at the intermission. Rupp vehemently encouraged his boys to play better, but the second half was just as tight. When "Wah Wah" Jones fouled out with 10 minutes left, the Wildcats were balanced on a 47–46 lead. Jones was disqualified and Groza was invisible, so Ralph tried to pull the game back together. He managed to keep the score close until the last four minutes when Loyola scored 9 straight points and took the game home, 67–56. The stunned Lexington sportswriters called the game "basketball's most fantastic and dramatic upset."

In the locker room after the game, the New York writers clustered around Rupp, looking for a columnful of cornball one-liners and a chance to step on a loose nerve. "We were flat," the Baron said abruptly. "Awfully flat. That's all there was to it." The writers were left to their own devices, and Rupp headed straight to his hotel room. In the sympathetic company of UK's athletic director, Bernie Shively, Rupp

LOYOLA (67)	G	F	P
Earle	3	3	9
Grady	0	1	1
Klaerich	1	5	7
Kerris	7	9	23
Bluitt	3	3	9
Dawson	1	0	2
Nicholl	1	3	5
Hildebrand	0	0	0
Nagel	5	1	11
	21	25	67

KENTUCKY (56)	G	F	P
Jones	1	2	4
Line	2	3	7
Barnstable	1	2	4
Groza	5	2	12
Hirsch	0	0	0
Day	0	0	0
Beard	6	3	15
Barker	6	2	14
	21	14	56

emptied a fifth of whiskey and poured out his heart. "I don't know," the Baron mourned. "Lordy. But I think there's something wrong with this team."

While Rupp was glooming over the possibilities, Beard, Groza, and Barnstable waited in a parked car on the other side of town for Nat Brown and their $1,500 payoff. During the flight back to Lexington, Rupp withdrew all of the ballplayers' diversions. The Baron wouldn't even let them play cards.

One week later, the Wildcats were back in New York to play in the Eastern Regionals of the NCAA tournament. UK trumped Villanova, 85–72, and Illinois, 76–47, to qualify for the finals in Seattle against Oklahoma A & M. Alex Groza scored 25 points and Rupp's boys took the Aggies, 46–36, to become only the second team in history to win successive NCAA titles. There was another parade of celebration in Lexington.

Two weeks after Ralph Beard's varsity career was concluded, he was given a dinner in Louisville's swank Kentucky Hotel. The keynote address was delivered by a local businessman, Dann Byck. "We are here," said Byck, "to pay tribute to a local boy who made good. We are here to admire him as more than an athlete, as more than a basketball, baseball, and football star. We are here to admire him as a young man whose conduct has surpassed his ability as an All-American. The kids in this town and this state think of Ralph Beard as something special." There were 350 in attendance, including Adolph Rupp, the chancellor of UK, and the acting governor of Kentucky, and they all rose to honor Ralph Beard, Jr., from Hardinsburg. Sue Beard wept as her son stepped to the podium.

"Thank you," said Ralph. "Words cannot express my gratitude."

During the summer of 1949, Ralph played minor-league baseball. He was an infielder and he hit .300 with power. But over the same summer, the details were finalized for the creation of a new franchise in the NBA: the Indianapolis Olympians. The team's featured attractions were Ralph Beard, Alex Groza, and Wallace Jones. Cliff Barker was the playing coach, and another one of Rupp's boys, Joe Holland, was a substitute guard. These five players, along with Lexington sportswriter Babe Kimbrough, also owned 70 percent of the ball club's stock. The players were paid $5,000 in salary and received a $5,000 bonus for signing.

The Olympians were placed in a Western Division especially designed by the NBA to take advantage of traditional rivalries. Besides Indianapolis, the division included the Anderson Packers, the Tri-Cities Blackhawks, the Sheboygan Redskins, the Waterloo Hawks, and the original Denver Nuggets. The teams traveled by station wagon, bus, and train, and the hometown customers saw their heroes win over 70 percent of the time. The league's average salary was $6,000, and the bit players had short, frantic careers. Before each game, there were invariably new teammates to meet. Sometimes the players were lucky to manage a cold shower after a ball game.

The only thing big league about the NBA in '49–'50 was the players: George Mikan, Dolph Schayes, Carl Braun, Dick

McGuire, Max Zaslofsky, Jim Pollard, and Belus Smawley. The Olympians won their division title but lost to Anderson in the second round of the playoffs. Alex Groza averaged 23.4 points a game and was selected to the NBA All-Star team. Ralph Beard averaged 14.9 and made the second team.

Beard and Groza had graduated, but the tradition of shaving points continued at the University of Kentucky. Walter Hirsch and Jim Line joined forces with holdover Dale Barnstable to do business with the Englises-Feinberg-Brown-Kaye gang. On December 12, 1949, Hirsch, Line, and Barnstable each received $500 to go under the spread against De Paul in Louisville. On January 2, 1950, the same three players were paid $1,000 each to shave UK's winning margin against Arkansas at Little Rock.

But the '49–'50 Wildcats repeated as SEC champs and carried a 25–4 slate into the NIT. In the first game of the tourney, the glory-bound Beavers outran the Wildcats, 89–50. The debacle shocked the entire state of Kentucky.

But the Baron recovered quickly. His next ball club, the '50–'51 Wildcats, would be one of his best. Seven-footer Bill Spivey plugged the middle, and the outlands were patrolled by Cliff Hagan, Lou Tsiropoulos, and Frank Ramsey. Dale Barnstable and Walt Hirsch were seniors, and Jim Line was one of Rupp's assistants.

Walt Hirsch would later testify that Bill Spivey came to him before the '50–'51 season and demanded to know if any games had been fixed the season before. Hirsch admitted that some had and Spivey said he wanted to be in on any similar arrangements made for the coming season. Hirsch testified to a meeting with Spivey, Jim Line, and Jack West in a cafeteria in Lexington.

JACK WEST TESTIFIED: "I offered a thousand dollars each to Hirsch and Spivey for a game against St. John's at the Garden on December 23, 1950. The offer was transmitted through Line, who stood to make another thousand dollars. But Spivey passed on the offer because he said he wanted to play his best against his main rival for All-American honors, Bob Zawoluk."

JIM LINE TESTIFIED: "Spivey talked with Hirsch and me before practically every game played in December 1950 and January 1951 about the possibilities and arrangements for deals. Spivey and Hirsch were offered twenty-five hundred dollars to go under the points in two games played in the Sugar Bowl tournament in December of 1950. We lost the first game to St. Louis, 43–42. Jack West complained to me that the game was so obviously fixed it was hard to get bookies to accept substantial bets on Kentucky games."

DALE BARNSTABLE TESTIFIED: "I missed a shot late in the St. Louis game and, when it was over, Rupp gave me the devil. He said that my miss had cost his friend, Burgess Carey, five hundred dollars."

The loss was the Wildcats' first of the season, but there were still twenty-seven games remaining. Rupp wanted to make sure his boys were happy, so he distributed $50 to each of them. Rupp knew that the SEC approved gifts of $250 to football players for expenses at bowl games, and the Baron decided that a basketball "bowl" game fit under the same rules. He would later claim that the money was left over from a fund used to send the UK players to the London Olympics.

JIM LINE TESTIFIED: "Then in January 1950, West promised me and Hirsch eight hundred dollars and Spivey a thousand dollars, to shave points against Notre Dame. But we ran up a 69–44 score and went way over the spread. West bet heavily on the game and I heard that he went broke."

The '50–'51 Wildcats went on to win twenty-one consecutive ball games before losing to Vanderbilt, 61–57, in the finals of the SEC Tournament. But a rule change instituted just prior to the season awarded an NCAA berth to the team with the best conference record during the regular season. Led by Spivey, Hagan, and Ramsey, the Wildcats cruised to Rupp's third NCAA championship, beating Kansas State, 68–58, in the final. The Baron was named Coach of the Year by the grateful sportswriters.

The '50–'51 season was also a fruitful one for both Alex Groza and Ralph Beard. The NBA was reshuffled and the Olympians wound up in a new division with the Minneapolis Lakers, the Rochester Royals, the Fort Wayne Pistons, and the Tri-Cities Hawks. Indianapolis finished fourth in the division and were eliminated by the Lakers in the first round of the playoffs.

But despite their disappointing play, the Olympians had a bright future. The cooperative franchise had all their bills paid, and they were left with $27,000 in the bank. The players once more received salary and bonus totaling $10,000, and stock in the club was worth another $10,000 a share. Alex Groza finished second in scoring to George Mikan and led the NBA in field-goal percentage. Ralph Beard scored 16.8 a game, eighth best in the league and one notch ahead of Bob Cousy. The '50–'51 NBA All-Star team included George Mikan, Ed Macauley, Bob Davies, Alex Groza, and Ralph Beard. The prospects were so good that Ralph abandoned his baseball career. "I was only twenty-two," said Ralph, "and I had never played better basketball in my life. I planned to play pro ball until my legs fell off."

When the Bradley players were arrested on July 25, they pointed Hogan's men to the Wildcats. The D.A.'s office was quiet for the next eight weeks, and on October 19, Ralph Beard was eagerly anticipating the opening of another NBA season. Beard, Groza, Jones, and Holland were en route to Moline, Illinois, where the Olympians were scheduled for a preseason game. The players decided to make a slight detour to see the Rochester Royals play the College All-Stars in an exhibition game at Chicago Stadium. The Baron was coaching the collegians, and his boys also wanted to pay their respects. After the ball game, as Ralph and Alex were leaving the arena, they were chested to a halt by a pair of detectives acting under the authority of the Illinois state attorney.

"Come with us," said Lieutenant James Oakey. "You're both under arrest."

Ralph and Alex were taken to the Cook County jailhouse and questioned without benefit of counsel for seven hours. At first, both of them spouted firm denials, but they were quick to confess when confronted with Nick Englises. "I'm so mixed up," said Ralph. "It's such a mess. It sounds stupid saying it now, but I wish I knew why I did it. I've been asking myself that, and it still doesn't make sense. The money was nothing. Yes, I took the money, but as God is my judge, I never did anything to influence the score of a basketball game. I had too much pride to do that and I was too win-oriented. People will say that I'm a lying SOB and that I'm the biggest crook on earth, but only me and the good Lord know the truth. And I don't care what anybody says, there were only three ball games, the Loyola game and two others down South. I've even forgotten which ones they were. I've tried to remember but I can't. I only know that I've had enough basketball to last me forever."

Dale Barnstable was arrested at his home in Louisville at 2:00 A.M. on October 20. He was taken from his wife, Willie, and his five-month-old twin daughters by five burly policemen. Barnstable readily confessed his part in the fixes and asked the public to be merciful. An hour after Barnstable was pulled in, his wife placed a call to Sue Beard.

"I'm so scared," said Willie Barnstable. "Something awful's happened to Dale and Ralph."

"What is it?" said Sue. "What happened? A car accident?"

Willie wept into her hands. "No," she said. "Something worse."

After he was interrogated, Ralph was tossed into the tank with "psychos and winos" and detained for a total of fifteen hours. When he was finally released, Ralph called his mother and then took a plane to Indianapolis. Sue met her son at the airport and drove him back home to Louisville.

"Mom," Ralph sobbed, "aren't you ashamed to be seen with me?"

"I've never been ashamed of you," said Sue Beard. "And I never will be."

The Baron jumped in headfirst in a rash attempt to defend Beard and Groza. "The Chicago Black Sox threw ball games," reminded Rupp, "but these kids only shaved points. My boys were the inexperienced victims of an unscrupulous syndicate." The University of Kentucky let it be known that Rupp would not be fired despite his revealed improprieties. An anonymous college official pardoned Rupp with claims that any other coach with a championship ball club would have acted the same way. But the Baron was reviled in public by Dan Parker of the *New York Daily Mirror*: "A coach who defends dishonesty of one type because it isn't as bad as dishonesty of another type is hardly the type to save basketball or mold a young athlete's character."

The NBA announced that Beard and Groza had thirty days to dispose of their stock and get out of town. A share in the Olympians that was once worth $10,000 had devalued overnight to $1,000. Maurice Podoloff, the president of the NBA, added that both players were permanently suspended from the league.

The NBA's surviving franchises threw a total of thirteen used ballplayers into a tub, and the Olympians' new owners selected replacements for their departed All-Stars. "Wah Wah" Jones couldn't get comfortable without his two running mates, and averaged only 7.4 points per game in his third and last NBA season. The revamped Olympians now featured a team of solid, workaday ballplayers. Leo Barnhorst, Bill Tosheff, Paul Walther, Joe Grabowski, and Bob Lavoy all averaged double figures, and the franchise gasped for life for another two years.

The first postscandal NBA season opened in mid-October at the Garden with the Boston Celtics paired against the Philadelphia Warriors and the Knicks against the Lakers. "Easy" Ed Macauley, Bob "The Houdini of the Hardwood" Cousy, "Big" George Mikan, Paul Arizin, and Nat "Sweetwater" Clifton were on display, but knowledgeable basketball watchers fearfully counted the crowd instead of the twinkling stars. The hometown Knicks lost to the Lakers, 80–73. The headlines in the New York papers ignored the score to proclaim a crowd of 16,127. The New York fans were officially hooked on the game, and the NBA had what any pro league has ever needed to survive and flourish—a successful franchise in the media capital of the world.

But even with the arrest of Beard and Groza, the NBA still hadn't quite gotten its tail feathers through the door. The new season was barely a week old when Assistant D.A. Vincent O'Connor announced that Sol Levy had been arrested and charged with conspiring with Salvatore Sollazzo to fix a total of six NBA games in 1950. For payments that varied between $400 and $900, Levy made certain that previously specified ballplayers were prematurely fouled out of the games. Sollazzo had winning bets on only half of the rigged games and wound up losing money on his NBA adventure.

Levy swore that he was innocent, and that he had been framed by Eddie Gard. But Levy was indicted for a misdemeanor instead of a felony only because there was no statute in the bribery sections covering referees. O'Connor asked the state legislature to pass a retroactive amendment so that Levy's crimes could be suitably punished.

AN EX-PRO PLAYER REMEMBERS: "Levy wasn't the only ref doing business, but all the other guys are safely dead by now. Even after the scandals broke, there were plenty of games dumped in the NBA. One of my teammates was a famous superstar who had an unstoppable pet move to the basket. Whenever he was doing business, he would take three dribbles away from the basket and throw up a low percentage hook shot. We heard he was making half his yearly salary every time he fixed a game. And he wasn't the only one either. Most of the coaches knew what was going on, but they tried to ignore it. Those were lean days for a guy trying to earn an honest living playing basketball."

Besides Beard and Groza, Hogan's office uncovered the names of two other NBA players who had worked with gamblers as collegians. Agents approached Podoloff with hard evidence, and with demands that both players be booted from the NBA; one of the players was a superstar and the other was a scrub. The owner of the star threatened to fold his franchise and go home if Podoloff touched his player. The star remained in orbit, while the lesser player was quietly expelled from the league early in the '51–'52 season. "If I had my way," Podoloff candidly told a friend, "I'd make everybody in the NBA take a lie-detector test. Going back to their college careers too."

The public wasn't unduly agitated by Levy's announced involvement. One sportswriter guessed that everybody expected shady dealings in the NBA. Levy was tried before a three-judge panel and was voted guilty by a margin of 2–1. The dissenting judge said that deliberately fouling out basketball players was not a punishable offense. The conviction was eventually overturned by a higher court, which held that Levy was a paid, independent contractor, and that the bribery laws applied only to gamblers and athletes.

In mid-October, two Connecticut schoolboys were offered $50 each to throw a football game between Danbury High School and Greenwich High School. On the same day, Clark County High School in Winchester, Kentucky, reported an attempt to bribe three of its basketball players. And there was more bad news for City College: three varsity players, Sheldon Thomas, Larry Meyer, and Howie Levinson, were ruled ineligible by the ECAC because they had participated in summer basketball games in the Catskills. Nat Holman was bent beyond his years. His English accent sometimes faded and his barking curses sometimes caught in his throat. Nat was still "Mr. Basketball," but now people addressed him with the majesty due to a genius who suffers unjustly. It was also announced that Herb Holstrom, the Beaver's co-captain, had been inducted into the army. Then on October 20, Judge Saul Streit sentenced the first round of confessed fixers.

Salvatore Sollazzo got eight-to-sixteen in a state prison and lived unhappily ever after. Eddie Gard received an indeterminate sentence of up to three years. Al Roth was sentenced to a six-month term in a workhouse, but the sentence was suspended with the approval of the D.A. when Roth promised to join the army. Irwin Dambrot received a suspended sentence because Judge Streit felt he had "realized the enormity of his misstep." Lou Lipman received a suspended sentence because His Honor was moved by Lipman's "good war record." Eddie Roman and Herb Cohen also joined the army as an alternative to six months in jail. Connie Schaff was given a six-months suspended sentence. Adolf Bigos, Dick Feurtado, Natie Miller, Leroy Smith, Floyd Layne, and Norm Mager were all permitted their freedom. But Ed Warner was slapped in the jug for six months.

A LAWYER REMEMBERS: "Streit considered Warner to be incorrigible and uncontrollable. Warner was too flamboyant and he also had a record as a juvenile delinquent. Streit believed in rehabilitation by deprivation."

Sherman White's lawyer failed to appear in court on the day of his client's sentencing, so Sherman stood alone before Streit with his head bowed in shame. The judge said that Sherman was a hardened criminal and a semimoron who didn't belong in college. The judge made several racial slurs. Streit also said that Sherman should be institutionalized and sentenced him to one year in prison. Sherman hired another lawyer, who immediately filed an appeal.

IKE GELLIS REMEMBERS: "The scandals were a healthy thing for college basketball. Everybody was forced to clean house. Coaches compiled scrapbooks and forced their teams to read them. People were alerted to the situation."

The '51–'52 college season officially began on December 1, and the Beavers played their inaugural game against the alumni. The varsity Beavers won, 91–45, and looked sharp. Their high scorer was Arnie Smith, a 6-foot-5-inch senior and a veteran of the "Cinderella Team." Observers of the basketball scene began to whisper about the possibility of Nat's pulling off another miracle. The day after the alumni game, CCNY officials announced that Arnie Smith and two other varsity players, Morris Bragin and Edward Chenetz, were henceforth prohibited from intercollegiate athletics because it had been discovered that their high school transcripts were altered. The players denied knowing of the forgeries and Nat cried "Woe!" once again.

On December 3, the decimated Beavers labored to edge puny Roanoke, 63–62. The Bradley Braves lost their season's opener to Vanderbilt, 55–51; Toledo lost to Niagara, 51–46; and Rupp's boys trounced Washington and Lee, 96–46. Long Island University fielded no varsity basketball team for the next six years.

On December 8, Judge Streit passed sentence on the Bradley fixers. Streit called Melchiorre, Mann, and Chianakas "repentant" and suspended their sentences because of their "excellent backgrounds" and because each had received an honorable discharge from the service. Streit also noted that the Bradley fixers were being very helpful in giving information on the activities of Jack West and Joe Benintende and would be available for testimony. West and Benintende had hired a common lawyer and were claiming they had been approached by "touts" who represented athletes willing to be bribed. The two gamblers denied making any overt moves to induce any of the athletes into a point-shaving conspiracy. But midway through their trial, West and Benintende changed their pleas to guilty and the testimony of the Bradley fixers was never required.

In announcing the Bradley sentences, Judge Streit also took the opportunity to issue a sixty-three-page document apportioning the blame for the scandals. The judge sprayed the guilt until it coated the gamblers, the corrupt players, the college administrators, the coaches, and the alumni groups "who participate in this evil system of commercialism and overemphasis." But Streit reserved some of his strongest comments for David Blair Owen, the president of Bradley University. "By his acquiescence in their subsidization and his extensive traveling with members of the team while their studies were being ignored, Owen gave official university sanction to their moral debasement." Streit charged that Owen believed "the basketball team to be the most important department in the university." Streit also held that coaches were given artificial titles of learning and that, in many instances, their tenure depended on their producing winning teams. Intercollegiate football and basketball are no longer amateur sports, the judge said. Scouting and recruiting violations are almost universal, and scholastic standards are evaded. Streit held that the "athletic scholarship" was a contributing evil and should be discontinued. "The answer," said Streit, "is not a reexamination of morals or of values or of standards. These are fixed qualities. And the time has passed for the appointment of committees, subcommittees, and commissions." Streit advocated the reorganization and revitalization of the NCAA, giving it increased powers to police and investigate the activities of its member schools. Streit warned the universities to regulate their own activities before the federal government began to take notice of the big business of intercollegiate athletics.

The judge's analysis of the situation was often naïve but it was fairly accurate. The reactions against his charges were models of righteous indignation and pious self-defense. Nat Holman called the charges completely unfounded. "I have been at City College for thirty-four years," said Nat, "and I can honestly say that our intercollegiate athletic program has

never led us into lowering our scholastic standards." Bobby Sand also challenged the inference that CCNY would "wink its eye" at the academic standards of its varsity players. Sand quickly added that he had absolutely nothing to do with the scholastic records of the City College athletes. Howard Cann denied having paid scouts and swore he had nothing to do with NYU's admissions office. "Judge Streit has told only one side of the story," Cann said. "We here at NYU have no training table and all our players live at home. We give our players only one meal, dinner after a late practice. Personally, I've tried to get help for our basketball players. Right now, for instance, I have four boys who live in Coney Island. That's a long trip home after a hard workout and I wish we could make it easier for them."

The judge's document roused every president, coach, and athletic director in the country. Southern Methodist University had a yearly budget that provided for 154 athletic scholarships. SMU's A.D., Matty Bell, said simply, "It isn't any of the judge's business." Clair Bee was entrusted with articulating the official stance of LIU. "We feel that a boy who plays on a team should get help if he needs it. Otherwise, only the boys who have money enough can afford to play. As long as the great majority of American universities help athletes with scholarships, tuitions, room and board, fees, books, and a job, we at LIU have to do it too. I would do it the same way again. The subsidization of athletes is traditional." The president of the University of Maryland, Dr. H. Byrd, also defended the dissemination of athletic scholarships. "Why should we make any change in a system that is working successfully just because of criticism from some obscure fellow in New York?"

But the officials at CCNY were stung by Streit's comments and they immediately broke into committees. "We have as our aim," said a spokesman, "the elimination of City College as an athletic power in the future."

When Streit was done with them, a Peoria judge sat and considered the Bradley fixers. His decision was to dismiss the indictments against Bill Mann and Mike Chianakas and to give Gene Melchiorre a suspended sentence and probation for a period of one year. After unsuccessfully trying to find employment in the Peoria area, Gene headed back home and settled in Highwood, Illinois. Gene beat the streets looking for work and finally landed a job selling insurance fifty miles away in Chicago. With only a week's training, Gene won two sales contests. He discovered that people liked him and were anxious to buy insurance from him. He was still a hero to those who really knew him. Within a few years, Gene became the president of the Highwood Community Center and the chairman of the local Community Chest Drive.

GENE MELCHIORRE REMEMBERS: "Everything could have been avoided if somebody at Bradley had warned us about gamblers and fixers. Especially when we got to the Garden. I guess they never thought it could happen. But I'm certainly not blaming the college. We let them down the same as we let everybody down. But at least the New York coaches were suspicious enough to warn their players. For whatever good it did. I don't know. I guess when it comes down to it, I can't blame anybody but myself. I know I made a bad mistake, and I know that fixes were going on for years. Sooner or later, somebody was going to get caught. We were the ones, I guess. But I'm still not complaining. You know, I was born and raised in a very religious home, but I never really got to know God until I got into all the trouble. Right after I was arrested, I met a man named Father Feeney. 'No matter what people say,' he told me, 'or what the newspapers print, what you did is not as bad in the eyes of God as they make it out to be.' After a while, I became convinced that my involvement in the scandals was the best thing that ever happened to me. It made me a better person."

14

Peace negotiations continued in Korea, but on January 1, 1952, Red jets bombed Kimpo airfield and Inchon harbor just west of Seoul. A poll conducted by *Radio-TV Daily* revealed that Imogene Coca and Arthur Godfrey were America's favorite TV personalities, while Tallulah Bankhead and Jack Benny were the best-liked radio stars.

Bill Spivey voluntarily resigned from the UK basketball team because of rumors around Lexington that he was a dumper. "I will not play again for Kentucky," said Spivey, "until my name is cleared of any suspicion."

On January 19, General James Van Fleet, U.S. 8th Army Commander, called the Korean War a "blessing" because it spurred the free world to become strong enough to "knock down" the Communists and "wipe them out on all fronts." On February 10, the French Army Command estimated that the Viet Minh rebels had suffered 45,000 casualties in "December-January" as against French Viet Nam casualties of only 5,135.

On February 20, Jim Line and Walter Hirsch were arrested and hauled to New York. The two ex-Wildcats gave testimony that implicated Bill Spivey. The 7-foot All-American came to New York to testify before Hogan's grand jury. A copyrighted story in the *Louisville Courier-Journal* quoted Spivey as saying he had twice been approached with bribe offers by a man named "George" but had refused to go along. Under oath before the grand jury, Spivey swore he had never ever been faced with an offer to shave points. Max Kase of the *New York Journal-American* won a Pulitzer Prize for his exposures of "bribery and other forms of corruption in the popular American sport of basketball, which exposures

199

tended to restore confidence in the game's integrity." On March 3, the Appellate Division of the New York State Supreme Court rejected Sherman White's contention that he had already been sufficiently punished, and upheld his jailing. "White was not merely a fixed player," the court ruled, "but he assumed the initiative in approaching another player." Sherman did his time on Riker's Island, a pile of rubble and refuse in the East River midway between Queens and Manhattan. Sherman grew a beard and refused to greet any uninvited visitors. It was several weeks before the reporters stopped coming after him. Then, one day, Sherman received a bill from the lawyer who had abandoned him at the sentencing, and the worm turned again in Sherman's soul.

SHERMAN WHITE REMEMBERS: "To this day, I believe there was some kind of collaboration between my lawyer and the prosecution. Riker's Island was supposed to have been built for rehabilitation, but it was the worst place in the world for a kid to try and straighten out his life. I often wonder why I never came out of there a criminal. With all the characters and perverts I met, it certainly would have been the easy way to go."

Sherman couldn't help growing hard around the edges and bitter in his core. Still, the love of his parents, his girl, and a few faithful friends helped to sustain him. Sherman played basketball during gym hours. He was popular even with the guards, and his job assignment was to turn on the showers. After a few months, Sherman began singing in the church choir and he was soon passing out the hymnals during services. And Sherman wondered if his girl really loved him. Or if all the publicity had just made her too ashamed to ditch him.

Paul Zeitlin was an old buddy of Sherman's who also happened to own a slaughterhouse in New Jersey. Zeitlin signed an affidavit guaranteeing Sherman a steady job and a living wage, and the imprisonment was commuted after nine months. Sherman was elated when he was first released. But then the best basketball player that anybody ever saw began working eight hours a day ankle-deep in smashed bones, bloody organs, and bleeding brains, in the midst of a putrid, bleating madness. Within a month, Sherman was feeling as wretched as ever. When he wasn't suspicious and paranoid, he groped through a baleful depression. He considered his aborted youth with sadness.

But then his girl did marry him. And Zeitlin formed a semipro basketball team called the New Jersey Titans that toured the East Coast playing the locals. Basketball was the perfect therapy for Sherman, and his instinctively unselfish game helped to flush out his heart. The Titans drew larger and larger crowds wherever they played.

In early March, after the '51–'52 Beavers had limped to a dismal 9–11 season, officials of CCNY tried to cry up an alarm. They pointed out that the Beavers' on-campus gym seated only 1,010 and that without the revenue from the Garden, it would be impossible for the college to continue its intercollegiate athletic program. The football team alone operated at an average deficit of $16,000 a year. The college urged the Board of Higher Education to let the Beavers play in the Garden next season. But the Board wouldn't hear of such nonsense and they ordered CCNY to foreclose its football team. Nat Holman's thirty-fourth basketball season at City College had been a continuing calamity, and the Board's tone led seasoned observers to guess that it might be his last. But for Adolph Rupp and his Wildcats, the '51–'52 season was still alive and promising lucky stars and fair winds.

In the afterglow of the scandals, the Baron became a coach without mercy and he ran up monster scores against his hapless SEC competition. Led by Cliff Hagan and Frank Ramsey, the Wildcats blasted Mississippi by 58 points, Florida by 47, Georgia by 40, Tulane by 49, Georgia Tech by 51, and Tennessee by 55.

ADOLPH RUPP REMEMBERS: "All those other SEC schools knew they couldn't beat me on the basketball court, so they said, 'Get rid of that SOB Rupp.' That only made me more determined than ever that, by gawd, I was going to have great teams. I said I'd get rid of all those SEC coaches who were against me, and, by gawd, there were fifty-six coaches in the conference from the time I came in until the time I left. I outlived them all. They didn't know it, but there was never any chance that UK would fire me. The board of trustees told me, 'Adolph, as far as we're concerned, you didn't know a damn thing about the fixes.' And they were right. How could I suspect my boys were working with gamblers when we were beating every damn team in the nation?"

Bill Spivey was barely missed as Rupp's boys coasted to another SEC title and beat Penn State, 82–54, in the semifinals of the NCAA Eastern Regionals. Then the Ides of March set a blue moon over the hills and cities of Kentucky. The Wildcats were dumped by St. John's, 64–57, in the Eastern finals, and the season came up empty.

On March 29, Bill Spivey was indicted for perjuring himself before the grand jury one month earlier. Spivey surrendered in New York, pleaded innocent, and was released on $2,500 bail. "I could not have been involved in such fixing," said Spivey, "because of my loyalty to my school, to the people who believe in me, and because of my love for the game." Spivey's trial was set for January 1953, but the University of Kentucky couldn't wait. The UK Athletic Board had been permitted to peruse confidential evidence and private minutes, and they declared that Spivey was part of "a conspiracy to fix Kentucky basketball games during the '50–'51 season." The board ruled that Spivey's retirement from the Wildcats was permanent.

Then on March 30, Judge Saul Streit sentenced the confessed UK fixers. Ralph Beard, Alex Groza, and Dale Barnstable received suspended sentences and indefinite probation. "Yes," said Ralph. "I'm guilty. Let me out of here. Let me die." Streit also issued another lengthy tome in which he branded UK as "the acme of commercialism and overemphasis." In a series of hearings held in his chambers, Streit said he had taken sworn testimony from the three players and from various UK officials. "I found undeniable evidence of covert subsidization of players, ruthless exploitation of athletes, cribbing on examinations, illegal recruiting, a reckless disregard for the players' physical welfare, matriculation of unqualified students, demoralization of the athletes by the coach, the alumni, and the townspeople." The judge offered a few new suggestions: do away with recruiting and postseason games, and do not allow freshmen to play varsity ball. Streit also continued his attack on the athletic scholarship: "It is the most fruitful racket yet invented to destroy the amateur code." On the very same day, the NCAA announced it was instituting an inquiry into UK's entire athletic program.

The citizenry of Kentucky reached for their muskets and their pens. Herman L. Donovan, the president of UK, said that Streit's report was "a harangue filled with misrepresentation. According to Judge Streit, all of the culprits live in Kentucky. The judge forgets that one of the rottenest gambling joints in the world, Madison Square Garden, is in his own bailiwick." Donovan added that UK was no more guilty than any other SEC school, and that to fire Rupp would be to admit to greater sin. But the Baron was leaving his own fortifications to launch an attack of his own. "I must say I'm getting a little tired of all this deemphasis business," said Rupp. "Do they want us to deemphasize a player's athletic ability? Or deemphasize the interest of the spectators? Or shall we deemphasize the winning of a ball game? I think it's time we deemphasized the deemphasis. And I am perfectly willing for the good people of Kentucky to be my judges."

President Donovan and Lawrence Wetherby, the governor of the state, issued a joint statement declaring that Streit had gone to "unnecessary lengths to blacken the reputation of UK." The statement placed most of the blame on radio stations, newspapers, magazines, and "college administrators and coaches throughout the land." Judge Streit's

203

only counterpunch was devastating. "All of my facts were obtained by me from the lips of the athletes, from coach Rupp, from UK's athletic director, and from the officials of the university."

In the late spring, the Manhattan College fixers appeared before the dock. Judge James M. Barrett confessed he was a basketball fan who had watched and admired the play of both Hank Poppe and John Byrnes. Then His Honor called the two players "traitors" to their school. He placed them on probation for three years and excluded them from professional sports forever. The gamblers involved in the case, Irving Schwartzberg, Benjamin Schwartzberg, and Cornelius Kelleher, were each sentenced to a year in jail. Judge Barrett also enjoyed the chance to air his own thoughts on the scandals. "There is no harm in athletic scholarships," he said. "But I think the colleges should be more careful in their selection of athletes. There would have been no scandal if the public did not want to gamble." The furor lingered into the baseball season.

On July 4, the Brooklyn Dodgers led the second-place New York Giants by 3 games, and the Yankees paced the Chicago White Sox by 2½. Frankie Baumholtz, Al Rosen, and Bobby Avila were all hitting over .330, and Ralph Kiner led both leagues in home runs. In the Bronx, Floyd Layne was hitting .400 with the semipro "New York Mohawks." The Mohawks played on Diamond number 4 in Crotona Park, where the dimensions were 330 down the lines and 300 to straightaway center. They also played in Van Cortlandt Park, which had no boundaries, and where groundballs sometimes went for homers. The Mohawks' most illustrious alumnus was Cleveland Indians' slugger Rocky Colavito. Rocky's brother, Dominick, still caught for the club. Floyd played first base and the outfield. Floyd ran fast, threw straight, played smart, always hustled, and hit rising line drives. The Pittsburgh Pirates flashed an interest in Floyd, and so did Cleveland. Under ordinary circumstances, Floyd would have been a hotshot prospect.

During the week, Floyd continued working at the Forest Neighborhood House. He was responsible for organizing and directing the basketball, volleyball, and boxing programs. He maintained the equipment, officiated, conducted tournaments and clinics, broke up fights, and sometimes swept the floor. Floyd's duties were soon expanded and he began counseling youngsters from age twelve to twenty-one. Floyd sought out the neighborhood lepers: the troublemakers, the unreachables, the late-bloomers, and the unteachables. Floyd ventured into alien playgrounds, into homes, and, painful as it was, into courtrooms. He talked with teachers, judges, parents, cops, and parole officers, doing anything to help a kid find a new chance. No one knows exactly how the fuel of honor burns and turns into love and redemption, but gradually, Floyd discovered he could control even the most stubborn situation by exercising only a quiet authority. When Floyd heard of an impending fight between two local gangs, he literally locked the gang members out of the gymnasium.

"Hey, man. We wanna play ball, Mr. Layne."

"Yeah. You can't keep us out. I'm a member, man. Here's my card."

"Yeah, Mr. Layne. I paid real money. . . ."

"None of you guys are playing basketball in here," said Floyd. "Until you forget about all of that gang-fighting stuff I've been hearing."

Floyd counseled troubled kids back into the mainstream of their passing adolescence. He bore witness that anybody could come back.

FLOYD LAYNE REMEMBERS: "The kids at the community center used to watch me play basketball. They wanted to know why I wasn't playing in the pros, why they couldn't see me on TV. I told them about the scandals and they said, 'How long are they going to keep you out? When are you going to get another chance?' They were too young to understand."

Then on a hot, wet morning in late July, Judge Saul Streit cleared his throat and imposed sentence on another group of fixers. Joe Benintende was awarded four to seven years in a state prison. Jack West got two to three. Jackie Goldsmith and his associates each received two-and-a-half to five. Nick Englises and Saul Feinberg were given indeterminate terms of up to three years. Tony Englises and Nathan Brown got six months. Instead of delivering another monograph, Judge Streit merely called the defendants "brazen and audacious brown rats."

On August 11, the SEC announced that Rupp's boys would not be permitted on the same basketball court with the loop's other schools for a probationary period of one year. The SEC was reported also to have demanded the Baron's head as the price for continued good standing, but UK took no such action. "We still believe Adolph Rupp to be an honorable man," said President Donovan. "We also feel the punishment we have received is excessive for the violations with which we have been charged and to which we have confessed. Violations which have also been committed by other members of the SEC in recent years." Kentucky's athletic director, Bernie Shively, hurriedly tried to patch the Wildcats' '52–'53 schedule. He called industrial teams, athletic clubs, armed forces teams, and Bible schools. But then the NCAA announced its own sanctions on UK. The NCAA's independent investigations supported most of Judge Streit's accusations, and the university was placed on total athletic probation for one year. None of UK's teams could appear in lucrative postseason ball games, and a spokesman for the school said the probation would cost nearly $150,000 in lost revenues. President Donovan yielded to the mounting pressure and reluctantly ordered Bernie Shively to scrap the Wildcats' entire '52–'53 season.

The president of the UK Alumni Association, William

Townsend, called the NCAA sentence "harsh." Townsend contended that "no body of men, reeking themselves with athletic halitosis, has any right to point an accusing finger at a speck on Kentucky's vest." Ed Hickey, the highly respected basketball coach at St. Louis University, also vented his anger at the NCAA's ruling. "The NCAA took much too long to make their decision," said Hickey. "Their sloth has hurt our school and other innocent bystanders." Hickey revealed that St. Louis had been scheduled to host the Wildcats on January 3, 1953—5,000 tickets had already been sold, and moneys would have to be refunded.

Then a Lexington lawyer named J. A. Edge filed a $500,000 lawsuit against Adolph Rupp. The suit alleged that Rupp had conspired with Ed Curd and the celebrated Frank Costello in a "debasing scheme" to gamble on college basketball games. "You cannot escape the idea," said Edge, "that something was going on between Rupp and the two mobsters. Why doesn't Rupp say he never asked Curd about point spreads? Why doesn't Rupp say he has no gambling connections? Why does he stay on while the boys have to leave? Rupp cannot escape justice simply because he is a coach. So far, Rupp has issued nothing but informal denials." The suit was dismissed in Lexington by Judge H. Church Ford, who claimed that Edge was only seeking "notoriety." Edge was also suspended from practice for a year.

Sherman White reported to his parole officer once a week and he continued playing for the New Jersey Titans. The team was doing so well that they began looking for a permanent affiliation. Sherman loved playing with the Titans, but his job at the slaughterhouse was getting on his nerves. Sherman had difficulty trying to locate something better.

SHERMAN WHITE REMEMBERS: "Society has a secret mean streak that not many people get to see. When a man is down, society likes to keep you down. I chased every lead and every suggestion, but I was constantly refused employment only because I was involved in this thing. I hoped to get into selling, because then I wouldn't have to be confined to an office. Through another friend, I finally wound up selling storm windows and house siding. It was a good living and I was able to pay all of my legal fees. But people recognized me wherever I went."

On August 16, Eddie Gard was released from prison after serving a nine-month stretch. The parole officer said that Gard was now "on the upgrade." Vincent O'Connor applauded Gard's cooperation, and the judge took into consideration the six months he had been held in protective custody. Gard already had a job, and he promised to live at home and attend night school until he earned his degree. Gard was placed on parole for two years and instructed to stay away from all sporting arenas.

Eli Kaye awaited his trial in a summer home he owned in Monticello, New York. But on August 22, Kaye suffered a fatal heart attack. All over the country, scores of businessmen, referees, teachers, coaches, CPA's, lawyers, candlestick makers, and professional basketball players rejoiced in the belief that Kaye's death had sealed the past.

The American Professional Basketball League was the oldest circuit in the country, having been founded in the early 1900s and revived in 1928. The league had franchises in small towns scattered through western New York, New Jersey, and Pennsylvania. The APBL competed with the upstart Eastern Basketball League for hometown favorites, undiscovered and overlooked talent, and NBA rejects. Paul Zeitlin settled his New Jersey Titans in Jersey City and signed Ralph Beard and Alex Groza to the squad.

ALEX GROZA REMEMBERS: "It was fun and it was invigorating. Sherman was a dream to play with. We started to believe we had lots of good basketball left in us."

In mid-October, the Titans applied for admittance into the APBL. But before the matter was adjudicated, the Elmira Hawks, one of the league's charter members in good standing, went out and signed Bill Spivey. The APBL traditionally garnered most of its gate receipts by sparring with NBA teams during the exhibition season. But Maurice Podoloff advised the APBL that he would never allow any NBA teams to play against convicted or suspected fixers.

On October 23, the Titans beat Elmira, 95–78, in an exhibition game played in Jersey City. High scorers for the home team were Groza with 32, Beard with 17, and White with 13. Spivey led Elmira with 22 points. While the game was being contested, the officials of the APBA were meeting in closed session. "I don't think it's right," said John O'Brien, the president of the league, "to ask the game to help players who have already hurt the game. In all our history, our league has never been tainted, and I don't want to start now." O'Brien offered his resignation, and the owners voted to disband the league rather than accept players involved in the scandals.

A week after the APBL folded, Bill Spivey signed a contract with a touring pro team called the Detroit Vagabonds. The owner of the Vagabonds, King Bring, refused to disclose Spivey's salary. "But I'll bet," said Bring, "it makes Spivey the highest priced nonleague basketball player in the country. Folks are sure going to hear about us."

In early November, Judge Streit sat up and took notice of the recent events. He responded with a telegram announcing that Beard, Groza, and Barnstable were prohibited from playing basketball during their three-year probationary periods.

RALPH BEARD REMEMBERS: "Streit said if I so much as touched a basketball in a YMCA, he'd throw my ass in jail."

With the Blackbirds in limbo, Clair Bee had the same need to continue coaching as the guilty players had to keep playing. On November 12, Bee replaced Chick Reiser as the coach of the NBA's Baltimore Bullets. The ball club was 0–3 when Bee took control. Don Barksdale, Paul Hoffman, Jim Baechtold, Ray Lumpp, and "Fat Freddie" Scolari were players of ample ability but abbreviated size. The college scandals had maimed Bee's enthusiasm, but he purchased total control of the Bullets several months later. Bee's career coaching record in the NBA was 34–116, and in 1954, he was lucky to clear out three days before the franchise collapsed.

If Clair Bee was anxious to get back into basketball, Nat Holman needed a vacation. Nat was sore from the scandals and he was only a few months away from retirement. He took off for Europe on a sabbatical leave from CCNY and left the team in the hands of Dave Polansky. For the first time in the history of Western civilization, a City College basketball team would not be coached by Nat Holman.

Then on November 19, the Board of Higher Education charged Nat Holman, Bobby Sand, and Professor Frank Lloyd with "unbecoming conduct, neglect of duty, and failure to cooperate fully with the 1951 basketball fix investigation." The three faculty members were suspended without pay pending a thorough inquiry by the Board.

ONE OF NAT'S BOYS REMEMBERS: "Nat thought he was invincible. Even after the scandal, Nat wanted City to stay big-time and continue playing in the Garden. But it was a new regime and the Board was out to fire him."

The bad news caught up with Nat in Madrid, and the personal nature of the attack flooded him with the feisty tonic of his youth. Nat took the first plane back to New York to defend his reputation. "I have a strong personal conviction," said Nat, "that I have been used as a scapegoat because the Board was unable to uncover the individuals who were responsible for tampering with the scholastic records of the involved players. I have always discharged my duties honestly and to the best of my ability. I defy any committee of basketball authorities to prove that any coach with integrity can discriminate between a poor performance and a deliberately dishonest effort. At no time, either directly or indirectly, have I had the slightest association with athletic irregularity. My conscience is completely clear."

Professor Lloyd, the chairman of the Physical Education Department, said he would establish his innocence at the forthcoming trial, but he also took a clue from Nat. "I will not shirk responsibility for anything I have done," said Lloyd, "but neither will I permit anyone to blacken my reputation as a face-saving device to cover the acts or omissions of others."

Bobby Sand made no immediate public response. While one of his colleagues was burning his files, Sand provided twenty-six pieces of evidence to the Board's investigating committee. "If I have to go, that's okay," Sand later told a reporter. "I'll offer my defense when the time comes, but I have no quarrel with an action that will finally clear up the situation. I felt a long time ago that basketball was the tail that wagged the dog here at CCNY. I can't think otherwise now that I've been hurt."

The Board of Higher Education hired a former FBI man to head its investigation. At CCNY, the "new order" took the game film of the Beavers' memorable 89–50 trouncing of the Wildcats and locked it in a safe.

Bob Schafer shot his free throws one-handed, and from the far right end of the foul line. Schafer's singular style would eventually angle him into a two-year career in the NBA. But on January 9, 1953, Schafer was a junior at Villanova and the team's star scorer. He had just eaten dinner and was comfortably wedged in his dormitory room, when the telephone rang.

"Bob Schafer?" asked a man's voice. "We have a package for you at the Villanova Post Office."

"Okay," said Schafer. "Be right there."

The post office had been closed for over an hour, but Schafer bundled up against the cold and went to claim his package. The postal building was situated off campus and it was dark when Schafer arrived. There was a car parked with its motor running just outside the entrance. A man jumped out of the back seat and approached the ballplayer.

"Hey," the man said. "You're Bob Schafer, ain't you?"

"That's me."

"Jeez," said the man. "I'm one of your biggest fans."

The man removed his glove and extended his right hand, and Schafer stepped up to greet him. As their hands meshed, another man popped out of the car, and Schafer was pushed inside. There were two other men waiting in the car, and Schafer thought he saw a gun. "What is this?" said Schafer. "Is this some kind of a prank? Hey, do you guys belong to Tau Epsilon . . .?"

"Shut up, kid," said one of the men. As they slowly drove around the campus, the abductors talked about basketball in general and Villanova's prospects in particular. Schafer thought they were "crackpot fans" and humored them. But when Schafer tried to bolt from the car at a red light, he was forcibly restrained. "Listen," one of the men said menacingly. "We want you to be less active in a couple of games. Understand?"

"What is this?" Schafer stammered. "Who are you guys?"

"Never mind," said the man. "Just think about what I said. And remember how easy it was to get ahold of you. You know what I mean?" When Schafer was finally released in front of the dorm, he raced upstairs and immediately called his coach. The phone didn't stop ringing until the FBI was involved. The area was Hoovered for several days but yielded no additional information. It was clear, however, that the 1951 basketball scandals had not discouraged the gamblers.

The Board of Higher Education specified its charges against Holman, Sand, and Lloyd:

1. In 1945 Paul Schmones was approached by teammate Leonard Hassman with an offer to throw a game. Schmones told Sand, who told Holman and Lloyd. Hassman was dropped from the squad but no report was ever made to the college administration. The charge was insubordination.

2. Between 1945 and 1951, the high school transcripts of fourteen CCNY athletes were changed to establish their eligibility for admission. The charge was fraud.

3. Holman, Sand, and Lloyd were all members of the Student-Athletic Guidance Council, which was really an illegal recruiting mechanism and which the Board claimed was instrumental in promoting an atmosphere of "cynicism and disregard of academic and ethical standards."

4. All three men were charged with participating in plans for a proposed tour of South America in 1950 that would have included illegal "kickbacks" to the players.

The Board also felt that Nat was either familiar with all the shaving and fixing, or else he was so naïve as to throw doubt on his fitness as a teacher. Then on January 23, Professor Lloyd received a Distinguished Service Award from the New York State Association of Health, Physical Education and Recreation. The Association's subcommittee on professional ethics simultaneously announced that it had examined the Board's allegations and found them to be unsubstantiated. The Association also asked its members to contribute funds for Lloyd's legal defense. With all due bureaucratic fumbling, the Board of Higher Education sorted out reports, findings, hearings, and soundings, and prepared to take its case to arbitration. But there was another trial already in progress.

Bill Spivey's fate was decided before a jury of his peers and Judge Saul Streit. The 7-foot All-American was never actually charged with fixing, only with committing perjury in his testimony before the grand jury. The hearing lasted for ten days, and through it all Spivey denied he had ever shaved a point or fixed a ball game. He testified he had once been offered $500 to doctor a game but had spurned the bribe. Spivey said he failed to report the incident because he thought the briber was a "crackpot."

Spivey's former teammates, Walt Hirsch and Jim Line, were the prosecution's main witnesses. The D.A. had also attempted to bring Jack West to the stand, but the convicted gambler refused to answer any more questions. "What do I have to do with any of this?" West balked. "My case is settled and I'm already doing my time. Leave me alone. What do I care if Spivey is guilty or not?"

"Testify," ordered Judge Streit, "or be held in contempt of this court." West opted for silence and the judge's disfavor.

The Spivey jury was out for ten and a half hours and returned with a 9–3 vote for acquittal on the grounds of insufficient evidence. The defense immediately asked for a dismissal of the indictment, and Streit heard arguments in his chambers. The judge subsequently revealed that the prosecution's star witness, Jack West, failed to testify; and that another key witness, Eli Kaye, was dead. Streit also felt that the credibility of Hirsch and Line was "uncertain" because of their own involvement. The judge dismissed the indictment against Spivey without any further comment.

Spivey's attorney called the decision a "vindication," and said that his client planned to return to school and continue his education. The lawyer failed to mention that Spivey also intended to make a formal application for inclusion in a forthcoming NBA collegiate draft.

The Beavers concluded their first "Nat-less" season with a surprising record of 10–6. Bradley was 15–12 and Toledo was 16–7: both Forrest Anderson and Jerry Bush were allowed to rebuild their teams for another swipe at the Golden Percentage. With the Wildcats idling on the sidelines, Bob Pettit carried LSU to the SEC championship. At LIU, a new president was more interested in initiating an intercollegiate boxing team than in revivifying the basketball team. Bob Leonard and Don Schlundt led Indiana to the NCAA title, while Seton Hall copped the NIT behind Walt Dukes and Richie Regan. The center on the consensus All-American team was 5-foot-9-inch John O'Brien of Seattle University. Then a month after the '52–'53 college season came to a close, Frank Hogan terminated his grand jury. There had been 33 players apprehended from 7 schools, and 49 fixed games played in 23 cities in 19 states. Ninety ball games had been discussed in advance by gamblers and players, and a total of $72,950 was paid in bribes. "There have been hopeful signs," said Hogan, "which indicate that colleges which have commercialized their athletic programs have taken to heart some of the hard lessons taught by this investigation." But the D.A. was wishfully whistling down a sewer.

The Board of Higher Education's trial committee commenced formal proceedings in June. Ballplayers were questioned, students were grilled, and faculty members were examined before three trial judges. The courtroom was circular and low-slung and could be reached only through a labyrinth of corridors in the basement of the Bar Association building in mid-Manhattan. In a preliminary interview, Nat Holman denied having knowledge of the "Sand-Warner" letter and swore he knew very little about CCNY's South American fiasco.

But Sam Winograd was one of the early witnesses, and he brought the letter with him to the seat of judgment. "Professor Holman knew all about the letter," said Winograd. "Professor Lloyd and I decided to put the letter in a safe-deposit box, but we had no intention of concealing it." Winograd's story added grounds of perjury against Nat. There was a movement afoot to convince Holman to either resign or retire, but Nat resisted. Anything but complete exoneration was tantamount to an admission of culpability.

Under oath for a second time, Nat admitted that he had in fact seen the letter. But Nat explained that whenever a problem arose in the department, the usual procedure was to go to Chairman Lloyd and "not go running across the street to the president's office." Nat said he had been furious with the thirty-eight-year-old Sand when he learned of the letter. "The warmth," said Nat, "went out of my relationship with the boy." Nat further testified that Winograd's plan was to hold the letter and use it in case Sand "got funny" sometime in the future. Nat's attempts to fire Sand had been overruled by Lloyd and Winograd, and Holman claimed that his two superiors were responsible for "suppressing" the letter. Nat concluded his defense by attributing the scandals to the lack of "moral fiber" in the guilty players. "I am not interested in athletic bums, or dividend athletes," said Nat. "My purpose is to turn out intelligent young men who will be a credit to the college and productive citizens in the community." Nat denied harboring even a suspicion that his boys were involved with gamblers.

Frank Lloyd removed himself from the Board's jurisprudence by resigning before he could be called to testify. "My decision concedes nothing," said Lloyd, "except that there may be some who might differ with me concerning the judgment I exercised in one, or at most two, incidents during my eight years of service at CCNY. Even in the event of my acquittal, it would no longer be personally desirable for me to return to my teaching position." Bobby Sand's testimony was brief. Sand confessed to using unseemly pressure in convincing Ed Warner to sign a flimsy affidavit. It was the only transgression with which Sand was charged.

After digesting the evidence, the trial committee recommended by a vote of 2–1 the dismissal of all charges against Nat Holman and his reinstatement with back pay. Nat had exhibited "poor judgment" in keeping "silent" about both the letter and the bribe proffered to Paul Schmones in 1945, but the tribunal found no misdeeds. The judges noted that Nat had always tried to persuade the newspapers from publishing point spreads. They were unanimous in considering Nat to be "a strict coach, a good one, and one who holds the respect of his players." The veteran jurors also determined that nobody could possibly detect deliberate bad play, and they thanked Nat for the generosity of his "full cooperation."

The vote was 3–0 to find Bobby Sand guilty. The panel suggested that Sand be suspended without pay for one year, and that upon reinstatement, he be reassigned outside the physical education department. No charges had ever been directed against Winograd, but the judges recommended he be reassigned to a teaching position and removed from his administrative duties. "The committee would like to congratulate Professor Winograd on his eager cooperation," said a spokesman, "on his loyalty to the college, and for his extraordinary administrative abilities."

The judgments seemed surgically clean yet painful enough to satisfy most responsible observers. Arthur Daley, of *The New York Times*, praised "the relentless and unsparing way that the City College authorities have pursued their investigation. There was no attempt at a whitewash, such as the University of Kentucky produced." For a while, an occasional reporter mentioned that Bobby Sand had borne too much of the guilt, but nobody was really interested. Small fries were supposed to fry. All that remained for the trial committee's recommendations to become official was the rubber stamp of approval from the twenty-one-member Board of Higher Education.

While the Board reviewed the findings, Sand helped a CCNY subcommittee cast new regulations for intercollegiate athletics. A student fee was initiated to replace the lost revenue from the Garden, and recreation replaced winning as the aim of the entire athletic program. Sand partially recompensed his suspended salary by coaching on weekends in the Eastern League. Sand also received financial assistance from an admirer, Abe Saperstein, the owner of the Harlem Globetrotters, and conducted clinics in Sweden, Indochina, and wherever else the clowns of basketball did their pratfalls.

In mid-August Joe Louis announced that he had remarried. On August 16, the NCAA restored the University of Kentucky to its good graces. Two days later, Joe Louis retracted his latest marriage. The "Brown Bomber" said the story was a "gag" to procure ringside seats to see Kid Gavilan fight Johnny Bratton in Chicago. On September 17, ex-beauty queen Marilyn Beard filed for divorce, asking custody of three-year-old Ralph Beard III.

RALPH BEARD REMEMBERS: "It wasn't Marilyn's fault at all. My life just disintegrated. I did manage to reenter UK and earn my degree, but whenever I walked around Louisville I hawked the passersby and avoided anyone who might talk to me about basketball. After I graduated, I moved from job to job. I laid pipe, I loaded trucks, and I sold cars. I lived in a void and I thought of myself as a complete failure. I wanted to go away and die. I was an absolutely unbearable person to live with."

Ralph didn't contest the divorce, but the wrench was still an affliction. Ralph also squirmed under Judge Streit's injunction against playing basketball. It seemed as though everything he had loved had been torn from him. A few months after Marilyn left, a friend named Joe Scott encouraged Ralph to start dating again. Ralph's first call was to Joe's sister, Betty. "She was very levelheaded," said Ralph. "She said I couldn't go through life mourning over that same mistake. She made me realize I had to live." Ralph and Betty were married on March 18, 1955.

Since Ralph was still on probation, he was automatically "U.S. Grade 1A Cannon Fodder" and he was drafted in July 1955 at the age of twenty-seven. But the army proved to be a blessing. The relentless routine imposed a continuity on his life. Then Ralph's probation lapsed and he was allowed to play ball. The familiar sounds, well-worn movements, and frenetic energy of the game helped Ralph to revive. He was shipped to Japan where he played for Camp Zama. "I knew they'd never let me back into the NBA," said Ralph, "but I also knew I had to keep on playing basketball."

Ralph was honorably discharged in 1957 and he got another job selling cars in Louisville. Ralph found that he liked talking to people. He was aware that nobody ever mentioned the scandals in his presence. The job paid adequately but it had no future, and Ralph went back to stalking the want ads and the employment agencies. He finally located a job selling pharmaceutical supplies. It was interesting and pleasurable work, but it kept Ralph on the road. After a year on the job, Ralph was offered a similar position by Kauffman-Lattimer, Inc., a pharmaceutical wholesaler. Whenever Ralph found himself on the East Coast, he would play in the Eastern League. Sometimes he made special trips to places like Sunbury, Pennsylvania, for important ball games. Jill was born in 1958, and a son, Scott, was born two years later.

RALPH BEARD REMEMBERS: "I worked on the road for fifteen years. Sometimes I worked from eight in the morning until ten-thirty at night. But I thought about the scandals all the time."

As soon as Scott was old enough, Ralph showed him the scrapbooks. Scott slowly read the clippings and saw his father's glory. Then Scott read the awful headlines from the summer of 1951. He saw pictures of his shamefaced father being handled by beaming policemen. "Hey, Dad," the youngster said. "What is all this?"

"Son," said Ralph, "it's all there. I did something wrong. And I've paid more than most people because I paid with my life."

Ralph slowly began to forget. During the summers he would play golf and shag fly balls with Scott. It got so that Ralph never even thought about the scandals in the summertime. But then the nightmares would return when the basketball season began.

Another basketball team came to Louisville in 1967, the Kentucky Colonels of the American Basketball Association. The business manager of the new team was Alex Groza, and Ralph rarely missed a Colonels' home game. Ralph's attendance became even more regular in 1973 when his employer promoted him to sales manager. At the same time, Ralph began scouting for the Colonels on weekends. When the ABA folded three years later, Ralph hooked up as a part-time scout with the NBA's Indiana Pacers.

The Beards live in a ranch-style home in the eastern section of Louisville where $50,000 homes are the norm. The family room is paneled and tastefully decorated with trophies and plaques. Ralph is only a few pounds over his playing weight. He wears golf shorts and a Ban-Lon shirt, while Betty wears a golf skirt. Jill is a freshman at UK and Scott wants to be a professional golfer.

"There was absolutely no justice," says Ralph. "They didn't catch all of them. The only thing I ever wanted was to be a professional basketball player and someday be in the Naismith Hall of Fame. That was my whole life, and it's gone. But I'm no longer interested in retribution. I realize we all have our own private guilt and our own private innocence. If taking the money makes you guilty, then I'm guilty. But if doing something to influence the score of a basketball game makes you guilty, then in my mother's eyes, I'm innocent. Yes, I took the money. We were always poor and financial insecurity was ingrained in my childhood. I needed the money and I wanted the money. But in my heart, I still know I'm innocent. I'm forty-eight years old now and I will never understand why it all happened to me. I thought I'd get over it when I grew too old to play ball, but I've had to learn to live with it like an alcoholic. I also realize that I've been lucky enough to be able to make another life for myself. In fact, everything's going along pretty good and I really can't complain. I don't even mind talking about it. All my dirt has already been dug up. There are plenty of days when I don't even think about the scandals. But, let me tell you something, partner. I know I won't be completely over it until they hit me with that spade."

On December 15, 1953, the Fort Wayne Pistons played the Celtics in Boston. The Celtics opened as 3½-point favorites, but the spread increased to 7½ and was subsequently taken off the boards. Boston won the game 82–75. On December 22, a businessman named Floren DiPaglia offered Ben Bumbry, a star player at Drake University, "several hundred dollars" to make sure Drake lost to Iowa State by at least 10 points. DiPaglia was arrested, tried, and under Iowa's stiff antibribery law sentenced to ten years in jail.

16

In addition to the Sol Levy case and a batch of undetected fixers, the NBA had several other bouts with scandal. In early December 1948, the NBA was known as the Basketball Association of America, and Joe Fulks of the Philadelphia Warriors was the league's leading scorer. A Philadelphia gambler named Morris ("Moxie") Fleishman offered Fulks "easy money" if he would "throw games." Fulks turned the offer over to the police and Fleishman was arrested. There was a state law covering the attempted bribery of athletes, but the Pennsylvania legislators had forgotten to include basketball within its scope. Fleishman had to be indicted on an ancient local ordinance that made it a misdemeanor to bribe, or attempt to bribe, an "employee." At the trial, Fulks was identified as an "employee" of the Arena Corporation, which owned the Warriors, but Fleishman was acquitted.

The NBA's sheets remained officially clean until January 1954 when Ike Gellis, sports editor of the *New York Post*, uncovered another gambling mess. Gellis received a tip from a bookie who operated out of a candy store on East 188th Street in the Bronx, that Jack Molinas, the Fort Wayne Pistons' rookie sensation, was doing business. Gellis had an honorary appointment from Maurice Podoloff to inform the NBA of point-spread fluctuations, betting irregularities, and hidden injuries. Gellis wrote a note of warning to "JM" in one of his columns and he reported the information to the league office. The newspaperman also advised Podoloff that in December 1953 and January 1954, New York bookies refused bets on several games involving the Pistons.

Detectives were quickly assigned to tap Molinas's telephone, and Podoloff promised Gellis the scoop and exclusive rights once the story was released. The Bronx-born Molinas was in cahoots with a gambler from his old neighborhood and the ballplayer was in fact dumping games. The eavesdropping detectives took advantage of their inside information by placing large bets on the ball games that Molinas worked. But Molinas became suspicious of the sudden influx of strange money and he began using public telephones to conduct his transactions. During a subsequent conversation over his home phone, Molinas communicated a false advertisement and the detectives bet on the wrong team. Molinas was arrested shortly thereafter. The story broke on a Sunday morning, nearly twenty-four hours after the *Post*'s weekend edition went to press.

IKE GELLIS REMEMBERS: "I was shut out with only a cursory thank you from Podoloff, may he rest in peace."

Molinas was eager to confess, but only to betting on his own team. "It's true that I bet on some of our games," said the Columbia graduate. "There were ten games in all, but I always bet on us to win. I have never done anything dishonest in my life." There was nothing illegal about Molinas's self-confessed wagers, but he was banned from the NBA for violating a standard antigambling clause in the players' contract. Maurice Podoloff was interested only in preserving the NBA, and he claimed that the Molinas situation was only "a personal psychiatric aberration that will not affect the league." Podoloff also comforted the fans by saying the gambling ring did not contain "a diabolical genius." Then the rotund basketball commissioner held his breath, crossed his fingers behind his back, and thankfully watched the public salute the tattered tale.

The fan-in-the-street admired the "forthright" way the NBA tackled the problem and the turnstiles never stopped spinning. The New York sportswriters could find nothing but glad tidings in the Molinas disclosures. According to Arthur Daley, "The disbarment of Jack Molinas should have a wholesome effect in impressing on all athletes the impropri-

223

ety of betting on themselves." Molinas wasted little time in suing the NBA for $3 million. Since he was innocent in the eyes of the law, Molinas claimed that the NBA owners were acting in conspiracy to deny him the means of earning a livelihood. After refusing a healthy settlement, Molinas lost his case in the courts.

On February 2, Clarence ("Bevo") Francis scored 113 points as Rio Grande defeated Hillsdale (Michigan) College, 134–91, in Jackson, Ohio. The heartless New York Giants traded Bobby Thomson.

Then, on March 4, the Board of Higher Education reversed the findings of its own trial committee. Nat Holman was now declared guilty of concealing and withholding the "Sand-Warner" letter, and of failing to report the 1945 bribe attempt to the college president. The Board also claimed that Nat had been "uncooperative," answering "only those questions he was asked and not availing himself of the opportunities to volunteer information." The Board of Hire and Fire commanded that "Mr. Basketball" be axed. The CCNY student newspapers backed Nat and accused the Board of using him as a scapegoat. But an on-campus demonstration sputtered out for lack of support. Nat's attorney called the decision an outrage, and an appeal was sent to Lewis A. Wilson, the State Commissioner of Education.

The Board voted to deliver a formal reprimand to Bobby Sand and to support the suspension of his back pay. But in appreciation of his "cooperation, his frank admission of guilt, and his expression of repentance," the Board also restored Sand to his faculty status. There were, however, two conditions: Sand would never be allowed to either teach or coach again. Sand was "temporarily" reassigned to planning and designing. He worked as a liaison between CCNY and the Board of Estimate. Sand was also rented to Queensborough Community College and Bronx Community College to help both schools map out new facilities.

A COLLEAGUE REMEMBERS: "Bobby worked in hidden offices, dusty attics, and damp basements. It was as though they didn't trust him around kids anymore. Bobby used to be bright, warm, and loving, but they cut out his heart."

Junius Kellogg did a second stint in the military after he graduated from Manhattan College. Soon after his release, he tried out for the Harlem Globetrotters. Junius was still only twenty-six and his athletic potential remained untapped. All Junius needed was more experience, and Abe Saperstein assigned him to the Globies' "B" team. The second string hit the bumpy roads and the backwater towns. They played in junior high school gyms and they traveled by car.

On April 3, Junius and a party of teammates and friends were motoring from Marianna, Arkansas, to Chicago to watch the Globetrotters' varsity play the College All-Stars. Driving the car was Boyd Buie, thirty years old, one-armed, and the comedy attraction of Saperstein's farm team. The three other passengers were former college teammates of Buie's, Luke Williams, O. B. Elders, and Norman Smith. They were just a few miles north of Pine Bluff, Arkansas, when Buie attempted to pass another car. The weather was clear, the sunshine pale, and the passing lane was a runway into the future. A tire blew out and the car overturned. The vehicle rolled over and crashed into a gully. Williams, Elders, and Smith were able to crawl away from the wreckage, pull out Buie and Junius, and climb up the embankment to hail assistance. Buie was awake and in pain, but Junius was limp. An ambulance arrived within minutes and the attendants tried to remove part of the front seat so their vehicle could contain Junius's insensible 6-foot-8-inch body. The attempt was unsuccessful, and as the ambulance screamed into Pine Bluff, Junius's feet protruded from the rear.

Buie was hospitalized with an injured hip, while Williams, Elders, and Smith were treated for minor cuts and bruises and released. X rays revealed that Junius had suffered a dislocated vertebra and a severed spinal cord. Junius was unconscious and, except for some slight movement in one arm, totally paralyzed. The attending physician held out little hope for his recovery. Junius's parents flew down from Portsmouth, Virginia, to be with their son and to pray at his side. Two days later, Junius was transferred to Veterans' Administration Hospital in Little Rock and his condition was listed as poor.

"Bevo" Francis was expelled from Rio Grande for excessive absences and he immediately signed to tour with the Washington Generals, the Harlem Globetrotters' ubiquitous patsies. Before the college season began, the NCAA had granted Frank Ramsey, Cliff Hagan, and Lou Tsiropoulos an extra year of athletic eligibility so the players wouldn't be personally penalized for UK's infractions. The '53–'54 Wildcats finished undefeated in twenty-five games and were top-ranked in the wire service polls. But Adolph Rupp declined postseason competition when the NCAA subsequently ruled his three graduate students ineligible for tournament play. Junius Kellogg continued to be listed in critical condition, but he showed marked improvement. Only two weeks after the accident, Junius was fully conscious and able to converse with attendants and visitors, and to pray along with his parents. Doctors said that the complete break in his spinal cord made surgery impractical.

Eddie Gard was spotted dressed in rags in a dinky bar in Brooklyn. He was having a difficult time adjusting to life as an ex-con. When Gard was prodded by a reporter, he delivered a prophecy. "I don't ever want to hear about basketball again," said Gard. "But, mark my words, all the rest of you will be hearing plenty about it. I've got to wonder if anybody ever stopped doing business. So it's only a matter of time. It'll all come out again someday and some other poor bums will do time in the can."

On August 27, Lewis Wilson, State Commissioner of Education, reversed the Board's reversal and ordered Nat Holman reinstated to his faculty post with full back pay. Wilson expressed sharp criticism of the ways in which basketball had been conducted at CCNY. Holman and others were certainly subject to "censure" for the degree of professionalism that dominated the sport. Wilson felt that Nat should have reported both the "Sand-Warner" letter and the 1945 bribe offer to the president, but since Nat's superiors knew, the onus was on them.

"Thank God there's justice in America," Nat rejoiced. "I thought the biggest thrill of my life was winning the double championship in 1950, but it isn't anymore. Today's vindication is my greatest victory." Junius Kellogg was removed from the critical list, but he was still completely paralyzed.

On October 15, after a forced absence of two seasons, Nat Holman greeted the '54–'55 Beavers. Nat's first official act was to sit his boys down and show them the collected clippings of the scandals. But practice was only a week old when the NCAA Council voted to lay one more stripe on Nat's back. The Beavers were prohibited from appearing in postseason tournaments for a year, a meaningless punishment since the college had already deemphasized intercollegiate sports. One of the announced reasons for the probation was the "Sand-Warner" letter describing the illegal scheme whereby the CCNY players would share in the profits of the proposed tour. The NCAA declared that the plan was made contrary to amateur rules, and "ostensibly with the knowledge of Nat Holman." Nat yelled libel and demanded a retraction. "I've just had my good name cleared," said Nat, "and now for them to bring it all up again is not cricket." Then Nat flung his own prognostication into the teeth of his accusers: "There is just as much gambling on college basketball games now as ever before. One of these days, some gambler somewhere is going to approach a kid and we're going to have another disaster on our hands."

Junius Kellogg's physical therapy progressed even more rapidly than his doctors had imagined. Within seven months,

Junius was able to sit in a wheelchair and to stand with support. It was evident that he would never be able to walk again. He'd never make the Globies or the Knicks, but his heart was still whole within his disjointed body. Within two years, Junius would be playing basketball in a wheelchair, organizing wheelchair teams and leagues, and talking rich corporations into sponsoring tournaments.

They were called fixers and dumpers, betrayers and jailbirds. Some of them turned around to face the whispered curses. Some pulled the pain into their bosoms like a sharp knife. Some tried to run away. Some were blighted, some remained confused, some were hopelessly numbed, and some were saved. They scattered like dice across the country, but their lives were inextricably tangled. Leroy Smith joined the marines and played basketball out of Camp Lejeune, North Carolina. He wound up in the Eastern League in 1954. Eddie Roman was stationed in Fort Eustis, Virginia, and was a first-team Armed Forces All-Star. When Eddie was transferred to the West Coast, he took several courses at the University of Seattle, earning nineteen credits of A, and four credits of B. Al Roth also served a two-year stint in the army. After Roman and Roth were honorably discharged, they were readmitted to CCNY and allowed to complete their degrees. Al went to business school, while Eddie majored in psychology. Both of them eventually surfaced in the Eastern League.

SHERMAN WHITE REMEMBERS: "I never went back to LIU. Sure, I would have liked to continue my education, and I did talk to some people about it. But what was the use? Who was going to let me teach? Why should I study something if I knew I could never put it to use?"

Sherman got a job as a salesman for an insulation company in Orange, New Jersey. In his spare time, he coached some kids in a Police Athletic League program in Tanglewood. On weekends, Sherman played in the Eastern League.

Ed Warner lived in Harlem and worked in an auto-assembly plant in Tarrytown. The pounding, clanging, dumb routine made his head ache. On weekends, Warner played in the Eastern League.

Floyd Layne played basketball for Camp Kilmer, New Jersey, and for Camp Pickett, Virginia, and joined Roman on the Armed Forces All-Stars. Floyd also played the outfield for a Fort Monmouth squad that reached the finals of the Armed Forces World Series. When he was honorably discharged in 1954, Floyd found an apartment in the Bronx, and a job as a recreation worker in P.S. 124's Evening Community Center. Floyd coached teens and preteens, conducted clinics and tournaments. He used the game as a tool to pry ghetto kids out of their lost lives. He spoke with Maurice Podoloff and with the Rochester Royals, but the NBA was closed to him forever, so he went back to City College and majored in physical education. During the summers, Floyd continued rapping out extrabase hits for the New York Mohawks. And in the fall of 1955, Floyd began an eight-year career in the Eastern League.

Even though its only competitor, the APBL, had folded, the Eastern League was still floundering. Allentown and Scranton were keystone cities but the other franchises were as substantial as coal gas. At one time or another, the EBL had teams in Pottsville, Lancaster, Easton, Hartford, Hazelton, Beverley, Reading, Hamden, Camden, Trenton, Cherry Hill, Wilmington, Baltimore, Monticello, Binghamton, Syracuse, and Brooklyn. At the conclusion of any given season, the owners would sniff around for a better deal—free use of the Boys' Club gym on weekends and reduced advertising rates in the local gazette. For the players, the Eastern League was to professional basketball as the Brooklyn Home for the Aged was to a hospital. Some of the players were incurably old, some had diseased jump shots, and some needed hand transplants.

Since the NBA's racial quota allowed only three Negroes to a franchise, many of the EBL players were also black. In order to try and salvage their brittle confederation, the EBL's owners finally voted to admit players tainted by the scandals. At first, the fans packed the gyms to vent their outrage and their righteousness. But the basketball talent was so outstanding that the ridicule was changed into admiration, and the curiosity seekers into fans. The league prospered and most of the teams generated money.

The ballplayers averaged $50 a game and didn't have to invest much of their time since the teams only played twice a week and never practiced. The defense showed it most: the Allentown Jets once scored 183 points in one game, 103 in the first half. Scores in the 150s were not uncommon. But most of the scandalous players had nowhere to go and they were grateful for the opportunity to play basketball in a public arena. Some of them, of course, felt otherwise.

AN EX-PLAYER REMEMBERS: "The Eastern League was very depressing. Every animal in the world was there. What team you played for depended on whose car you drove down in, but we were all losers. There was always some lunatic I barely knew at the wheel and everybody else was always asleep. We were just a bunch of guys trying to recapture some dead glory. I played one season but I quit before it was over. The whole situation was very threatening to me."

In '55–'56, Jack Molinas led the EBL in scoring, and the Hazelton Bullets featured the first all-black starting team in professional basketball: Tom Hemans from Niagara, Jesse Arnelle from Penn State, and the Fort Wayne Pistons, Fletcher Johnson, Sherman White, and Floyd Layne. The coach of the team was Bobby Sand. Throughout the years, several EBL players made it into the NBA: Bob Love, Mike

230

Riordan, Ray Scott, Bob Weiss, and Harthorne Wingo. Upon occasion, an NBA team would farm a player out to the Eastern League. In most cases, the NBA club illegally subsidized the player's per-game salary. When he was the coach of the Seattle Super Sonics, Bill Russell once exiled John Brisker to the Eastern League to shame the ballplayer into behaving. But the EBL continued bouncing checks and shuffling its hobo franchises.

In 1976 Steve Kauffman was a twenty-seven-year-old lawyer from Philadelphia who was very much interested in the EBL. Kauffman was moved to ask Scranton coach, Stan Novack, how he could get involved in the league. Kauffman thought perhaps he could do something like keep score. Novack got back to Kauffman the very next day. "Mr. Kauffman? How would you like to be the commissioner?"

17

KEN NORTON, BASKETBALL COACH AT MAN-
HATTAN COLLEGE: "Only an idiot would say
that it can't happen again. All of the elements are still
there: the betting, the gamblers, the bait, and the temptation. We've got to keep people aware of what happened.
We can't let them forget."

None but those who were tragically involved seemed to
glean a lesson from the scandals of 1951. And the seeds
continued to germinate. On March 6, 1955, Charley Hoxie of
Niagara University was tendered a bribe and reported it to his
coach. At the same time, a Kentucky schoolboy named
"King" Kelly Coleman was tearing up the state, averaging
46.8 points a game in his senior year at Wayland High School.
Adolph Rupp called Coleman the greatest high school player
he had ever seen. "He's a combination," said the Baron, "of
Cliff Hagan and Frank Ramsey." Wayland High School won
so often and by such huge margins that gamblers took to
betting on how many points Coleman would score. One
night, the coach of Hindman High School bragged that his
team would hold Coleman to 21 points, and the local
gamblers established a betting line of 35. "I had 39 at the
half," said Coleman. "When I walked out of the gym, the
gamblers all lined up and shook my hand. And every time I
shook a hand, I pulled back a $20 bill and put it in my pocket."

When Coleman graduated in June 1956, he was inundated
with scholarship offers. He was given a car, credit cards, and
sufficient clothing to outfit everyone he knew. One university
tried to recruit him with a gambler who spouted a list of illegal
ways in which Coleman could make money at Varsity U. But
Coleman opted for Eastern Kentucky, moved on to Ken-

tucky Wesleyan, and five years later he was playing in the Eastern League.

In 1957 the Bradley Braves made it all the way back to win the NIT. The sins of the past were rendered invisible by forgetfulness, and even hard-boiled cynics were afraid to look back. Then Adolph Rupp's '57–'58 boys helped restore a degree of the familiar by roaring forth from a subpar 19–6 regular season record to capture the NCAA championship. "The Fiddlin' Five" were paced by Vern Hatton, Adrian Smith, and Johnny Cox. The Baron had his fourth Blue Ribbon, a record unequaled until John Wooden's days of glory at UCLA.

Then the NCAA announced that Memphis State and Seattle University were being placed on probation for lowering their academic standards and providing financial aid for their basketball players. Besides losing the lucrative privilege of playing in Bowl games and postseason tournaments, the guilty schools came under brand-new NCAA prohibitions: The number of basketball scholarships they were allowed to disperse was greatly reduced, and their varsity teams could not appear on national television. The resulting financial deprivation was severe, but an unnamed NCAA official revealed that 13 percent of the membership continued to illegally coddle their athletes. The NBA also had a frightening season, and everyone expected that another scandal was imminent.

A BOOKIE REMEMBERS: "We had to take a total of ten NBA ballgames off the boards that season. The word was around that there was business going on."

Then on December 21, 1959, Dr. Edward Sebastian, a one-time dental instructor at the University of Pittsburgh, tried to bribe two Pitt basketball players, John Fridley and Dick Falenski. Dr. Sebastian tempted the players with free dental scholarships and half of his own winnings, but the offer was relayed to the police, and nobody cared. A federal law was passed a few months later making it illegal to telephone betting information across state lines, and the famous Minneapolis Clearinghouse went out of business. But the bettors had to be fed, and the "morning line" joined the chorus line in Las Vegas. The First Amendment to the Constitution allowed Jimmy "the Greek" Snyder to syndicate betting information to newspapers all over the country and the big business of gambling became show business. In late 1960, Bill Spivey sued the NBA for $820,000 in damages, contending that the league was blacklisting him. While the suit was being settled out of court, Spivey averaged 32 points a game for the Baltimore Bullets of the Eastern League.

The other sneaker finally dropped on March 17, 1961. Frank Hogan's office announced the arrest of a pair of gamblers who had made arrangements to throw basketball games with one player from the University of Connecticut and two from Seton Hall. The particulars were distressingly familiar: payoffs of $1,500, shaved ball games turning into dumps, daily bulletins of new teams and new players, and tall young men ducking their faces from photographers. Before Hogan was finished, 37 players, 22 colleges, and 44 ball games were branded with the same iron used ten years before. The list of colleges included NYU, St. John's, Brooklyn College, Columbia, Tennessee, Mississippi State, St. Joseph's, La Salle, and North Carolina.

Ray Paprocky played guard at NYU. He was married, his wife was expecting, and his father had just died. In addition to playing basketball, Paprocky carried sixteen credits, commuted three hours to and from school, and worked an eight-hour shift in a fruit cannery. "I was aware that what I did was wrong," said Paprocky. "But if I were in the same circumstances, I'd do it again. Not because I'd want to, but because I'd be forced to. It was better than robbing a grocery store."

Fred Portnoy played for Columbia. He was from the Bronx and grew up playing in the same school yard with Jack Molinas. "I knew it was morally wrong," said Portnoy, "but I just didn't think of it as criminally wrong. I know I never would have done it if there had been the real threat of jail. But I didn't have too much loyalty to Columbia. I knew we didn't have a good team, so what difference did it make if we lost by five points instead of ten?"

Gamblers were collected, tried, fined up to $21,000, and sentenced to fifteen-year prison terms. Jack Molinas was arrested, tried, and given ten-to-fifteen for being the "master fixer." In addition to conspiring to fix at least twenty-five games, Molinas also had players he knew introduce him to other players. Connie Hawkins and Roger Brown were two of Molinas's unwitting contacts. The two players from Seton Hall asked to be placed in protective custody, but none of the other guilty ballplayers was ever arrested.

IKE GELLIS DISAGREES: "College basketball scandals in 1961? What are you talking about? It's news to me."

The public was weary of corruption. The only headlines that appeared on the front pages heralded plane crashes, wars, rapes, bludgeonings, and gangland slayings. The second scandal produced the same pious reveries as the first, and the same invisible results. Over the course of the next few years, the NCAA broadened its investigative capacities and crusaded to prevent recruiting atrocities. Colleges placed on probation for basketball violations included: Miami, South Carolina, La Salle, Clemson, McNeese State, North Carolina State, Canisius, St. Bonaventure, Florida State, Pan American College, Minnesota (twice), Sam Houston State, Long Beach State, Stephen F. Austin College, Illinois, Centenary College, Western Kentucky, and New Mexico. The list of schools punished for overturning the rules in favor of football players was twice as long. Southwestern Louisiana University was charged with 120 code violations, including making cash awards to its basketball players. Cornell used university funds to pay application fees for twenty-three prospective basketball players. Tampered high school transcripts were discovered at Wichita State and Tennessee. But athletic budgets ballooned. Recruiters climbed fences and hid under beds. The colleges started coming after 6-foot-10-inch Wayne McKoy when he was fourteen years old. It was business as usual on all fronts.

In early January 1965, three basketball players from the University of Seattle, Charlie Williams, Peller Phillips, and L. J. Wheeler, were asked to dump a ball game against the University of Idaho. The hopeful briber owned a bar in Chicago and had been a junior college teammate of Phillips's. The three ballplayers refused the offer but failed to report it to the college authorities. When the bribe was eventually uncovered, the players were expelled and the college officials crowed their own innocence. "I don't think we failed in any way," said a member of the athletic board. "The university is definitely not at fault," said the athletic director. "We took all the necessary precautions," said the freshman coach. "The fault lies with the gamblers," said the varsity coach.

Despite the official blindness and the institutionalized greed, the scandals did have some minor results. When college basketball was at its peak in the late forties and early fifties, bets on college games constituted about 80 percent of a bookie's handle. With the continuing revelations, irregularities and bountiful rumors, the total dropped to 20 percent. Several coaches also made personal attempts to prevent a third visitation of scandal. Frank McGuire was the coach at St. John's in the middle of the 1951 scandals, and he subsequently left for the University of North Carolina in 1953. Several members of McGuire's Tar Heels were incriminated in the 1961 scandals, and the coach moved on to the University of South Carolina in 1964. Every season since then, McGuire has the FBI talk to his players and warn them about gamblers. When his ball club is on the road, McGuire screens all incoming calls. "You can't be an ostrich about this," says McGuire. "It's an awful thing, but you have to be realistic."

Chuck Daley, the coach at the University of Pennsylvania, sends half his team to dinner with an assistant coach, and the other half to dinner with the trainer. "It's just a precaution," says Daley. "I don't want any gamblers poisoning my team."

Lou Carnesecca is the coach at St. John's, and he conducts his own yearly ritual. Carnesecca shows his players clippings of the scandals and makes them sign pledges to report any attempted bribes. "You take five cents and you're hooked," says Carnesecca. "Nobody is above suspicion. Nobody."

Adolph Rupp grew older and more frail. He needed surgery to correct a twisted back that prevented him from moving, and he had an operation on his stomach to repair what he called "a blowout." But Rupp remained garrulous, irresistible, and as popular as only a consistent winner can be. Rupp was voted Coach of the Year in 1966 for the fourth time in his career. He received plaques, awards, and salaams: "For Adolph Rupp, a man who has done much for college basketball over the years." The Baron's glory was crowned on April 4, 1969, when he was voted into the Naismith Hall of Fame.

During the '71–'72 season, Rupp teetered at seventy, the mandatory retirement age for all UK faculty members. A painful gout condition forced him to oversee practice sessions with his foot propped on a chair. The '71–'72 Wildcats were once again the SEC champs, but the UK board of directors was making plans to retire Rupp. Most Kentuckians couldn't even imagine the Wildcats playing without Rupp and his ever-present brown suit warming the first seat on the bench. Students and faculty petitioned the authorities to change the rules to accommodate Rupp. "If I'm forced to retire," Rupp threatened, "then I'm going to run for Congress." But on March 29, 1972, a spokesman for the college pronounced the end of Rupp's career. The Baron had coached at UK for forty-two years and he left a legacy of 4 national championships, 27 SEC crowns, and 25 All-Americans. His lifetime record was 874 wins in 1,064 games, an amazing percentage of .821.

Rupp hung around the campus to help ease in his hand-picked successor, Joe Hall, and he also dropped by to see the ABA's Kentucky Colonels. But Rupp studiously avoided Madison Square Garden until March 13, 1976, when the Wildcats played in the NIT. Surrounded by an admiring clique of reporters, Rupp delivered his opinions and discussed his place in history. "I was never afraid of New York," the Baron said. "I always believed in doing things on the road just like at home. Why, I once took my boys out to see Sophie Tucker at the Copa. There never was anyplace like the Garden. There was that coach at Rhode Island State, Frank Keaney. He would put a smudge pot in his gymnasium so his boys could get used to the smoke and smell of the Garden. I was the best coach in the country and I was the most vicious recruiter in the world. Almost ninety percent of my players came from Kentucky. I also had a different practice schedule from anyone else. My players knew exactly how long it was. Every day—every day, you understand—we had thirty minutes of shooting drills. The first seven minutes were for free-lancing. Then fourteen minutes for dribbling and hook shots under the basket. Then drills for the centers and forwards, then drills for the guards."

Rupp smiled at the busy pencils and condescended to talk about the scandals. "People told me I should have known what was going on," he said. "Hell, we won the NCAA and the NIT and we sent the team to the Olympics with those same players. If I was supposed to know what was going on when a team like that is winning, then why doesn't a coach of a losing team think his players are fixing games?" Rupp mentioned Nat Holman and Clair Bee and observed that many of the game's greatest coaches came from New York. "Most of them worked with Jewish ballplayers in those days. They were all smart ball handlers, the best I've ever seen. But the color of the game has changed." Then the Baron addressed the writers with the pungent air of a man chiseling his own epitaph. "I want to be remembered as a man who didn't shirk responsibility. As a man who always did his best.

I was always blunt. But I was always right. Time is the greatest proof."

Six months later, the University of Kentucky was placed on probation for two years for basketball and football violations. The NCAA revealed that UK had offered high school prospects cash, clothing, free transportation, the free use of cars, trips to Las Vegas, lodging, theater tickets, and, in one instance, a thoroughbred racehorse.

Adolph Rupp died of cancer in Lexington on December 10, 1977.

Alex Groza continued as business manager of the Kentucky Colonels. In November 1970, Groza was interim coach of the ball club until the departed Gene Rhodes could be replaced by Frank Ramsey. Groza retired undefeated in two games. In 1972 Groza shifted to another ABA franchise, the San Diego Conquistadors. He began as general manager of the new team and soon was appointed vice-president as well.

"Groza residence," says a little girl.

ALEX GROZA REMEMBERS: "When the San Diego franchise folded, I got into professional volleyball. But I wasn't too happy so I left after a few months. Now I'm trying to get back into basketball on an administrative level. People have been very gracious to me. And as far as I'm concerned, the scandals are gone from my life. It's happened and it's behind me. I have no other comment to make."

Al Roth sells insurance and lives in a suburb north of New York City. He is reputed to be a very wealthy man.

AL ROTH REMEMBERS: "People talk about the double championship to my face, but they never mention the scandals where I can hear them. I'm sorry that my name makes people remember the scandals. A sportswriter called me recently to ask about the two Bradley games. We talked about nothing else. When the article came out, it was all about the scandals. I'm not bitter, but I can't see what good can come from any more publicity. I don't live with it anymore. I would just as soon be left alone to hope that people will forget about what happened. Sorry."

Nat Holman resumed his coaching duties at CCNY after his final exoneration by Commissioner Wilson. Nat's boys were 8–10 in '54–'55; they were 4–14 the following season, the worst record in Nat's career. Nat left on another sabbatical after the embarrassing '55–'56 season. Before he left, he noted that he had applied for the leave before the season began. Nat spent most of the next two years traveling around the world. He conducted basketball clinics in Mexico, Israel, Japan, Turkey, and Hawaii, sometimes under the sponsorship of the State Department. Nat returned to City College and coached the '57–'58 Beavers to a record of 6–12.

Under the deemphasis, the Beavers were regularly beaten by the likes of Rider College, Hunter, Panzer, and Yeshiva. Nat began the '59–'60 season but he came down with a respiratory ailment after only the second ball game. There was a flurry at CCNY when Floyd Layne was proposed as Nat's successor, but the job went to Dave Polansky. Polansky was one of Nat's boys from 1938 to 1940, he had been City's frosh coach for years, and had compiled a 40–30 record as interim varsity coach. The freshman team was given to one of Dave's boys.

Nat retired on June 5, 1960, leaving behind a 421–186 career record, a Cinderella memory of March 1950, a tradition, a myth, a brown suit, and a pair of spotless hands. "The scandals are things of the past," said Nat. "Any boy with talent knows what's ahead of him. There's big money to be made in the professional game these days. A boy would have to be mentally sick to jeopardize his future. We have the pros to thank for that."

Nat is now eighty, but his life remains full and productive. He is the president of the United States Committee for Sports in Israel. Every day Nat takes the bus from his apartment on East Seventy-third Street downtown to the office building. He hobbles on an arthritic hip, but he says he wants to postpone a ball-bearing operation until he's "older." Despite the pain and discomfort, Nat also makes several fund-raising trips every year.

In 1946 "Mister Basketball" was presented with complimentary season's tickets to see the Knicks play at the Garden. Red Holzman was always Nat's star pupil, and Nat enjoyed watching one of his boys coach the Knicks to NBA championships in 1970 and 1973. But Nat's tickets were taken from him in 1976 in one of a series of economy measures imposed by the Knicks' new owners. Nat was much too proud to show his hurt. "I watch the Knicks' games on cable TV," he said. "I don't have to walk up ramps, buck crowds, get cabs, and fight the snow. But I do miss meeting people I know at the games."

Nat's eightieth birthday was celebrated by a gala $60-a-plate testimonial dinner at the New York Hilton in December 1976. A few of his boys came to pay their respects. Most stayed away. Nat knew that his future was growing short but he held on to one more sustaining dream: to attend the Maccabiah Games in Israel in 1977, and to march behind the athletes in the opening-day ceremonies. "I've had a pleasant life," said Nat. "I've been lucky."

At eighty, Nat answers the phone shyly and without a trace of an accent. His voice is resonant and his words are crisp and alert. "I'm by myself," Nat says. "I have no secretary. Writers are after me all the time and I have to protect myself. You understand? Why don't you write me a letter explaining all the things you want to discuss? And also, if you would, please have your publisher send me a note." The letters of reference and intent are speedily forwarded and the telephone rings two days later: "This is coach Nat Holman. I'd like you to call my brother, Aaron, about our interview."

Brother Aaron is a lawyer and he is anxious to reminisce about the days and joys of his childhood. "But the scandals are a ticklish situation," Aaron says. "Nat doesn't want to be quoted. He feels it would affect his relationship with the boys. They are friends of his. He feels he can't give you anything you can't get from the newspaper clippings. The boys are all grown men who have established decent lives. Nat wants to leave it lie."

"Yes, this is Eddie Gard. . . . Who? . . . What? . . . No, no. I'm sorry. I can't help you. I'm just trying to make a living. Whatever anybody says about me is true."

Eddie Roman now has 270 pounds spread over his 6-foot-6-inch frame and he is periodically troubled by phlebitis. Eddie is a psychologist in a ghetto school in Brooklyn, and he feels he can now understand why society treated a small group of erring postadolescents so harshly. "The American people have a romanticized view of athletics," says Eddie. "They want to identify with the entire fantasy that the world of sports has come to represent. Whenever you break a moral code that people think they are supposed to believe in, you are confronted with a stronger wrath than any burglar or common thief ever faces. It was also a period of rampant McCarthyism so there were a great many self-protective reactions. All of the coaches, for example, yelled their innocence from the rooftops. We were left defenseless and we took the rap. But I don't feel guilty anymore. The most damaging thing was that it prevented me from playing professional basketball. But the Eastern League was good for my self-esteem and I learned to compromise. The scandals changed the course of my life and interfered with my intellectual development. But I got over my bitterness and anger many years ago. I'm finally going after a Ph.D., and I have so many other things to get into that the scandals don't mean that much to me. Above all else, I've learned that the entire universe of sports is based on illusion."

Eddie Roman hasn't touched a basketball in years and there is a touch of relief in his voice when he mentions his son's total lack of interest in the sport. Eddie's deeds are now more private than rebounding, setting picks, and popping from the corner: he is helping kids in slums adjust to what the rest of the world calls reality. Eddie Roman has become a clear-thinking and profoundly sensitive man.

"So much depends on the coach and the school," Eddie says. "The coaches are still under tremendous pressure to win and the same old double standard remains in operation. Colleges offer all kinds of illegal inducements to the players, and the kids are expected to be as pure as the driven snow. Basketball is just as commercialized as ever and the kids know it. I can't see that we're at all immune to another scandal."

The phone is picked up after ringing only once. "Hello . . .? Yes, this is him. What can I do for you? . . . Are you kidding? Why the hell would I want to talk about that stuff? My kids don't even know. I'm sorry."

Bobby Sand continued doing paperwork for CCNY and the Board, and he persisted in his battle to find legal redress. Finally, nine years after his suspension, a State Supreme Court Justice directed that his status be reviewed. The procedure occupied another year, but in April 1962, the Board revoked the ruling that prevented Sand from holding a teaching position. "Mr. Sand has shown himself to be not only completely reliable and conscientious but also very able in the discharge of administrative functions involving thousands of detailed actions and millions of dollars." Sand was readmitted to the classroom and allowed to coach intramural teams on his own time.

"I was never involved," Sand says over the phone. "I never bet on a game in my life. I tried to clear it up but nobody would listen. I'm still in purgatory. I've gone twenty-eight years without a promotion. There's no question that I was a scapegoat. It's still too painful. . . . My wife's a sick woman. . . . I'm sorry. I can't help you."

Sam Winograd has moved to Southern California where he earns a living in real estate law. Ed Warner works for HARYOU-ACT, a self-help organization for Harlem residents. Warner specializes in drug counseling, and he plays in an over-forty league on weekends. "If it happened today," says Warner, "we all would have gotten off scot-free."

AN EX-PLAYER REMEMBERS: "I'm an optimist. If one area is closed, I can find four areas to work in. I've discussed my involvement with my kids and I think the whole experience has taught me a great deal. I see it now as a sign of weakness, a moral lapse. Just one stupid mistake. I never did anything dishonest before or after that. I'm a much more tolerant person these days. I refuse to condemn or criticize anybody. But I got lucky in life. I've become a very straight person. I don't smoke and I don't drink. I never think about it now. I remember the good times."

Salvatore Sollazzo served twelve years in prison and he was too old to be dapper when he was released. Jeanne had divorced him to marry a jewelry manufacturer who used to sell wholesale to Sollazzo in the old days. Sollazzo makes a decent living selling groceries to retailers, but he is a horse-player and he still bets on every rumor that's presented to him. Sollazzo is broke, but he knows a lot of jockeys.

He spears and eats his chef's salad with the efficiency of a man who knows that a lunch hour lasts only forty-five minutes. "We were guilty," he says, "but not as guilty as everybody made us out to be. There are pro boxers and baseball players who are deserters and rapists. We wound up playing basketball for personal advancement, for what we could get. It stopped being fun. The totality of the basketball universe kept us young and immature, but I have to take the full blame on myself. I had the opportunity to refuse and I didn't. There are no extenuating circumstances that can ease that fact or ease the pain."

He neatly nips the corners of his mouth with a napkin. He drains a glass of soda and enjoys a backhand belch. Then he finishes his dessert, puts down his fork, and leans across the table. "But I never tried to run away from it," he says. "I stayed and confronted myself even though it hurt. I've asked myself 'Why?' a million times, but I don't think I've come up with an answer that makes any sense. I try to be flexible. I know I have to forget, but I know I never really will. I have grown to feel very private about myself, about my past. But I do have the memory of my athletic accomplishments. Nothing can take that away from me."

Junius Kellogg learned to accept his physical limitation and to redirect his energies and abilities. He is in the forefront of the civil rights movement currently being promoted by the physically handicapped. In 1970 Junius joined forces with another paralyzed athlete, Roy Campanella, to back an attempt at organizing a taxi company operated solely by physically handicapped people. Junius is also an assistant commissioner for the Community Development Agency in New York City. He still lives in the Bronx, only minutes away from the campus of Manhattan College. Junius makes regular public appearances to boost the National Wheelchair Basketball Association and its annual tournament.

"Another scandal is highly unlikely," he says. "I'm in the streets every day working with kids and with young athletes. We have a pretty good dialogue, me and the players there. They're the ones playing on high school and college basketball teams all around the city. If there was anything brewing, I'd be able to pick it up. And I haven't. There's a much healthier atmosphere for ballplayers today. Today's kids aren't just basketball players. They have moral character and a social consciousness that gives them a better view of things. Another factor is that most of their coaches have made a point of talking to them about the scandals. There's also just

246

too much money to be made in the pros for a kid to do anything foolish. I definitely believe it was the coaches' fault that it all happened again in 1961. Not enough of them warned their kids about it. But the times have changed too much for there to be another scandal. And more importantly, the kids have changed."

Al McGuire played for St. John's University from 1947 to 1951. "I believe the next great scandal will be with the agents," he says. "There are guys who pay a kid while he's in college—up to two hundred dollars a month over his junior and senior years—just for the privilege of getting ten or fifteen percent of the kid's pro contract when he graduates. The agents are the Achilles' heel of all college sports. I'd be in a nunnery if I thought that none of these kids were betting once in a while. You go to a summer league game and you have to use a pole vault to get past the agents."

In 1958 Sherman White began selling liquor displays to retail stores, and he settled into a lifetime job. Sherman has also been doing volunteer work in the Neighborhood Community Development Corporation in Orange, New Jersey, since 1973.

"I talk to a lot of kids here," Sherman says. "Some I can help. I'll tell a kid about my involvement in the scandals if I think it will do him any good. But I don't dwell on it. I'll tell a kid to be careful who he hangs out with. I think that certain supervision could have prevented the dumping. I also feel the law officials dropped the whole weight on us. We were used by a lot of people. That's why you don't hear too much about the scandals these days. A lot of people just want to let things alone."

The summer day is hot and Sherman discards his jacket and tie and unbuttons his collar. His waist is thickening but he lounges in the tiny folding chair with an unmistakable athletic grace and suppleness. His words are friendly and reflective.

247

Sherman knows more than he reveals, but he embraces every question and he readily explores the ramifications of his answers. Sherman White has learned that he is worth loving and respecting. The promise of his youth has been bestowed on his manhood. Sherman's eyes are tired and experienced, but they have nothing to hide.

"I'm on my second marriage now," says Sherman. "I jumped into the first one and it didn't work out. I don't go to church very often but I know there is a God and I think that my involvement has served a purpose. It made me a much stronger person. It's allowed me to help other people. My life is full and I enjoy it. I have no more room for bitterness or shame. I'm proud of who I am."

"It's been a long time," he says. "But, sure, I'll answer a few questions." Then his wife picks up the extension and begins to scream. "Leave us alone!" she says. "I've got high blood pressure! Hang up the phone and don't bother us." He excuses himself and puts down the receiver to argue with his wife. The muted sounds of their battle sputter across the open wire. "I'm not a little boy," he tells her.

A few minutes later he is back on the phone. "You can see the problems I have," he sighs. "We were just kids back then. We were so young. . . ." His wife shrieks again in the background. "I'm sorry," he says.

19

Floyd Layne played in the Eastern League for eight years. He learned to economize and to save a half-mile every ball game. He was thirty-three in 1962 and still in superb playing condition. But there was persistent gossip about the Eastern League's obtaining farm-system status from the NBA, and pressure was suddenly applied to the fixers. They all started having trouble getting contracts, and their salaries began to shrink. "If you don't like it," they were told, "you can quit." One by one, the players retired, but Floyd wouldn't be bullied and he continued playing for the reduced wages. When Floyd hired a lawyer to investigate the situation, his money ran away. "The deck was stacked against us," says Floyd. "We were exploited, used to make money for somebody else, and then dumped. When I left the Eastern League I was by no means ready to leave."

It was still another trauma, another bitterness. But Floyd knew what he wanted. His vision was locked onto the final victory of social acceptance. And his heart was large enough to absorb and digest every negative experience. "Basketball is war," says Floyd. "And I'm a warrior."

Floyd continued working in community centers, organizing clinics for the Bureau of Community Education, and coaching a hundred kids a year. He graduated from the New York Mohawks to the New York Bombers. The major-league scouts loved him but his "history" was common knowledge. Floyd closed out his baseball career with the highly respected New Rochelle Robins. Floyd also found time to earn a B.S. in education from CCNY in 1957, and an M.A. in recreation from Columbia Teachers College a few years later. When it was too late for Floyd to dream of playing in the NBA, he began the quest to find a job as a collegiate basketball coach.

He mimeographed a five-page vita and an eloquent letter of application and sent them everywhere a college coach was fired, retired, or resigned. Floyd got back nothing but carbon-copy refusals.

One day in 1960, Floyd happened across a frail twelve-year-old playing on a "midget" team in a community center in the South Bronx. The youngster had an obvious gift for the game but he was very quiet and sometimes sullen. As usual, Floyd held an informal clinic after the game, designed to calm aggressive young spirits, repair wounded egos, and perhaps teach a crossover dribble or a rocker step. The twelve-year-old's name was Nate Archibald and he studied every word, every move, and every one of Floyd's smiles.

For the next few months, Nate managed to show up on one of the many age-group teams that Floyd coached. Floyd taught Nate to discipline his game and his life. Nate improved rapidly but he couldn't get along with the coach at De Witt Clinton High School and he never played high school ball. Floyd kept after the youngster and routed him to summer leagues, winter leagues, and springtime tournaments. Floyd was instrumental in getting Nate a basketball scholarship to the University of Texas at El Paso. In 1973 Nate Archibald led the NBA in minutes played (46.0 a game), assists (11.4), and scoring (34.0).

"I don't know too much about the scandals," says Nate, "but I do know that Floyd was a tremendous influence on my life. He was our community director and he ran a great basketball program. Floyd was directly responsible for keeping me off the streets and out of trouble. He encouraged me to apply myself, to succeed in high school, and to go on to college. There's no way I can adequately express how much I owe him."

One of the more exotic features of any recreation program headed by Floyd Layne was the star-studded scrimmages he would arrange. At regularly unspecified times, the basketball

250

courts at J.H.S. 120, P.S. 124, or P.S. 18 would be sanctified by the appearance of NBA and EBL players like Wilt Chamberlain, Satch Sanders, Leroy Ellis, Sherman White, Ed Warner, Ray Felix, Walter Dukes, Ray Scott, Walt Simon, and Calvin Ramsey. Floyd would also invite a few selected guests and a couple of neighborhood hotshots to join the "run." The workouts were popular in late August and early September, before the NBA's training camps opened, but they were absolutely sensational for a solid six weeks after the season was over.

Floyd continued to play his life one ball game at a time, but the form letters of rejection sometimes got him down. "I couldn't get a coaching job," Floyd says, "strictly because of the scandals. Everybody figured they would be taking a big chance if they hired me. It's easy to get used to being turned down, and I had to decide whether to keep fighting or to break from the strain. Some of the other guys stepped back, slid out, and tried to maintain a life of obscurity. That's up to them. I chose to fight. I've told the other fellows many times that our names will never be cleared until we can establish a positive image. For me, the only way to do it was to stay in basketball."

In 1964 Floyd was presented with the opportunity to teach and coach at the College of the Virgin Islands. He became an instructor of physical education, the director of intramural athletics, and the coach of both the baseball and the basketball teams. Floyd's family was originally from Barbados and he thoroughly enjoyed the opportunity to explore the Caribbean. "There is a kind of freedom and a sense of peace to be found there," says Floyd. "A release from the self." Floyd returned to New York in 1965, refreshed and ready to resume the lifelong battle for respectability.

Floyd began coaching in Harlem's famous Rucker League during the following summer. In those days, the ball games were played on an outdoor asphalt court on East 138th Street.

The bleachers were always a scramble of ragamuffin kids in sneakers, jeans, and basketball jerseys; shaven-headed men with thick necks and floppy white hats; other ballplayers; and an occasional scout from the NBA. They watched spellbound while NBA stars risked their legs, knees, careers, and reputations against every young gunslinger in the territory. They gawked at the antics of "Dr. J," "The Hawk," "Tiny," "The Dipper," and Herman "Helicopter" Knowles. The ball games themselves were reckless and spectacular. But Floyd demanded that his players attend practice sessions and learn set plays. The players resisted, especially the older ones. Floyd's strength of character could usually establish a proper tone of comradeship, bemusement, and wisdom, and he could convince the players to execute orders, give up the ball, and play defense. "The old game is my system," says Floyd as he snaps his fist into his open palm. "The team game. Give and go, pick and roll, do things without the ball. Everybody makes a contribution. I don't like some of the modern-day selfish ballplayers who think they are bigger than the team. It's a slovenly attitude, and I blame it on their upbringing. In spite of them, I know the old game will survive."

When the Boston Celtics drafted Dave Cowens out of Florida State in June 1970, Red Auerbach shipped the rookie off to the Rucker League to be coached by Floyd. Cowens played for the "Bronx Celtics" and Floyd helped him smooth out his game and prepare for the NBA. The complete list of professional basketball players either coached or counseled by Floyd is over one hundred names long and includes Austin Carr, Jim McMillian, Jim Brewer, Gary Brokaw, Billy Paultz, Wilt Chamberlain, Charlie Scott, Dean Meminger, Jimmy Walker, Tom Henderson, John Shumate, Campy Russell, Rick Sobers, and Earl Monroe.

Dave Polansky's teams at City College were well drilled, respectable, and mediocre by mandate. The low-key Polansky had a lifetime coaching mark of 126–129 when he decided to move on in the spring of 1970. It became the responsibility of CCNY Physical Education Department to hire a new coach. In the past, protocol demanded that an outgoing coach select his own replacement while the department merely signed the proper forms. Polansky nominated Floyd to become the third varsity basketball coach in CCNY's history, but the Physical Education Department rejected Floyd and chose Jack Kaminer instead.

Polansky was sufficiently irked by the breach in tradition that he decided to stay on for another year in the hopes that Floyd would have another chance. Joe Galiber, Sonny Jameson, Irwin Dambrot, and Eddie Roman formed an ad hoc committee to meet with the department chairman and convince him that Floyd was worthy of the position. They pointed at Floyd's experience as a teacher and as a coach. They mentioned how much work Floyd had done in the Harlem community and how popular he was there. "Sorry," said the chairman. "The reality of the situation is that CCNY wants nothing to do with Floyd Layne because of his involvement in the scandals. There are still several old-timers in the PE department whose votes will never be swayed."

The committee of friends and ex-teammates also met with CCNY's new president, Buell Gallagher. "I agree that Floyd would be good for the school," said Gallagher. "He has my support, but I am constitutionally unable to overrule the Physical Education Department in this matter."

"It's not to my benefit to say how much hatred I felt," says Floyd. "I think it fluctuated day by day. But there was always the constant realization that the world was an awfully hypocritical place. If you told the truth, you were crucified, but if you lied and maintained an air of respectability you could ride right through and everything would be okay. It destroyed my image of what's right and what's wrong. I was always led to believe that if you do something wrong you should feel bad about it and seek to tell the truth. But I've discovered that people can look right at you and lie without feeling a thing. I might lie but I would certainly suffer for it."

Over the years, an old buddy of Floyd's named Alfred Kahn had evolved to the chairmanship of the Physical Education Department at Queensborough Community College. When the Queensborough basketball coach took a leave in 1970 to pursue a graduate degree, Kahn offered Floyd the position. Floyd stayed at Queensborough for two years, molding notoriously meager talent into competitive ball clubs.

As usual, Floyd also became personally involved in the lives of his players and the life of the community. He organized and advised a Black Students Basketball League. He brought the varsity team into neighborhood centers and conducted open clinics. At Queensborough, Floyd continued to demonstrate that basketball was a viable alternative to the criminal temptations of the street. But when Queensborough's incumbent basketball coach completed his degree in 1972, Floyd was dismissed.

He resumed mailing letters of application whenever there was a coaching vacancy, and he formed a short-lived company with Nate Archibald. It was a soul agency, designed to counsel high school and college ballplayers and to protect them if and when they turned pro. The company was named after the only player under contract, Nate Archibald Enterprises. Floyd now had an office, a secretary, and a wall full of good-luck autographs from famous players. But the secretary had nothing to type and Floyd had grilled-cheese sandwiches sent in every day for lunch. Floyd's efforts to land a coaching position continued to no avail. Columbia University turned him down, saying Floyd lacked sufficient coaching experience on the high school level. Floyd's pain was much closer to the surface than at any other time since the scandals.

"Whatever I've done through the years never seems to count," he said. "No matter how many youngsters I've been able to salvage I just can't establish myself as a responsible, upright person in the eyes of the public. And it's only because the public is not well informed. There was such a thin line drawn between shaving points and actually throwing a ball game. I never would have gotten involved with dumping.

That requires a different kind of person. But no distinction was ever made. The public doesn't think about weighing good and evil, so the evil tends to dominate. Whenever they hear my name, people remember the scandals. I'm not to be touched. Maybe I'm wrong in not wanting to shake a few limbs. Maybe I'm wrong in not saying a lot that perhaps ought to be said. The nice approach certainly hasn't helped my career. Maybe I should start jumping up and down on tables and make people sit up and take notice. I don't know. I'm like the picture of Dorian Gray. On the outside I look fine, but on the inside I'm ripped apart."

But Floyd's consciousness had already found that the present was a healing place in which to live. His latest disappointment was gradually integrated into his life and he carried on. Then in the spring of 1975, an advertisement appeared in *The New York Times*: "Varsity basketball coach wanted. Experience a must. Send resume to Box #2022. An Equal Opportunity Employer."

Jack Kaminer knew he would never get tenure at CCNY because he wasn't pursuing a Ph.D. So when a better-paying, tenure-bearing high school coaching job was offered to him, Kaminer had no choice but to resign. There were 275 inquiries after the vacated position, but the Physical Education Department narrowed the candidates to a one-time CCNY varsity player named Teddy Hurwitz, Floyd Layne, and Bobby Sand. Sand offered to coach the Beavers for nothing. Since the varsity teams at CCNY were no longer budgeted for meal money and transportation costs, Sand proposed that his salary be used to reimburse the ballplayers. The Board of Higher Education relented and allowed Sand to coach a quasi-team that represented CCNY's School of Business for the next couple of years. But neither Sand nor Hurwitz were seriously considered for the varsity job.

The CCNY officials reasoned that Floyd was sufficiently "rehabilitated," and that his appointment would provide good publicity for the school. Since Floyd was not interested in obtaining a Ph.D., his appointment had the further advantage of being necessarily short term. A press conference was called and Dr. Julius Shevlin, the chairman of the Physical Education Department, took pains to emphasize that CCNY had no intention of returning to big-time athletics. "Floyd was hired," said Shevlin, "because of his educational experience and his background as a coach. There will be no difference between this year's program over last year's program."

Then a few crusty sportswriters scratched suspiciously at the corners of their eyes as Floyd stepped up to make a short speech. "Coaching at City College has always been a lifelong dream," said Floyd. "Words cannot describe my feelings at this time. The shortest distance between two points is a straight line, and I've traveled in a wide circle. But I finally got back home."

During the '75–'76 season, Floyd coached the Beavers to a record of 16–14, the most victories posted by any ball club since the "Cinderella Team." The Beavers were also asked into the NCAA's Small-College Tournament, but were eliminated in the second round. But Floyd's rookie year remained an unqualified success, and the team grossed close to $20,000 in road-trip guarantees. "A figure," said a college spokesman, "not to be ignored in these budget-crunch days." Then late in the spring of 1976, it was announced that New York's financial crisis would require its public universities to trim their services and their faculties. Minority groups anguished, picketed, and petitioned, but tuition was raised and teachers were fired throughout the system. CCNY lost over fifty instructors, including a Black Studies teacher, thirteen members of the Physical Education Department, and Floyd Layne. The minute Floyd heard the news, he sat down and started stuffing envelopes with job applications.

Then, a bare two weeks later, the provost of CCNY, Dr. Egon Brenner, made a startling announcement: Floyd Layne was being retained to coach the varsity basketball team and to perform "administrative work in the intercollegiate athletic department." Floyd would be paid through a special appropriation from CCNY's "discretionary funds," which consisted of nontaxed moneys contributed by alumni. Floyd would be paid $18,000, a sum equal to his first year's salary. The special appointment marked the first time that a CCNY basketball coach was not a member of the faculty. The other twelve Physical Education teachers were not rehired. "The money was made available through the president for the express purpose of hiring a basketball coach," said Provost Brenner. "It was a matter of using the money for that purpose or not using it at all. Basketball is the premier sport at City College. It's very important to the college and to the students."

The announcement swept up another momentary protest. Barry Poris was one of the fired Physical Education instructors, and he also had coached the baseball team. Poris claimed that Physical Education chairman Shevlin had advised him that winning should be the most important consideration for any coach at CCNY. Having a winning record was the best way to gain "prestige" with the college's administration. "I've got nothing personally against Floyd," said Poris. "He's a fine person and a fine coach. It's just what Floyd's rehiring represents. I'd like to know what the administration is trying to accomplish. Are they looking for basketball to support the entire athletic program? Are they looking to start giving scholarships? Maybe there's a job open for someone to travel across the country to recruit players. If you're going to play big-time basketball, why not go all the way? When were the scandals? Twenty-six years ago? What have they learned?"

Floyd ignored the latest hullabaloo. He knew it would pass. "I'm pleased to be back coaching here at City College," said Floyd. "It's nice to be working again."

The old Wingate gymnasium now houses administrative offices, and there is a new athletic complex on the CCNY campus. Convent Avenue is barricaded to traffic so that wrecking crews can demolish Lewisohn Stadium. But the massive smoky-red-brick classroom buildings are still standing, with their terraces and battlements lined in whitewashed brick. "Raymond the Bagel Man" still hawks his salted pretzels just inside the main gate. "Yeah," he rasps. "I remember you. Ya big stiff." Raymond shakes open a bag. "How many?" he asks. Then he sells the first two pretzels his hand touches and he makes change while he scans his next customer. "Pretzels," he croaks into the wind. "Get your Southern fried pretzels."

If the campus is more or less the same, the students are totally different. They seem more assured and more buoyant than the ghosts in the cafeteria. There is still graffiti peppering the walls, but the slogans now hail Puerto Rican Independence, Women's Lib, Black Power, and Gay Liberation. Even though the sun is hidden, there are several knots of students lounging on benches and lawns. Everybody who's on the move moves fast. Few of them turn to look as an ambulance goes sirening down Convent Avenue.

The athletic center is a monolith of cinder blocks and poured-concrete walks, but half its glass doors are boarded with plywood. The building's entrance corridor must be traversed before reaching the gym, the pool, the classrooms, or the suite of faculty offices. There are a series of glass cases built along one wall, containing a dazzling display of polished athletic hardware. Inside one case, resting beside a football trophy, are a pair of cracked and shriveled leather basketballs.

CCNY - 69	CCNY - 71
BRADLEY - 61	BRADLEY - 68

The opposite wall is lined with plaques commemorating the athletes in the CCNY Hall of Fame. Nat Holman is honored there; so, too, is Red Holzman. Irwin Dambrot was admitted into the select company in 1973.

Floyd Layne shares an office with the soccer coach and three other teachers. There are framed pictures set on the wall behind Floyd's desk of basketball players familiar and obscure. There are group portraits of several tournament-winning teams flying the colors of the Sportsmen Athletic Association, and there is a picture of the "Cinderella Team."

Floyd is forty-six years old and his carriage is as regal as ever. There are no webs of distress pulling at his arching, glossy-brown cheekbones. His mouth is full and ready to smile. He laughs easily and his eyes twinkle with mischief as he teases a colleague about his weight. "Let's go down to the gym," says Floyd. "I want you to see the new court. It's a rubberized surface. I had to have the kids do some special stretching exercises until they got used to it. . . . Me? . . . I'm feeling fine. I'm always ready to go. Sometimes I run on this stuff, but I try to run on wood, and I never, ever, run on concrete. I'm still playing in the Old-Timers' League. In fact, we've got a game this Saturday in Atlantic City. You got your sneakers in your car?" He laughs in rolling monosyllables.

Floyd is a Pied Piper as he walks through the halls. At least half of the passing students toot him with friendly greetings. Floyd salutes them each by name. The gym is empty and the new floor hums under a bluish light. The lines and circles are black and the entire court is shaded in a light lavender. Floyd involuntarily snorts at the plastic odor.

"I don't think too much about the scandals," he says. "But it does come up from time to time. I've come to realize that this has already happened and that I can't reshape it. Being a Pisces I'm supposed to be a dreamer but there's no way to dream the scandals away. I always tried to look at it realistically. . . . What does what happened make me? And where do I go from where I am? But it took me years to develop this kind of attitude."

Floyd walks around the apron to the other side of the court. Every so often, his eyes take aim and shoot forth sparks of pride. "I'm not ashamed of the Floyd Layne that existed back then," he continues. "He was basically decent, a good athlete, and fairly obedient in the home. I think he was a worthwhile individual. But the newspapers were too harsh. The writers were not mature enough to deal with the situation. They were too wrapped up in their own personal at-

259

tachments to sports. A lot of them figured if they could lay the full blame on us, they could keep a lot of other stuff from getting out. We certainly didn't invent point shaving, that's for sure. Through the years I've developed a feeling of compassion for those players who were involved but never named. Not that I was ever vindictive. I would never wish what I went through on anybody. The only thing that I'm still peeved about is the way the authorities tried to make us the complete villains. They shouldn't have come down so hard on us. If they wanted to save the sport, that's fine. No one feels any stronger about that than I do. We made very serious and very tragic mistakes, but we were only kids. Nowadays, I think more about the future than I do about the past. I always wanted to play on the highest level and now I want to coach on the highest level. I am definitely interested in coaching in the NBA. It represents a different kind of challenge. There's more continuity in personnel. You can go out and find a specific part for a team. A power forward. Or a ball-handling guard. The whole strategy is much more sophisticated. . . ."

Floyd pauses to chide himself with a quiet laugh, then his eyes get serious. "I'm very glad to be at City College," he says. "At this point in my life, I'm very glad to be anywhere."

Epilogue

In 1970 Richard "Digger" Phelps became the varsity basketball coach at Fordham University. Phelps was a fine coach, and a dynamic recruiter even on a tight budget. His primary inducements were New York City and the anticipation of playing for such a nice guy for the next four years. In Phelps's first season, the Rams played until the semifinals of the NCAA's Eastern Regionals and finished with a handsome record of 23–6. The players were incredibly talented and fiercely loyal to their coach. A few days after the season was over, Phelps was offered the basketball coachingship at the University of Notre Dame, the Vatican of American colleges. Phelps wrangled out of his contract with Fordham, and the press hailed his wit, intelligence, and charm.

In 1972 the NCAA made freshmen eligible to play varsity basketball and football. Colleges now receive a four-year return on their deposits instead of three. High school seniors like Moses Malone, Darryl Dawkins, and Bill Willoughby are thrust into the NBA. Jimmy "the Greek" reports of a new long-range electronic device that can cause a player to drop a ball.

We are absorbed with gate receipts, lucky numbers, won-and-lost records, seven-figure salaries, shooting percentages, vicarious living, and vicarious dying. We have abdicated our responsibility to protect the kids in short pants who play the game. We are clinging to an athletic code initiated in England to govern competition among the landed gentry of the nineteenth century. We have already forged ourselves a new reality. Let's reforge our own native set of athletic mores. Let's start by accepting the professionalism of all major American sports. Let's make amateurism an option. Let's worry about our children and forget about our country's performances in ecopolitical events like the Olympic Games.

Like the rest of us, the ballplayers were afraid of what the future would cost. Most of them spent precious little of their bribe money. They salted it away in bank accounts, shoe boxes, dresser drawers, and flowerpots. But when the buzzer suddenly sounded, they were strangers to themselves. The scandals have left many lingering scars and easy questions. But questions can only lead to other questions. It makes little difference who was to blame, or who got away free. Scars are part of living people, so they can heal and be healed.

"No matter what I do," says one ex-player, "I can't forgive myself. What good is all of this going to do?" Some of his brothers have learned that guilt is just another commodity. Some have been able to forget, and some have not. But they were all marched to the edge of the abyss at an earlier age than most of us. And they have already encountered what most of us have yet to see. Each of them has gained a special wisdom that is, at the very least, sobering, and at most, inspiring. Their lives can give us warning, self-doubt, and pangs of hope. Theirs is a precious heritage, painfully wrought. We can learn to forgive each other only when we learn to forgive ourselves.

"Hello? . . . Yes . . . Speaking . . . The scandals? Hum! I don't know. That's still a very touchy subject. . . . Yes . . . Yes, I know. I was there and I know everything that happened. I can tell you about things you'll never find in the newspapers. . . . I don't know. It really doesn't sound like a good idea. . . . I don't think so. . . . But wait a minute. Let me ask you a question. . . . What if I tell you everything I know for five hundred dollars . . .?"

Rosen, Charles.

Scandals of '51

DATE			